PRAISE FOR
SURVIVOR INJUSTICE

"By identifying rape culture's political systemic roots—omnipresent regardless of political affiliation—Cheung provides the anticapitalist analysis lost when the mainstreaming of #MeToo led to a whitewashed movement. *Survivor Injustice* serves as a reported modern history . . . connecting survivorship to patriarchy and carcerality, pushing for reproductive justice, and looking for better answers in social justice-oriented ideologies and traditions."

—LEXI MCMENAMIN, politics editor at *Teen Vogue*

"A searing indictment of the ways that gendered violence—which, as Cheung intentionally explains, is horrific in and of itself—exacerbates inequality and violence within democracy and our broader social structures. Cheung skillfully dissolves the veil between the personal and political in her reporting and her prose, and the result is shattering, even for those who are deeply familiar with these issues. This is an urgent read."

—BECCA ANDREWS, author of *No Choice: The Destruction of Roe v. Wade and the Fight to Protect a Fundamental American Right*

"Kylie Cheung exposes how domestic abuse and sexual violence targeting women of Asian descent is frequently overlooked, downplayed, and rendered invisible. A compelling and important book for these times."

—MICHELE GOODWIN, author of *Policing the Womb*, host of *Ms.* magazine's *On the Issues* podcast, and Chancellor's Professor at UC Irvine School of Law

"*Survivor Injustice* is beautifully threaded with Kylie Cheung's lived experience, depth of knowledge, and expertise. Kylie creates an easy-to-follow roadmap, helping readers to understand how we got here and where we're going. This book could not be more timely and powerful. As a survivor, I felt so seen and held in Kylie's words. If you are a survivor yourself, or you love a survivor, this book is for you."

—ALISON TURKOS, survivor-activist

SURVIVOR INJUSTICE

STATE–SANCTIONED ABUSE, DOMESTIC VIOLENCE, AND THE FIGHT FOR BODILY AUTONOMY

KYLIE CHEUNG

North Atlantic Books
Huichin, unceded Ohlone land
Berkeley, California

Published by
North Atlantic Books
Huichin, unceded Ohlone land
Berkeley, California

Cover design by Jess Morphew
Book design by Happenstance Type-O-Rama

Printed in the United States of America

Survivor Injustice: State-Sanctioned Abuse, Domestic Violence, and the Fight for Bodily Autonomy is sponsored and published by North Atlantic Books, an educational nonprofit based in the unceded Ohlone land Huichin (Berkeley, CA) that collaborates with partners to develop cross-cultural perspectives; nurture holistic views of art, science, the humanities, and healing; and seed personal and global transformation by publishing work on the relationship of body, spirit, and nature.

North Atlantic Books's publications are distributed to the US trade and internationally by Penguin Random House Publisher Services. For further information, visit our website at www.northatlanticbooks.com.

CONTENT DISCLAIMER: This book contains material that may be triggering, including references to self-harm, sexual abuse, or trauma.

Library of Congress Cataloging-in-Publication Data

Names: Cheung, Kylie, 1998- author.
Title: Survivor injustice : state-sanctioned abuse, domestic violence, and
 the fight for bodily autonomy / Kylie Cheung.
Description: Berkeley, CA : North Atlantic Books, [2023] | Includes
 bibliographical references.
Identifiers: LCCN 2022051199 (print) | LCCN 2022051200 (ebook) | ISBN
 9781623179083 (trade paperback) | ISBN 9781623179090 (ebook)
Subjects: LCSH: Women--Violence against--United States. | Women--Crimes
 against--United States. | Abused women--United States. |
 Feminism--United States. | Reproductive rights--United States.
Classification: LCC HV6250.4.W65 C537 2023 (print) | LCC HV6250.4.W65
 (ebook) | DDC 362.880820973--dc23/eng/20230508
LC record available at https://lccn.loc.gov/2022051199
LC ebook record available at https://lccn.loc.gov/2022051200

1 2 3 4 5 6 7 8 9 KPC 27 26 25 24 23

This book includes recycled material and material from well-managed forests. North Atlantic Books is committed to the protection of our environment. We print on recycled paper whenever possible and partner with printers who strive to use environmentally responsible practices.

CONTENTS

INTRODUCTION

When my sisters and I were growing up, our parents would tell us stories of grandparents and great-grandparents and great-aunts nearly sold away as child-brides, stories of young women of previous generations who were accorded no power, worth, or determinism in their marriages and in society at large. They told us these stories for the same reason immigrant parents often tell their children family stories—to not-so-subtly guilt us into gratitude for our comparably much cushier lives. At the time, I didn't make too much of family lore, but now and then, I found myself mentally returning to the story of my mom's grandmother, who had locked herself in a closet for days as a teenager to escape marriage to an older, abusive man. It's a story I continue to think about today.

All these stories I heard as I spent my formative years coming of age in a quiet Silicon Valley suburb. Like many of my peers, throughout high school I struggled to keep my head above water amid a pervasive mental health crisis across schools like mine. On top of the at-times debilitating pressure to achieve academic perfection, if such a thing is possible, when I was sixteen, I also struggled to care for myself and navigate the trauma of experiencing sexual assault—starting with even acknowledging what had happened to me.

Eventually, through years of reflection, campus anti-rape activism, and learning from and healing with others who have survived sexual violence, I came to meditate on the unique experience of Asian American victims and survivors like me. And as I did, the stories my mom once told me became more real, less distant—stories of a great-aunt, now deceased, whose husband was physically abusive if she gave too much money to their church or to unhoused community members, and controlled her spending and access to a car; stories of another aunt whose husband stopped her from volunteering in the community, and later, from leaving the house. Eventually, the individual anecdotes of relatives both distant and close, sexually abused as girls, beaten or controlled as wives, blended into one greater story—a pattern, a broader culture of normalized domestic violence.

Drawing on my own experience as well as the stories of women in my family, I've witnessed how Asian American survivors are forced to navigate a difficult space: We face cultural erasure from the white-washing of dialogues about sexual violence and victimhood; we face the hypersexualization of Asian American feminine identity in white and Western spaces; and we face the often conservative, sex-shaming politics of immigrant households at home and in our communities. These dynamics can expose Asian American victims to intensified victim-blaming, and certainly force many to hide our pain and struggle within a culture of silence and invisibility.

Stereotyping and fetishization of Asian women originate from Western imperialist conquest in the Pacific throughout the nineteenth and twentieth centuries that resulted in the trafficking and rape of thousands of Asian women, inspiring persistent, targeted violence against us. In March 2021 a white man went on a shooting rampage exclusively targeting Asian massage parlors in Atlanta, Georgia, and killing six Asian women, and explained to police that they were a "temptation" to him and his "sexual" addiction; he had targeted the women because of his perception of them as sex workers, a conclusion he drew from their race and class as Asian women service workers. Other violent acts against Asian women, which have seen a pointed surge since the 2020 COVID pandemic, are erased by model minority mythology that sweeps anti-Asian oppressions under the rug and silences victims of abuse.

I'll never forget how I felt when, in the fall of 2019, Chanel Miller published her simultaneously devastating and healing memoir, *Know My Name*, recounting her experience as the plaintiff in the notorious

Stanford rape case of 2016, which saw Brock Turner, a white man, jailed for three months for raping Miller. Specifically, I'll never forget seeing Miller's face in her 2019 20/20 interview, my shock when I realized she was an Asian American woman and not a white woman; I'll never forget reading about her family like mine, her schooling and upbringing in a Bay Area suburb like mine, her grandparents like mine, her school's mental health crisis like mine. Her identity forced me to question my instincts and my own white-washed assumptions, and why nearly all the victims we hear about or are socialized to sympathize with are middle-class white women. Miller's story also made me consider other narratives and preconceived notions about sexual abuse and society, about anonymity, race, gender, class, about the heard and the unheard stories of violence and exploitation, and the differences between them. Her story prompted me to recognize my identity as not just an Asian woman and a survivor, separately, but an Asian woman survivor. And it made my once isolating, lived experience with sexual violence less lonely.

The most visible victims of abuse are middle-class, straight, cisgender white women, yet it's women of color, queer women, and trans and nonbinary people who are more likely to experience sexual and domestic violence—and who are subjected to greater pressure to be silent due to fear of hostility and punishment from law enforcement, and who lack resources and support to protect themselves or be independent from abusers. Jennifer Kelly, a Black woman and US Navy veteran, reported her white ex-husband in the Air Force for physically abusing her three young daughters and herself—at one point, allegedly sexually assaulting her with a knife—and subsequently lost custody of them and faces criminal charges in Alaska for briefly running away with her daughters in 2020. Today a restraining order prohibits her from even contacting her daughters. In an interview with me in 2022, Kelly insisted that "stories like mine are not uncommon."

As an Asian American woman and a journalist, activist, and author, I've researched and reported on rape culture, feminism, public policy, and racial justice for almost a decade. My reporting has spanned from an emergent new wave of campus survivor justice organizing in the early

2010s to the rise and persistence of the mainstream MeToo movement in 2017; the COVID-era crises of heightened domestic violence; the swell of violent attacks on Asian women since 2020; and both most recently and perhaps most devastatingly, the overturning of *Roe v. Wade,* empowering the state to become the ultimate abuser in 2022.

Within mere days of *Roe* being overturned and the wave of state abortion bans that followed, Republican lawmakers were making threats to ban birth control, Plan B, and IVF methods. Amid an ongoing legal battle to block Louisiana's abortion ban from taking effect post-*Roe*, one woman was forced to endure a painful, hours-long delivery to birth a dead fetus, because the ban temporarily went into effect and her doctor wasn't allowed to provide a simple, fifteen-minute abortion procedure. Months before this, an abortion ban in Texas forced one woman to carry a dead fetus for two weeks after doctors refused to give her emergency care out of fear they could be bankrupted by lawsuits as a result of Texas's civilly enforced six-week ban, placing her at risk of severe infection and death.

A week after *Roe* fell, a ten-year-old rape victim in Ohio was forced to travel across state lines to get abortion care in Indiana, because she was slightly more than six weeks pregnant—in violation of Ohio's newly minted ban. What followed was a gutting, dehumanizing media circus of politicians and legacy newspapers claiming the tragic story was a "hoax" perpetuated by abortion rights activists, implicitly questioning a child rape victim's credibility. Indiana's attorney general announced he would investigate and possibly prosecute the doctor who had offered the child abortion care—emblematic of the dystopian, fundamentally carceral society that the end of *Roe* had ushered in for survivors. It was a lesson for liberal abortion rights advocates who relied on respectability politics in vain attempts to change hearts and minds: There's no story, no experience deemed sympathetic enough to ruthless anti-abortion lawmakers and their supporters, who simply do not care about the suffering they're inflicting.

For me, reporting on these moments and movements put faces to the nearly one in five women in the US who have experienced sexual assault, and one in six men who have experienced some form of sexual abuse.

Notably, this is a higher rate than that of men who are supposedly "falsely accused" of sexual violence, a fact "men's rights" activists purporting to care about men often ignore. (Speaking of the myth of endemic false accusations targeting men, in its 1996 report compiling police data indicating 8 percent of rapes are falsely reported, the FBI marked rapes and assaults that didn't involve a weapon or were reported by people with prior relationships with their assailants—a sizable chunk of assaults—as "false reports."[1] Something to keep in mind!) I've heard the diverse range of stories of the nearly one in four pregnant-capable people who have had abortions, some to escape abuse (homicide, often by abusive partners, is the leading cause of death for pregnant people[2]), some because they couldn't afford kids, some because they didn't want them—all equally important, all equally valid. And I've heard the stories of those who were forced to remain pregnant and give birth by the government, acting as an abusive partner, a phenomenon that 2020 reports about ICE performing nonconsensual hysterectomies on detained migrant women put in stark, jarring relief. A 2022 US Senate investigation into ICE-perpetrated abuses said the ICE gynecologist performed "excessive" and "invasive" procedures on dozens of detained migrants between 2017 and 2020.[3]

In 2022 I reported on the steady disappearance of rape exceptions to state abortion bans—a shift for the worse from the last decade. Within months of the fall of *Roe,* lawmakers in Tennessee introduced a bill that would add a rape exception to the state's abortion ban—but threaten people who "lied" about being raped with up to three years in prison, while requiring rape victims who are able to access abortion to submit embryonic remains to the state government for possible criminal investigation.

The Tennessee bill exposed the reality that, truthfully, these exceptions have always been little more than a ploy for anti-abortion lawmakers to save face and appear more humane: Most rapes aren't reported to police, which most rape exceptions require, and these exemptions function to separate "good," worthy abortions from "bad," frivolous ones, to essentially measure survivors' trauma with a yardstick. I've also interviewed activists like Analyn Megison, a mother who chose to give birth after being impregnated by rape and was eventually forced to fight her rapist in court to keep custody of her daughter. She continues to make child support payments to her ex-husband, who has sole custody of her first child and once beat her so severely while she was pregnant that she miscarried. When she called the police, Megison told me, they "didn't take the report because they said my husband and me 'were one flesh, you can't beat yourself.'"

Throughout my career, I've sought to expose the human toll of gender-based violence through storytelling, to shine light on the prevalence of compelled silence in a society where men and abusers overwhelmingly hold power, and coming forward about surviving sexual violence is implicitly and explicitly met with skepticism, blame, and punishment—thus, an estimated 80 percent of sexual assaults are unreported, per the National Sexual Violence Resource Center.[4] And I've always been particularly drawn to understanding where rape culture and white supremacy intersect, and why gender-based violence and its wide-ranging consequences are so often depoliticized in society. Asian Americans are broadly represented as the passive, apolitical "model minority," despite how many are on the front lines of activism for racial justice, immigrant justice, and other innately political issues. And alternatively, in wealthier Asian communities, Asian Americans are often on the front lines of conservative political activism—against affirmative action, wealth redistribution, protections from gentrification, and other progressive policy issues. Similarly, while acts of sexual and domestic violence know no political party or affiliation, gender-based violence is an inherently political issue, too, through its substantial impact on elections, representation, and who has the power to change policy and culture.

Domestic violence and the lasting impacts of any sexual trauma can severely restrict or entirely deny someone's ability to participate in democracy or be active in their communities. Abusive partners might control their victims' voting abilities, prevent them from leaving the house to attend political events, deny them contact with other people to organize in their communities, or control their ability to volunteer with or even donate to social causes, and certainly their ability to run for office or organize mass movements.

With this in mind, I set out to interrogate the fundamentally political roots and impacts of victimhood within one's own home, culminating in this book. State violence, which all too often creates the optimal conditions for interpersonal violence, entails the policies and law enforcement apparatuses that deny resources to and even criminalize and incarcerate disproportionately non-white victims of abuse. And it can range from police killing a person of color to states enacting full abortion bans in post-*Roe* America. Even prior to the fall of *Roe*, Texas's 2021 abortion ban, SB 8, was notably enforced by citizen policing, compelling people across the country to sue anyone who may have helped someone have an abortion for a prize of *at least* $10,000. The law, reproduced in several other states before *Roe* fell, placed rape and domestic violence victims who have abortions at disproportionate risk, encouraging their vengeful partners or rapists to stalk them and possibly extract a fortune off their pregnancies. It's critical to recognize how state-sanctioned reproductive coercion extends from the same well of misogyny as any other interpersonal acts of gender-based violence, with the same long-term consequences. Per a March, 2023, *Texas Tribune* report, one man took legal action against his ex-wife and three women who helped her obtain an abortion, seeking $1 million in damages shortly after *Roe* fell.[5]

The policing of pregnancy has also frequently yielded criminalization, in some cases leading to the worsening of the sexual assault survivor-to-prison pipeline, where survivors are at greater risk of being criminally charged and incarcerated. Since *Roe* was decided in 1973, Pregnancy Justice (formerly National Advocates for Pregnant Women) has documented nearly 2,000 instances in which people were criminalized for their pregnancy outcomes or self-induced abortions; they were disproportionately people of color and low-income, and some were criminalized for losing their pregnancies after experiencing violence.[6] In the fall of 2022, new reporting revealed a county in Alabama had jailed dozens of women—without trials or convictions—for indefinite amounts of time because they were pregnant or postpartum and alleged to have used substances. As this book will explore, victims of gender-based violence are more likely to be harmed than helped when they turn to law enforcement: A shocking number of women who call the police to report intimate partner violence are deemed the abuser and themselves arrested, while, again, most incarcerated women, who are primarily women of color, experienced sexual violence before entering the system. Legislative loopholes allowed police officers to legally rape detained individuals with impunity until very recent legislative action by Congress. The prison-industrial complex—the inherently racist system through which the government and private sector profit off locking up marginalized people—thrives and profits from rape culture.

State violence plays a significant role in politically disempowering and dehumanizing victims of abuse, working in tandem with interpersonal violence. Yet we rarely encounter broad recognition or criticism of capitalist policies—which force low-income victims of abuse to rely on abusers for health care coverage and housing, and result in sexual assault victims who go to the emergency room being charged thousands out-of-pocket as further punishment for what was done to them[7]—as pieces of a greater framework of state violence, just as we rarely encounter broad recognition of the political and electoral impacts of domestic violence, overall. Domestic violence, in fact, is not just political, but quite literally a feature and consequence of greater systems of state violence: State and interpersonal violence are inseparable from each other, feeding each other in an endless cycle. Capitalist policies allow domestic abuse to thrive. Denied living wages and universal health care, many victims are entrapped in abusive relationships because their abuser provides them health insurance, shelter, or money in general, and the state does not. "One of the reasons why I tended to go to abusive situations was looking for financial stability," Kelly told me, pointing to her history of abusive relationships prior to her marriage to a man in the Air Force who abused her and her kids.

The personal and political are unfailingly intertwined, and for me, writing this book was no exception. The rape allegation that surfaced against Joe Biden in March 2020—at the height of COVID and amid a worldwide surge in domestic violence—shocked me in how much its varying details reminded me of my own traumatic experience with sexual violence as a young woman. I was not particularly shocked by the frustrating predictability of a powerful man being accused of abuse, but the allegation forced me to confront how I'd continued to carry the resulting trauma of my experience for years, in ways I hadn't even been conscious of before gauging my reaction to the news. That, of course, is the thing about trauma, about the impacts of rape and abuse that stay with you long after the perpetrator is gone from your life: Trauma can be invisible, not just to others but even to you, until the emergence of jarring and unexpected triggers.

For years, I repressed my adolescent experience of sexual assault because I didn't see it as "that bad" compared to the graphic rapes that are normalized by mainstream media as the only legitimate forms of sexual violence. Often I tried to convince myself that what had happened was just a misunderstanding, and I let my pain become invisible because it failed to meet societal gatekeeping standards that are informed by rape culture. Sometimes I'll even allow myself to believe I'm fully healed, until I'm periodically confronted by inescapable cultural reminders of how much further I—and society at large—still have to go, to heal from the experience of sexual violence and navigate the day-to-day violence of rape culture as it exists all around us.

Reporting and writing on gender-based violence have never been easy, and shouldn't be for anyone, regardless of lived experience. It's a line of work that has become especially gutting more recently: Amid these reactionary years since the mainstream rise of MeToo, backlash against any movements toward survivor justice, in any capacity, has spiked—a trend very much cemented by specific, landmark moments, starting with the confirmation of accused sexual assailant Brett Kavanaugh to the US Supreme Court in 2018, all but setting the stage for Johnny Depp's defamation lawsuit against ex-wife Amber Heard in 2022.

The trial, examining whether Heard had defamed Depp by accusing him of abuse, was rife with scorched-earth tactics deployed by his legal team, as well as harmful myths about domestic violence (for example, that victims retaliating in any way against abuse or failing to sufficiently behave as "perfect victims" amounts to "mutual abuse") that will inevitably help abusers across the country for years to come—already, a quarter of women who called police to report experiencing intimate partner violence said in a 2015 survey that they were the ones who were arrested or threatened with arrest.[8] The idea that self-defense or other ostensibly "inconsistent" behaviors from a victim constitute "mutual abuse" has quite literally cost victims their lives: In 2021 Gabby Petito was killed by her boyfriend shortly after police officers who confronted the couple declined to help her, perceiving *Petito* as the abuser for fighting with her boyfriend. The following year, women celebrities who supported Depp doled out lengthy social media posts detailing anecdotes of all the times Depp had been wonderful to them or their children, meaning he couldn't possibly be violent with someone else since their individual experience with him must be universal—after all, if a man didn't rape or abuse every woman in his life, surely he didn't rape or abuse *any* woman? Depp and Heard's trial held up a mirror to the era through which we're currently wading, an era in which advocacy for survivors and survivors' right to even publicly speak about their experiences are being met with almost unprecedentedly violent, misogynist retaliation, ranging from costly defamation lawsuits to threats to their lives.

Through all of this, I've realized that recognizing and validating our own pain as survivors, in all its often unexpected waves, can be a vital step toward healing. In the months after the aforementioned allegation against Biden had entered the mainstream, I would find comfort, even joy, when I saw an almost triumphant portrait of Chanel Miller on the cover of a new edition of her memoir published in fall 2020. It was in that portrait that I glimpsed myself in her resiliency, her power as an Asian American woman and survivor: Never had it been more tangible to me how white supremacy and patriarchy had invisibilized my identity as a survivor, how urgently we need voices like Miller's—perhaps even voices like mine—to create change.

It always frustrates me when I or others face pressure to talk about our own experiences, in the often vain hope that doing so will make cruel people and a crueler society care or see us and our experiences as real and human. No one should be pressured or forced to publicly rehash their traumas for validation and respect, or to prove to privileged skeptics that survivors do, in fact, live and exist all around them.

To that end, I've written this book, both an effort to expose the massive social, economic, political, and electoral consequences of domestic abuse that exist in plain sight all around us, even as abusive acts are often private by nature, as well as a call to action. This is a book about democracy, political power, and gender-based violence—how domestic abuse impacts democracy by restricting who can safely and autonomously vote and participate in public life; how the election and appointment of abusers in every tier of our government, across the political spectrum, perpetuate cycles of abuse, and further harm women and survivors through dehumanizing policy outcomes.

This is also a book about the political ideologies that normalize domestic and sexual abuse; the massive, capitalistic inequities that force victims to stay with abusers or lose health care and housing; a carceral system designed to punish rather than help abuse victims, helmed by police officers and law enforcement agents who are often abusers themselves; and the broader electoral system that disproportionately empowers politicians who produce harmful policy outcomes for women and survivors. State-by-state data on domestic abuse, to be explored later in this book, reveals that said system accords disproportionate electoral power to ideologies and policies that harm women and survivors. And while voting can be a powerful tool within democracy, the crises of racist, patriarchal state violence, of a government that systematically disempowers and entraps abuse victims, require an even deeper commitment to activism than voting alone to be addressed. It's on each of us to ensure victims of abuse can get the support they need through mutual aid and community organizing, because electoral and policymaking systems consistently, deliberately exclude and fail them.

I've written this book to shine new light on the politics of abuse, the politics of our identities as survivors, and, most importantly, to inspire change that politically empowers us—because we simply do not have the luxury of holding depoliticized identities. Change necessarily begins with knowledge, with the fundamentally political act of knowing, itself— knowing about the gendered, violent horrors unfolding behind closed doors, and knowing that state violence in its wide-ranging forms creates the conditions that empower these realities.

1

THE INVISIBLE THREAT

Tawni Maisonneuve, founder of the domestic abuse support group the Purple Owl Project in Toledo, Ohio, has survived several abusive relationships and marriages over the course of decades. At one point in her life, Maisonneuve had worked as a manager in her state senator's office and was deeply involved in her community as an activist. But the abuse she endured in her relationships took a toll: Several of her partners blocked her access to political information and coerced her to vote in a certain way, or stopped her from voting at all. The toll of this abuse had lasting impacts: "My divorce was final in 1994, and I didn't even vote after that for the simple fact that I didn't want to run into him at any polls, I just didn't want to deal with any of those dynamics," she told me in 2020.

In her next relationship, Maisonneuve said she "felt if I didn't vote the way he did, or I didn't agree with those political views, it would really be a physical issue" threatening her safety. When she did go to her polling place to vote, she said, her abusive partner would accompany her, tell poll workers, "Oh, she's slow, I gotta walk her through it," and proceed to vote on her behalf.

Stories like Maisonneuve's aren't uncommon—they're part of an alarming trend that's largely invisible to pundits, poll workers, and the country at large.

The first time I thought about domestic abuse and its potential to impact elections, I was reading a 2018 essay by author and cultural critic Rebecca Solnit, in which she reflects on anecdotes shared by campaign organizers and canvassers, about wives answering the door only for their husbands to intervene and send them away. Solnit writes:

> *Husbands answered the door and refused to let the wife speak to canvass-*
> *ers, or talked or shouted over her, or insisted that she was going to vote*
> *Republican even though she was a registered Democrat, or insisted there*
> *were no Democrats in the house because she had never told him she was*
> *one. A friend in Iowa told me, "I asked the woman who answered the door*
> *if she had a plan for voting, and a man appeared, behind her, and said,*
> *quite brusquely, 'I'm a Republican.' Before I could reply, he shut the door*
> *in my face."*
>
> *Another friend reported, "A woman I texted in Michigan told me, 'I am*
> *not allowed' to vote for the candidate." Many canvassers told me those*
> *experiences were common.*[1]

As a frequent canvasser myself since I was a college student, I've experienced this sort of interaction up close, and for years my instinctive reaction was fear and discomfort at being snapped at by an intimidating, older man. But Solnit's analysis stayed with me because, as she points out, what we see at the doorstep of an abusive household is just the surface, just one visible layer that almost inevitably hides far worse behind it. If someone is willing to block their partner's access to political information in front of volunteers at their door, what else could they be doing, behind that door?

Every now and then, I would think about Solnit's essay as I knocked on doors or pondered whether there was more to the story when polling data showed women voting in large numbers for political candidates who had built their entire platforms around denying women, survivors, and preg-nant people bodily autonomy and dignity, through policies criminalizing reproductive care or otherwise harming and punishing sexual violence victims. That said, it can't be overlooked that white women often play an active role in voting and organizing to uphold white supremacy, even sometimes at the cost of their reproductive rights—a steep price to pay for any pregnant-capable person, regardless of wealth or any other privileges they may hold. Research has shown being denied abortion care substantially increases someone's risk of experiencing long-term domestic violence,[2] and certainly their risk of homicide—a leading cause of death for pregnant people—from abusive partners.

Nonetheless, even prior to the 2022 overturning of *Roe v. Wade*, abortion bans like the aforementioned SB 8 in Texas have underscored how white supremacy exists at the heart of abortion bans, singling out abuse victims of color for even deeper harm. SB 8 allowed anyone in the country to sue anyone who may have helped a Texan have an abortion, for at least $10,000 in damages. The ban has rendered domestic violence victims with vengeful exes—and the disproportionately Black, Latinx, and migrant people who are more likely to have abortions in Texas— especially vulnerable to this citizen-policing. Relatedly, a 2022 report from reproductive justice legal advocacy organization If/When/How found the majority of cases in which pregnant people faced criminal charges for self-managed abortion in the past two decades were first reported to law enforcement by doctors and acquaintances, specifically friends and intimate partners.[3]

Citizen-policing historically traces its roots to the period of American history when lynching by white-supremacist citizen militias targeting Black people was more overt; the legacy of this violence has persisted to this day, between the citizen-perpetrated killing of Trayvon Martin, a seventeen-year-old Black man in 2012, and Ahmaud Arbery, killed by a white-supremacist militia in 2020. The architects of Texas's abortion ban, including numerous white women in the state's anti-abortion-majority legislature, were surely aware of this legacy.

Pursuit of the benefits and protections that white supremacy extends to white women is certainly one explanation for why most white women vote Republican[4]—and an important one, too. Still, my casual searches for existing research or data on the matter of why women may vote for or support anti-women politicians, and the potential role domestic violence plays in creating these outcomes, often came up empty, and the topic would eventually slip my mind until the next canvassing shift, or the next round of frustrating exit polls.

And then came the spring of 2020.

By March 2020 the field of contenders in the US presidential election had been narrowed to two wealthy white men both accused of devastating acts of sexual abuse. And, of course, while all that was happening, reported domestic violence cases had skyrocketed as a direct result of the global COVID pandemic. Experts and the public increasingly demanded that voting in the remaining primary and general elections during the pandemic take place at home by mail—and while this will always be an important option, home isn't a safe place to vote for everyone. Domestic violence is an inevitable factor in electoral outcomes that shape who holds state power and consequently shapes policy, yet domestic violence is rarely if ever analyzed in the context of elections, let alone state violence broadly.

STATE VIOLENCE, DOMESTIC VIOLENCE, AND DEMOCRACY

Interpersonal abuse isn't just a byproduct of state violence, which occurs when victims are denied the material resources to protect themselves and leave abusive situations—it also directly feeds state violence: Victims are criminalized and incarcerated for seeking help from law enforcement or practicing self-defense against their abusers. In this way, abusive partners and the state, acting as an abuser, are in frequent collaboration with each other.

By nature, domestic violence isn't visible in public life—that doesn't mean it's apolitical. Conversations about gender and safety from violence often center around mythologized ideals of stranger-danger and violence in urban public landscapes. And these fears, particularly among women, femmes, and queer people, aren't unfounded, given the prevalence of dehumanizing street harassment and attacks. As feminist geographer Leslie Kern writes in her 2020 book *Feminist City*:

> A woman alone is presumed always available to other men. It links back to notions of women as men's property. If a woman out in public isn't clearly marked as property by the presence of another man . . . then she is fair game. Women instinctively know that the quickest way to deter a man's unwanted advances is to tell him you have a boyfriend or husband. Men will respect another man's property rights more readily than they'll respect a woman's simple "no."[5]

But the cultural fixation on public, street-based acts of urban violence over the statistically more prevalent threat of intimate partner and domestic violence in the home is deliberate—a choice to bolster popular support for policing, surveillance, and carceral methodologies to target supposed threats to urban safety along lines of race and class. And just as importantly, to bolster public faith in the capitalistic, heteronormative suburban nuclear family and keep women within the ostensibly safer confines of the home. As Kern writes:

> Domestic violence, sexual assault by acquaintances, incest, child abuse and other "private" yet much more prevalent crimes receive far less attention. From a feminist perspective, this difference in attention serves to direct women's fear outwards, away from the home and family, reinforcing patriarchal institutions like the nuclear family and women's reliance on heterosexual partnership for the appearance of security. In a vicious cycle, this stigmatizes violence experienced within the "safe" space of the home and drives it further out of sight. . . .
>
> Fear restricts women's lives. It limits our use of public spaces, shapes our choices about work and other economic opportunities, and keeps us dependent on men as protectors.[6]

Contrary to the depoliticization of domestic life, there's almost nothing more political than the ability to be safe in one's home, the ability to leave and have a life outside one's home, the ability to engage with society and have a political identity without the threat of violence from one's partner or family members. There's nothing more political than being unable to leave an abusive marriage or family living situation due to financial constraints, or fear of losing housing or health insurance coverage.

Thus, the 2020 elections during the pandemic presented a perfect storm: COVID, which disproportionately ravaged communities of color, exacerbated domestic abuse cases, and upended voting norms to give abusers unprecedented political power over their victims—during a presidential election cycle in which the two main candidates were both alleged sexual predators. Many victims were trapped at home with abusers, cut off from employment, income, or even just an excuse to safely leave the house. At the same time, political events, community events, and even information about voting and elections were largely shifted online to the confines of our homes, where abusers maintained full control of their victims' access to all of this, or the outside world at all. And all of this took place in the shadow of a general election itself tainted by allegations of gendered violence.

There's virtually no way to gauge the prevalence and full breadth of domestic abuse–driven voter suppression and its impacts. Every year, more than 12 million people in the US report experiencing domestic abuse, while 200 million people are registered voters.[7] But because of the inherently private nature of both domestic abuse and voting itself, it's almost impossible to say exactly how many people have had a partner block them from political information or directly control their vote in any other way.

Even in the best-case scenario, if victims can flee their abusive relationship at all, there arises the problem of abusers using voter registration information to stalk and threaten them years later. In many states, victims who escape their abusers can protect themselves and their ability to vote safely and confidentially with options including registering to vote with temporary, fake addresses. Different states have different voter confidentiality laws, and more than half of them offer some protections to victims of stalking and domestic violence, according to the National Coalition against Domestic Violence (NCADV). Unfortunately, most states don't widely advertise these options and resources, leaving many victims without them. The government simultaneously fails victims of abuse by neglecting to provide sufficient resources and protections, as well as neglecting to inform them about those that *are* available to them.

Political coercion and controlling a partner's vote are rarely discussed as forms of domestic abuse, meaning many victims could be subjected to such behaviors without even realizing that what they're experiencing is abuse. For a May 2020 article I wrote for *Dame* magazine, Ruth Glenn, president of the NCADV, told me that in addition to domestic abuse being notoriously underreported, those who do report their experiences might omit cases of their partner controlling their access to political information, or controlling their voting and political behaviors broadly. "That may just be one part of other actions and behaviors they see as more urgent to report," Glenn explained.[8]

After all, victims in abusive relationships and marriages may face a wide range of violent, threatening acts, of which political coercion is just another item on a long, excruciating list. And there are virtually no protections or safe options for recourse offered by the state—in a country that only first recognized marital rape as a crime on the federal level in 1986. As recently as 2019, seventeen states still didn't allow for a spouse to be convicted of raping a partner who was unconscious, drugged, or otherwise incapacitated. In 2010 one study found fewer than half of surveyed police officers said they were likely to believe a woman who said her husband had raped her; of course, other research suggests (at least) 40 percent of police officers are domestic abusers themselves.[9] One of the two officers who pulled over Gabby Petito and her boyfriend in 2021, and perceived Petito as the "primary aggressor," was accused of threatening to kill his then-girlfriend in a lawsuit the following year.

Like voting coercion, reproductive coercion is another oft-erased form of domestic violence that victims may not even recognize as abuse. In 2021 California state Senator Dave Min introduced a first-of-its-kind bill to include acts of reproductive coercion, including tampering with a partner's birth control or forcing them to have or not have an abortion, in the state's civil definition of domestic violence. The bill would also recognize an abuser taking out loans as their partner, entrapping them in debt, and consequently forcing them to stay in an abusive relationship because of their debt, as domestic violence, and the bill would offer survivors legal recourse. Domestic violence experts have said economic sabotage (for example, deliberately tanking a partner's credit score) ranks among the top tactics used in abusive relationships.[10] Sometimes abusers take out massive loans in their victims' name to entrap them in the relationship, or abusers attach their own debt to their victims, also as a means to entrap them. Some important history on this: An early 2000s federal program meant to help those with student debt made economic sabotage even easier for abusers by allowing married couples to consolidate their student loans to pay a lower interest rate. But once their loans were merged, couples were given no avenue to separate them—even if they were divorced, and even in cases of domestic violence. It's why student debt cancelation is a vitally important survivor justice issue.

But outside this legislative effort from Min in 2021, these acts of reproductive and economic coercion aren't readily understood by the public as domestic violence, and victims and survivors are accorded virtually no legal protections as a result. It's also important to note that reproductive and economic coercion are inseparable—being forced to carry an unwanted pregnancy can make someone three times more likely to experience poverty and four times more likely to stay in an abusive relationship.

"We have a societal conception of sexual violence as stranger violence, and it's hard to comprehend when someone who says they love you is also someone who denies your autonomy and sexually violates you," Jane Stoever, a law professor and director of the University of California, Irvine, Domestic Violence Clinic and the university's Initiative to End Family Violence, told me in 2021 for a reported feature I was writing on the cultural and political erasure of reproductive coercion as a form of domestic violence.[11] Stoever has worked closely with domestic violence victims who have experienced reproductive coercion and didn't realize this amounted to abuse.

Shortly after the overturning of *Roe*, one doctor said in an interview with Jezebel that she's previously offered abortion care to several people in abusive relationships who otherwise would have wanted to continue the pregnancy if it felt safe to do so. In July 2022 a Missouri man was sentenced to life in prison for killing his wife, who had been six weeks pregnant. Police revealed that before she went missing, she had searched on her phone: "what to do if your husband is upset you are pregnant." This gutting story is not an outlier: Homicide is, again, a leading cause of death for pregnant people, often perpetrated by abusive partners; the overturning of *Roe* and inevitable rise in forced pregnancies fathered by abusive men exacerbate this crisis.

Abusers often aren't strangers but rather the people with whom we share homes, sometimes even children. Notably, also in the summer of 2022, one Louisiana woman who said she had been impregnated by her rapist as a teenager sixteen years earlier—when she was sixteen and he was thirty—lost custody of her child to her rapist. A judge had granted full custody of Crysta Abelseth's teen daughter to John Barnes, the man Abelseth identified as her rapist, and even required her to pay Barnes child support—all because Barnes alleged that Abelseth had given her teenage daughter a cell phone.

Abelseth recounted facing stunning mistreatment from the legal system for years, as well as routine threats from Barnes, who sought to intimidate her by citing his "connections in the justice system." According to Abelseth, after filing criminal charges against Barnes in 2015 when she learned about an exception to the statute of limitations for child sex crimes, nothing happened in the subsequent seven years: "It was never assigned to a detective, and nothing was ever investigated," she told a local news outlet, which reported that court records about Barnes, Abelseth, and her charges against him were "mysteriously under seal." Police inaction and the local judge's decision to give Barnes custody were all the more suspect given Barnes's relationship with local law enforcement.

Abelseth's story wasn't an isolated incident. That same year, I interviewed one woman whose rapist sued for custody of the child she had conceived in 2011, and he was granted joint custody. Darcy Benoit has been forced to co-parent in some capacity with her rapist to this day. After local police initially refused to even accept a report from her in 2011 and 2012, she says police interrogated her for almost two full days and questioned her rapist for thirty minutes. Benoit told me an officer looked her in the eye and said, "'I believe you *think* you were raped.'"

While Crysta Abelseth eventually won custody of her daughter again, Darcy Benoit has exhausted every legal option available to her for the last decade, and remains entrapped in an ongoing custody war with the man who raped her. She's still fighting an abuser who wielded state processes and institutions to punish and control her over the course of a decade. Notably, a 2017 study found that when mothers alleged domestic violence in custody cases, fathers won custody 73 percent of the time, and when mothers alleged child abuse, fathers won 69 percent of the time, no matter how much evidence corroborated it.[12]

Where else is she to turn for help?

Even the Violence Against Women Act, the famous federal law that presents itself as a resource to victims, is more likely to criminalize or harm victims based on their race, class, immigration status, or other facets of their identity, if they seek help by reporting to law enforcement. In 2022 the San Francisco Police Department was exposed for quite literally using a victim's rape kit—evidence of her rape collected from her body—to charge her with another crime years later. It wasn't until that same year, 2022, that Congress closed a loophole that had long enabled police officers to sexually abuse people in their custody and defend themselves from charges by simply claiming the encounter was consensual. Between 2006 and 2016, at least 26 of 158 law enforcement officers who had been charged with "sexual assault and unlawful sexual contact" with people they had detained had invoked the "consent defense" and were acquitted, Buzzfeed News found.[13]

Especially for abuse victims with children, there is a persistent history of mothers being criminalized for purportedly putting their children at risk of violence from their abuser. One Oklahoma woman was convicted under the state's "failure to protect" law requiring parents to shield their children from physical harm from other adults; she was imprisoned because her boyfriend killed her infant child while she was at work. Experts have said failure to protect laws are disproportionately weaponized against mothers rather than fathers because of sexist cultural expectations about parenting responsibilities. As a result, mothers with abusive partners are frequently subject to criminalization.

The impact of intimate partner abuse on not just elections but democracy broadly is potentially threefold, as it shapes who can exercise political autonomy of any kind, from voting to community organizing. It shapes who can hold elected office or any leadership positions. And consequently, it shapes policymaking and agenda setting within movements, leading to legislation that often further empowers abusers over their victims, and advocacy movements that aren't equipped to respond.

Domestic abuse especially impacts electoral outcomes when candidates are alleged sexual abusers, and all too often rely on tired rape culture tropes and rape apologism to defend themselves. When people who are sympathetic to sexual abusers, or are abusers themselves, are elected to positions of power, they can use that power to enact policies that further perpetuate cycles of abuse. They can harm and deny political agency to victims and survivors—from abortion bans that enforce nonconsensual pregnancy; to neoliberal health and economic policies that have proven to force victims to stay in long-term abusive relationships for survival; to the agenda of the carceral capitalist police state, in which 90 percent of incarcerated women are survivors,[14] 60 percent of prison sexual assaults are perpetrated by guards,[15] 40 percent of cops are (known) domestic abusers, and there are greater profit incentives for the state to police and imprison victims of abuse than offer them resources and support. Eighty percent of incarcerated women are mothers and sole caretakers of children.[16]

Legislation is determined by electoral outcomes; electoral outcomes are determined by who can and can't vote. And a considerable amount of the electorate—one in three women and one in four men—consists of victims of domestic abuse, who may not be able to vote safely, independently, or even at all.

THREATS TO DEMOCRACY BEGIN IN THE HOME

In the early days of March 2020, I was among millions of people who made the urgent trek home to shelter in place with their families at the start of the "novel coronavirus" pandemic. Social media platforms were simultaneously rife with harrowing images of both overcrowded airports, teeming with people rushing home from travels, and scenes of hauntingly empty airports, drained of countless people who had canceled trips and become rightfully wary of travel. The photos made it clear how visibly and inescapably the pandemic had changed day-to-day life as we'd once known it. And of course, as time wore on, we would come to learn the many less visible, not-so-photographable ways it had more intimately altered our lives, too.

After spending the first months of the year in Washington, DC, where I'd briefly moved for a new job, I went to shelter in place with my family in my childhood home in the Bay Area. It was supposed to be a temporary trip—I still had big plans to return to DC, adopt a dog, plan my first trip to Europe for the summer, and more. But the gravity of the new world we live in dawned on me the moment I landed, as the first stay-at-home orders were rolled out, and the pandemic dominated nearly all cable news segments that my retired parents watched 24/7. Like many young people with a certain amount of privilege, home, with my parents and siblings, was a safe place for me—the rules of this new normal at the onset of the pandemic were inconvenient and isolating, but not life-threatening. For me, staying home at the height of COVID meant teleconferencing for work, trying new recipes, scheduling regular FaceTime calls with friends and family. Home was a non-oppressive, seemingly non-political space.

But home—during the pandemic more than ever—*is* political. Safety and lack of safety are inherently political. The pandemic, which had claimed well over 1,000,000 American lives by mid-2022, had no upsides or surprising benefits—but it did bring many unsettling revelations. It shined light on the countless systemic inequities that deny millions of Americans health care and housing along lines of class and race, putting many low-income people and people of color at greater risk of contracting and dying from the virus.

Enforcement of stay-at-home orders often resulted in racist policing that targeted and criminalized Black communities and communities of color for "loitering" if they convened in public spaces or were experiencing homelessness. Per Kern's research in *Feminist City*, new, luxury condominiums, which are significant purveyors of gentrification, capitalize on urban racism to advertise particularly to young adult women by emphasizing their extensive security measures that safekeep women from external, street-based violence. But Kern notes this dynamic "wasn't going to make life any safer for the women who would be displaced by this form of gentrification," and it served to make "safety a private commodity in the city . . . less and less available to those who lack the economic means to secure themselves."[17] In contrast, funding for affordable housing, or social housing, is increasingly and routinely being gutted, in many cases robbing domestic violence victims of what could be their only means for safety and independence from abusers. Further, the capitalist housing market is fundamentally unconducive to multifamily or cooperative housing setups that can provide safety and supports like child care and community, and alleviate the gendered norms and divisions of labor that standardize the oppressions of women and non-cis, straight men in single-family homes. Options for communities, multigenerational households, and non-single families to live together, in general, are dwindling in a market saturated with increasingly expensive single-family homes, as well as ever-increasing incentives for ambitious Airbnb hosts to purchase homes solely to rent out to wealthy travelers.

Throughout 2020 we faced near-constant reminders of the reality that social inequities allow some of us but not others to be safe in our homes. Acts of police violence, often targeting non-white neighborhoods and public spaces, surged that year as protesters mobilized across the country following the police killings of George Floyd and Breonna Taylor. Yet the home itself has never been a safe space by default for groups including LGBTQ youth who may face intolerant families; people with disabilities who are especially vulnerable to exploitation and abuse; women and girls of color who are more likely to experience sexual and domestic violence; and Black and brown families who are systematically targeted by police, or, like Taylor, killed in their own beds by law enforcement. Stay-at-home guidelines and rhetoric insisted home was the safest place, as the deadly global pandemic spread far and wide. This was true for some of us—but it also erased the millions of domestic violence victims for whom home is a place of danger and disruption rather than safety.

At the onset of the pandemic in March and April 2020, law enforcement agencies across the United States reported domestic violence cases almost immediately rose by nearly 33 percent.[18] This rate paralleled similar increases in countries around the world, per data shared by the United Nations in March that year. These numbers foreshadow a February 2023 report from the CDC collected during the thick of COVID stay-at-home orders in 2021, which revealed a 27 percent increase in sexual assaults targeting teen girls.[19] And all of this was consistent with research that's shown that incidents of domestic violence increase after natural disasters, as perpetrators often have extended access to their families, support services for victims are stretched thin, and home life can become increasingly tense and stressful for families. Additionally, further research has linked men's experiences with underemployment and economic hardship with an increased likelihood of practicing abusive behaviors.[20] My initial discovery of this study left a bitter taste in my mouth—many men who experience economic marginalization do not become abusive, and certainly, the many women and especially women of color who experience economic marginalization often don't become abusive toward their partners. But the study overall reminds of the institutionalized violence committed by capitalist governments through dehumanizing neoliberal policies, like the gutting of the social safety net, and for-profit health care and housing markets, as well as the grim reality that violence does, in fact, produce violence. In many ways, interpersonal violence is foremost an extension of institutionalized state violence. It's often a result of being left behind, overburdened, or persecuted by a state that's more likely to punish the poor than offer relief. Those who are offered no other options, or pushed to the brink by poverty and marginalization, may be more likely to harm and endanger themselves and others.

As if a public health crisis and its massive economic fallout didn't make matters urgent enough, the high-stakes 2020 presidential campaign pushed forward almost without skipping a beat—even as we all should have slowed down to consider public health concerns. But while numerous state elections for the contentious Democratic presidential primary were postponed, others attempted to shift voting exclusively to vote-by-mail.

In Wisconsin, state Supreme Court justices, who debated cases remotely for safety purposes, voted to prohibit a switch to vote-by-mail for the primary, which forced hundreds of thousands of voters to put their health and safety at risk to either vote in person or not vote at all. It was, of course, no accident: High voter turnout has always favored progressive outcomes. Later, ahead of the general election that year, the US Supreme Court—stacked with three right-wing justices appointed by the former president—ruled that mail-in ballots not received by election night could be dismissed altogether.

Voter suppression is often—and importantly—understood as a problem of structural racism, enacted through racialized gerrymandering and voter ID and registration laws that target Black, Latinx, and immigrant communities. And it comes in the form of not only discriminatory policies and voting requirements but also inaccessible voting hours on weekdays and poorly run polling places, which ensure that hourly workers who are disproportionately low-income people of color are unable to vote if they can't miss work. It certainly wasn't an accident that following Donald Trump's decisive electoral loss in November, largely due to Joe Biden narrowly flipping Wisconsin, Michigan, Pennsylvania, and Georgia, the lame-duck president railed against "illegal" votes cast in Milwaukee, Wisconsin; Detroit, Michigan; Philadelphia and Pittsburgh, Pennsylvania; and Atlanta, Georgia. These cities allowed Biden to win their respective states, owing to higher proportions of more progressive Black voters and voters of color, whose votes Trump and Republican operatives implicitly dismissed as "illegal."

But voter suppression is also a gender-based violence issue. After the disastrous Wisconsin primary election that had sparked an outbreak of COVID cases,[21] politicians—in some cases across party lines—and national health agencies alike rightfully demanded universal vote-by-mail options for the remaining primary elections, as well as the presidential election in November. At the time, vote-by-mail was undoubtedly the safest option during a public health crisis as urgent and unprecedented as the one we faced. But the reality remained that for much of the electorate, home isn't conducive to safely voting and exercising political autonomy. Vote-by-mail has long been a prevalent voting method, meaning countless abusers may have stolen ballots or other voting-related materials sent in the mail. Abusers have always had the ability to prohibit their partners from attending local political events and rallies or leaving the house to vote; I've talked to survivors of domestic violence who have experienced all of this.

Ruth Glenn of the NCADV told me what she understands as the underlying motive of these extensive, arduous efforts to deny political agency. "In our democracy, if you can vote, it's one of the ultimate forms of power. Stripping that away from someone is taking away their power," she said. "It's what abusers have always done." Reliance on the internet for electoral processes has vastly increased across the board, all the more so at the height of COVID, as campaigns could no longer hold in-person rallies and town halls or knock on doors amid stay-at-home and social distancing policies. As a result, many abusers suddenly had almost total control over victims' access to information about candidates and elections.

Spending more time at home, abusers had exponentially greater ability to intercept victims' mail—vote-by-mail ballots, political mailers, voter registration forms, and notices on upcoming elections—and overall greater ability to supervise and coerce victims.

ENTRAPPED BY THE PRIVATIZED, CARCERAL HEALTH SYSTEM

The pandemic disproportionately harmed communities of color, who are already marginalized by the health system—and particularly domestic violence victims within these communities. People who are struggling financially or lack their own health insurance or secure housing are more likely to be entrapped in abusive relationships, and are more likely to be women of color as a result of systemic racism and sexism. Among those who lack health insurance, uninsured sexual assault survivors can be especially cruelly punished by our privatized medical system: A 2022 study found that out of about 112,000 sexual assault survivors who sought emergency care after their assaults, 17,000 faced bills averaging nearly $4,000.[22] The study of national data from almost 36 million visits to the emergency room in 2019 found costs for sexual assault-related visits averaged $3,551 for all victims, while pregnant victims faced even higher average charges: $4,553. Medicaid was the expected payer of 36 percent of visits, but 16 percent of patients were expected to pay out-of-pocket, and the average cost for these self-paying victims rose to $3,673. The majority of the victims who sought emergency care after an assault were young—women between eighteen and forty-four, thus more likely to be low-income and uninsured.[23] The study's findings are also a reminder of the extensive financial ramifications that follow sexual assault, which include being forced out of jobs, forced to drop out of school, forced to move homes, and possibly facing costly defamation lawsuits—on top of the exorbitantly high medical bills. A separate study found that rape costs victims more than any other crime, with total estimated costs reaching $127 billion per year.[24] Years after experiencing abuse, women have health care costs that are 19 percent higher than costs for women who haven't been abused.[25]

In the first month of the pandemic alone, 60 percent of those who reported unemployment were women of color. By May 2020, 40 million Americans had reported unemployment and an estimated 27 million lost health insurance. The economic fallout of the pandemic likely forced many victims to remain dependent on their abusers, as millions lost jobs, health care, and paid leave and were left without options. Resources for survivors were stretched impossibly thin, while family members and friends whom victims might otherwise have turned to lost their own jobs, savings, or even their homes, too.

Two years into the pandemic, the overturning of *Roe* and banning of abortion in states across the country cemented abuse victims' disenfranchisement. When pregnant people are unable to get abortion care for any reason, ranging from legality to economic barriers and lack of insurance, they're put at greater risk of being forced to stay with or even being killed by abusers.

Even prior to the overturning of *Roe*, for decades, medically unnecessary and purely political restrictions on abortion and reproductive care surged—including requirements for clinics to have hospital admitting privileges (formal agreements between clinics and nearby, sometimes Catholic, anti-abortion hospitals to provide certain services)—leading to massive shutdowns of abortion clinics, and 90 percent of all US counties being left without a provider. These political attacks have immeasurably violent, even fatal consequences when pregnant people, and especially poor people of color, are unable to get the care they need. The US has the highest maternal death rate among wealthy nations,[26] with even higher death rates in states with more restrictions on abortion access. According to the Centers for Disease Control and Prevention (CDC), Black pregnant people are three to four times more likely than their white counterparts to die from pregnancy or birth-related causes.[27]

States like Texas have aimed to make this crisis even deadlier: In response to the Biden administration's guidance reminding doctors of their obligation to provide abortion care in emergency medical situations after the fall of *Roe*, Texas successfully sued the administration, seeking a national injunction for the distinctly "pro-life" right to let pregnant people die rather than have an abortion—a possible death sentence for those who experience complications. The legal complaint claimed the Emergency Medical Treatment and Active Labor Act (EMTALA), which requires doctors to provide stabilizing, emergency care to people amid pregnancy-related complications, doesn't guarantee a right to abortion, because "abortion does not preserve the life or health of an unborn child." In other words, per Texas's interpretation, "people" aren't already-born, living pregnant people, with loved ones, hopes, and dreams—"people" are fetuses.

The lawsuit, which also formally recognized the act of providing abortion care as a crime, is a reminder that the end of *Roe* means people will die, not because self-managed abortion is unsafe, but because doctors are afraid to provide life-saving care, or don't know when they can legally intervene to save someone. Pregnant-capable people will die when pharmacists won't fill prescriptions for certain life-saving medications that are deemed "abortifacients," known to increase risk of miscarriage. They'll die when they become pregnant, can't get abortion care, and their abusive partners who don't want to have kids take dire action.

COVID and its economic fallout shuttered low-income victims' access to health coverage. Two years later, the fall of *Roe* opened the door for the state itself to become the ultimate abuser, for the carceral system to infect the health system, for the most marginalized victims and pregnant people to pay the price.

CRIMINALIZING PREGNANT PEOPLE AND SURVIVORS

There are few obvious solutions to a crisis like endemic domestic abuse that remains almost entirely invisible to the public eye. We can support abuse victims and their ability to safely and autonomously vote by donating to shelters and mutual aid networks that provide services and support to victims. Political campaigns and local elected officials can invest time and resources in outreach to shelters for domestic abuse victims, people experiencing homelessness, and all displaced and unhoused people, to ensure they have access to information about elections and the means to vote. Expansive, community-based networks of mutual aid already exist, and have always existed, all around us. Whether or not you've heard of them, they need you.

And, of course, those of us with the means to do so must organize, vote, and apply pressure to our representatives—particularly on the state and local levels that carry the greatest impact on our day-to-day lives—to redistribute wealth and politically empower victims of abuse. The onus is on us to fight for the rights, freedoms, and safety of those who have been denied the power to fight for themselves—denied by abusive partners, and by a government that has neglected to provide them with basic resources and protections. Until such time as elections and electoral politics in general become a safer space for survivors, and a more effective means to bring forth survivor-centric policy change, we should particularly aim our efforts toward mutual aid and collective care to fill the gaps left by decades of patriarchal, neoliberal economic failures.

The fact remains that the most effective long-term solutions to protecting and empowering victims of abuse are policy changes that would grant victims reliable access to health care, housing, livable income, paid sick leave, child care, and safety from criminalization. Yet bureaucratic impediments on the federal level, lack of leadership from Democrats as a serious "opposition party" against Republicans, and general inaction have stalled meaningful, nationwide, progressive economic legislation for decades. As a result, too many victims are forced to stay in dangerous, traumatizing relationships solely for economic reasons, in a country where poverty can be a death sentence, and those who experience poverty are disproportionately policed for "survival crimes"—what we call being punished by the state for its own failure to invest in community resources, and its reliance on commodifying and profiting off incarcerating the most vulnerable.

Despite how frequently cases of rape and domestic abuse are invoked to justify policing and prisons, women who are victims of abuse face more severe punishment for "enabling" child abuse, pregnancy loss, or even surviving abuse, broadly, than their abusers do. The many documented cases of this include Marshae Jones, a Black woman in Alabama who was jailed for fetal homicide in 2019 after miscarrying from being shot in the stomach. Sex workers who report being victimized are disbelieved and often criminalized by police officers themselves (a 2007 study found 44 percent of police officers said they were unlikely to believe a report of rape from a sex worker[28]), while the rapes and sexual violence cases of Black and Indigenous women and girls are chronically ignored by police departments and media. Victims of abuse with the least resources and social capital are more likely to face punishment than anything else when they seek help from authorities, rendering it more likely they would seek criminalized means to protect or provide for themselves.

In too many documented cases that disproportionately implicate people of color, pregnant people are criminally charged for ostensibly endangering fetuses—for example, due to substance use struggles—and even prior to the overturning of *Roe*, for self-managed abortions. Many pregnant people have faced charges or incarceration for miscarriage or stillbirth, and even for harms inflicted on them while they were pregnant, like Marshae Jones.

This is in part because about forty states have feticide laws that were written with the intention of protecting pregnant people from domestic violence. It's an important crisis to address, given how high homicide rates targeting pregnant people are. Yet all too often, feticide laws are co-opted and misused by anti-abortion activists and prosecutors to criminally charge pregnant people who lose their pregnancies. Misuse of fetal homicide laws has contributed to the nearly 1,300 criminal charges for pregnancy loss doled out between 2006 and 2020 alone—a number that's tripled from 1973 to 2005, according to research from Pregnancy Justice. Let's not forget that it's police officers who are the primary enforcers of abortion bans, a role they've enthusiastically stepped into: In February 2022 the city of Louisville paid a police officer $75,000 in settlement fees almost a year after the officer was suspended for protesting outside a local abortion clinic while armed and in uniform. After being suspended with pay for almost half a year in 2021, the officer sued the city for supposedly violating his constitutional rights while off-duty and discriminating against him for his "pro-life" views. The incident is part of a long history of police officers either ignoring or enabling violent anti-abortion protesters at clinics, and apparently even joining protesters themselves.

Fetal homicide laws are just one example of legislation that accords unborn fetuses with legal personhood rights, resulting in extensive legal risks for pregnant people, and particularly those who experience abuse. Dana Sussman, deputy executive director of Pregnancy Justice, told me in 2022 that there's "simply no way to grant fetuses 'personhood rights' without subjugating the rights of pregnant people by creating a false tension between the rights of the fetus and the rights of a pregnant person." When a pregnant person's "rights are secondary to the fetus, or at odds with the fetus, that lends to an environment in which violence—whether it's state violence like imprisonment, or interpersonal violence—can be committed against pregnant people with far less accountability."[29]

Per Pregnancy Justice's research, there have been numerous legal cases of a pregnant person being prohibited from traveling out of state due to their partner's custody claims over their fetus—some cases went so far as to regard pregnant people's interstate travel as "kidnapping." The child welfare system, which systematically singles out and persecutes Black families and families of color, has "found people to be 'neglectful' or 'abusive' parents before there's even an actual baby," Sussman said, because of their actions during pregnancy.

Certain groups are disproportionately punished and criminalized for the violence they experience. Migrant women and girls from Latin America—60 to 80 percent of whom experience rape and sexual assault in the process of crossing the border[30]—often face criminalization and detention upon entering the US. Many are fleeing violence and abuse in their home countries. Upon starting new lives in the US, undocumented women who experience rape or sexual and domestic violence are often unable to report their experiences or seek safety, resources, and improved working conditions out of fear of deportation, criminalization, or family separation; abuse is normalized as an indelible part of their job, a condition of their living here. In several documented cases, minors impregnated by sexual violence and held at migrant detention centers have been denied abortion care.[31]

As a consequence of the militarization of the US-Mexico border, rape is so prevalent that one border patrol official spoke to the Associated Press in 2018 about the increasingly common phenomenon of migrant girls as young as twelve being coercively put on birth control pills, "because they know getting violated is part of the journey."[32] That same year, the Intercept reported that of the 1,224 sexual abuse complaints filed at detainment centers between 2010 and 2017, only 43 led to investigations.[33] According to a report by the Department of Justice in 2019, in four years between 2014 and 2018, the federal government received more than 4,500 complaints about sexual abuse of immigrant children held at government-funded detention facilities. These complaints notably saw a pronounced increase in 2018 under the Trump administration's migrant family separation policy, which deliberately separated detained migrant children from their families. And of these 4,556 cases, just 1,303 "deemed the most serious" were referred to the Justice Department, the *New York Times* reported.[34]

Like sexual violence at the border and in detention centers, sexual violence in the streets that targets sex workers is often performed with impunity. According to research by the Urban Justice Center, a US-based organization that offers legal advocacy to sex workers and survivors of human trafficking, 80 percent of street-based sex workers who were interviewed reported being threatened with violence while working, and when asked about reporting violence to police, they said that police "did not take their complaints seriously and often told them that they should expect violence."[35] One sex worker told the organization, "After a girl was gang raped, [police] said 'Forget it, she works in the street.'" Reporting to law enforcement isn't a safe option for sex workers, so long as sex work remains criminalized. Additionally, 30 percent of sex workers interviewed said they had been threatened with violence by police officers, and 27 percent reported experiencing violence by police, including beatings and rape. Eighty-seven percent of sex workers interviewed were homeless or in unstable housing, reflecting the importance of accessible housing and living resources for all as requisite to victims' safety.

Women of color and other migrant and marginalized women, queer, and trans folks learn early on from experience that policing, prisons, and the carceral system at large don't solve violence but rather perpetuate it; they know from experience that the state doesn't protect them but rather targets and criminalizes them and their families. They know that reporting sexual and domestic abuse all too often implicates and criminalizes them, more so than their abusers. One previously mentioned study found 24 percent of surveyed women who reported sexual assault and intimate partner violence were either arrested or threatened with arrest after calling the police to seek help. They know police may charge them if they respond to violence with self-defense, or charge them with child neglect if it's found that they "failed" to shield their children from violence from their abusers.

Victims who are ultimately incarcerated are then exposed to the prevalence of prison rape from guards. In November 2022 New York state enacted a law to expand the statute of limitations for sexual assault victims, including those assaulted in public facilities—within days, one law firm filed individual lawsuits for 750 different, formerly incarcerated women.[36] If they're pregnant, they may be incarcerated in one of the thirteen remaining states (as of 2022) that permit the shackling of incarcerated pregnant people, called "a barbaric practice that needlessly inflicts excruciating pain and humiliation" by the American Medical Association. Perhaps they're carrying an unwanted pregnancy and are incarcerated in one of the 67 percent of prisons—often in rural areas, far from abortion clinics—that require the pregnant person to pay for both the abortion and all associated costs, including not just gas and transportation fees but "officer time" for those who escort them.[37] Worse, they may be incarcerated in a state that's totally banned abortion post-*Roe*. In 2023, at least three pregnant women incarcerated at an Arizona-based prison said the prison induced their labor early against their will, per *Arizona Republic*.[38]

As Judith Levine and Erica R. Meiners write in their 2020 book *The Feminist and the Sex Offender*, "Interpersonal violence and the violence inflicted by the state are not opposing actors in a moral or political war. Rather, the abuser or rapist and the criminal legal system are a team, the former the bad cop, the latter the good."[39]

Invoking (needlessly) partisan ideals in any dialogue about domestic abuse, survivor justice, and elections feels strange, even inappropriate, considering abusive behaviors exist across the political spectrum and know no single political ideology. Still, in Rebecca Solnit's essay that I reference at the beginning of this chapter, she writes that she "did not find stories of the reverse phenomenon—wives dominating their husbands, or husbands pushing their wives to vote for the Democratic candidate." Solnit adds, "Of course I talked to people canvassing for Democrats, and domestic violence takes place across the political spectrum, but the bullying seemed to be mostly either to oblige the wife to lean to the right or to not participate at all."[40] She questions why, in nearly all the anecdotes she hears, husbands are turning away canvassers from Democratic and progressive campaigns, and whether this is strategic, to disproportionately benefit conservative political candidates whose policy platforms hurt women and survivors. Solnit's analysis makes a compelling case for the influence of gender power dynamics in who is more often on the receiving end of political coercion.

When some of the most vocal, virulently anti-women politicians—from President Donald Trump to former Mississippi state Rep. Douglas McLeod, who punched his wife in the face for not taking off her clothes quickly enough before a sexual encounter, to the famed alleged child sexual abuser Alabama US Senate candidate Roy Moore—have been accused of grotesque acts of sexual violence, it's tempting to make assumptions. Conservative ideologies are inherently rooted in controlling and enacting violence on feminized bodies, and a scan of rates of reported domestic abuse cases reveals states with anti-women and anti-victim policy landscapes often have higher rates of documented abuse.

That said, it can't be stated enough how limited the research on this subject matter is, and that abusive behaviors transcend party affiliation and always will. Many abusers perform as vocal progressive advocates and feminist allies, for a variety of reasons—to evade suspicion, to expand their power over victims. Many abusers and rapists identify as pro-choice—at least until it comes to the individuals they choose to hurt. Ultimately, because of the very limited data on intimate partner violence and its impacts on voting, there may be a compelling statistic or particularly attention-grabbing case of an anti-abortion politician accused of abuse, here and there, but there's no data to definitively confirm that domestic abuse–driven voter suppression necessarily hurts or benefits one political party more than the other.

That said, there are plenty of anecdotes that suggest conservative, anti-women politics may benefit from prevalent domestic abuse and the voter suppression driven by it. Several politicians with records of domestic and sexual violence—only a fraction of whom have been exposed to the public—have records of introducing or supporting bills that would ban and criminalize abortion care, thus denying survivors a health procedure that's essential to their liberation from abusive relationships, and even threatening to jail them.

Over the last couple of decades, several states have floated and nearly passed laws requiring a pregnant person to obtain their partner's consent to access abortion care. And in more than half of all states, laws require parental involvement for minors seeking abortion care, which can be devastating for young people—and especially LGBTQ youth—who have abusive parents or guardians. Elected officials also hurt survivors by slashing funding for victim resources, threatening access to health care and affordable housing, or, on the local and state levels, prosecuting and incarcerating women who are disproportionately victims and survivors of color for trying to survive.

But politicians with records and allegations of sexual violence are performatively progressive, self-identified pro-choice leaders, too. The 2020 presidential election, again, came down to Joe Biden, a Democrat who identified as pro-choice, and Donald Trump, a Republican anti-abortion zealot. Both men were accused of sexual abuse. In addition to the sexual assault allegation, Biden helped expose Anita Hill—a Black woman who accused then-Supreme Court Justice nominee Clarence Thomas of sexual harassment in the 1990s, and whose experiences came to define modern understandings of sexual harassment—to ruthless, sexist political attacks before the Senate in 1992. His authorship of the 1994 crime bill and its crackdown on drug use and emphasis on incarceration and policing also harmed survivors—who, again, comprise 90 percent of incarcerated women—and women and victims of color. Trump has been accused of sexual misconduct and rape by dozens of women over the course of decades, and spent his presidency enacting campus sexual assault policies that supported rapists; defending, sympathizing with, and appointing known abusers to positions of power; and defunding and advocating for the criminalization of reproductive health care.

More examples of pro-abortion-rights and anti-abortion politicians accused of sexual misconduct abound on both sides, up and down the political spectrum—and again, these are just what we, the public, know of. In a country where one in four women and girls experience sexual abuse, and most sexual assaults are unreported, what we know likely just scratches the surface.

There's almost no better example of politicians with abusive records on both sides of the aisle than the 2020 election, up and down the ballot.

On the same day that Biden was elected president, Kansas voters of the state's 37th state House district elected nineteen-year-old Aaron Coleman, a self-identified Democratic-socialist who shared a twelve-year-old girl's nude photos when he was fourteen, pressured a girl to commit suicide, and as recently as 2019, allegedly choked and assaulted his ex-girlfriend. On the right, voters in North Carolina's 11th Congressional district elected the twenty-five-year-old neo-Nazi Madison Cawthorn, also accused of sexual assault. Both Coleman and Cawthorn, elected in the same cycle as some of the youngest people to hold elected office, reflect how sexual violence and misogyny aren't bound or limited to a single political party. Their public politics and private behaviors reflect how violent right-wing misogyny and progressive, redistributive stances can both be attached to perpetrators of violence and abuse.

Our political and electoral systems accord survivors few protections from abusers and offer even fewer candidates whose policies afford survivors real, material supports, or candidates who aren't abusers themselves. Our economic system neglects to give survivors enough resources to liberate themselves from abusers. Our social norms erase, minimize, even mock survivors' pain and experiences, and justify and maintain vast spaces for abusers.

These realities are further compounded by our post-MeToo cultural era, in which scorn is surging for survivor justice movements and advocacy, perceived as threats to male hegemony. This new and growing cultural hostility to abuse survivors is inseparable from our electoral system—as domestic violence survivor Tawni Maisonneuve framed it to me, controlling a partner's vote is perhaps the ultimate act of dominance in an ostensibly democratic country, because if someone "can control the way you vote in your community," they know they "really have control of you at home."

2

CARCERAL FEMINISM AND THE VIOLENCE AGAINST WOMEN ACT

In 2018 an eighteen-year-old woman in New York testified that two officers raped her in their police van after arresting her. The officers claimed she had consented, and prosecutors subsequently dropped the sexual assault charges. The men were sentenced to just five years of probation after pleading guilty to separate charges unrelated to the rape.

There are laws in thirty-five states that allow police officers to claim that a person in custody consented to sex with them, a loophole that wasn't closed until Congress passed the appropriately named Closing the Law Enforcement Consent Loophole Act in 2022. But before that, as previously noted, between 2006 and 2016 at least 26 of 158 police officers who had been charged with unlawful sexual contact with people they had detained were able to successfully invoke the "consent defense" to have their charges dropped or be acquitted.

Thanks in large part to the Violence Against Women Act—supposedly the definitive federal law to address sexual and domestic violence, passed in 1994—cops have been tasked and culturally entrusted with the role of protecting women and abuse victims. The damage of this to victims, particularly poor, non-white, queer, or non-citizen victims, is immeasurable. In January 2021 a Louisiana woman working with local police entered a drug house wearing a hidden microphone and camera to help police gather information about the dealer. Once inside, the Associated Press reported that the woman's police handlers essentially abandoned her, allowing the dealer to rape her twice as he threatened to put her "in the hospital."[1] Police were able to use the intel gathered by the woman to arrest the drug dealer on charges of second-degree rape, false imprisonment, and distribution of meth. But weeks after the sting, they arrested the woman who had been their informant and charged her with possession of drug paraphernalia—after she had been raped while successfully helping them build a case against a drug dealer. In defense of the incident, an officer who helped lead the operation told the AP: "We've always done it this way. She was an addict and we just used her as an informant like we've done a million times before." One local official who saw footage of the assaults described it as "one of the worst depictions of sexual abuse I have ever seen."

The operation itself is a jarring display of incompetence that resulted in a woman being raped, while officers' flippant language shrugs the woman off as "an addict," her trauma a minor mistake they can "learn from" to "do better next time." Her subsequent arrest is a stark reminder, too, that criminalized and incarcerated people are often survivors of sexual assault, further harmed by law enforcement agencies that—as in this Louisiana woman's case—do nothing to protect them.

If galling stories like this surprise you or challenge any of your preconceived notions about law enforcement, then pro-cop propaganda, or copaganda, might just be to blame. It exists all around us, with tremendous implications for how the public understands (or rather, misunderstands) gender-based violence and all violence. Copaganda starts early—think children's shows like *Paw Patrol*. Growing up on dramas like *Law and Order: SVU* and *Castle*, even iconic comedies like *Brooklyn Nine-Nine*, I'm one of many Americans who was socialized to see law enforcement and the court system as being decisively, nobly on our side, the be-all and end-all for justice and community safety. You probably wouldn't guess from watching *SVU* that a significant amount of cops are domestic abusers and perpetrators of sexual violence themselves, and many are openly hostile to victims: As noted earlier, a 2010 study found fewer than half of surveyed police officers said they were likely to believe a woman who said her husband had raped her, despite how marital rape is illegal in all fifty states.

Even more tellingly, a 2014 study found most surveyed officers believed most rape reports are false, and 80 percent believed false rape reports were more common than the estimated 2 to 8 percent statistic put forth by most researchers—which is already an inflated rate, given that police departments have often classified rapes that don't involve weapons or were perpetrated by romantic partners as "false reports."[2] When false reports do happen, they predominantly involve male district attorneys or police officers pressuring victims to identify a certain man as their rapist or attacker in order to close a case and inflate their safety records. And calling police for help with a situation involving intimate partner violence often leads to victims being arrested or threatened with arrest.

This issue—of abuse victims being seen as perpetrators by authorities who lack proper training to intervene in abusive situations—is inevitably worsened by myths about "mutual abuse," which cast victims who defend themselves or retaliate against abusers as abusers, themselves. Ruth Glenn of NCADV has said mutual abuse, or equating victims' physical or emotional reactions to abuse with abuse, amounts to victim-blaming. "Sometimes victims respond with violence, or even encourage the violence so they can get it over with, knowing that it's going to happen," Glenn explained to me in 2022 in my reporting for Jezebel. "It's so complex, and that term, 'mutual abuse,' is very harmful." Per Amanda Kippert, director of editorial at Domestic Shelters, the term is "by and large not supported by most domestic violence advocates as being valid, because the core of domestic violence is to have power and control over another person." She told me, "What is far more likely is that most victims accused of being mutually abusive are just having emotional or even physical reactions to the abuse that they're suffering. Abusive partners will then accuse their victims of being abusive, in order to shift the blame as a form of gaslighting."

This innately victim-blaming mythology certainly contributed to the jarring outcome of Johnny Depp and Amber Heard's 2022 defamation trial. It was a civil rather than criminal case, but it too exemplifies a legal system fundamentally at odds with justice for survivors. The predominantly male jury ruled that an op-ed in which Heard didn't name Depp while identifying herself as a domestic violence survivor and advocating for other victims constituted defamation. When one male juror elaborated on why he had voted this way, his reasoning was practically dripping in misogyny: "The crying, the facial expressions that she had, the staring at the jury—all of us were very uncomfortable. She would answer one question and she would be crying and then two seconds later she would turn ice cold . . . Some of us used the expression 'crocodile tears.'" In other words, because Heard couldn't meet this individual man's precise threshold of what constitutes an appropriate emotional display for a victim, she was lying.

Exemplifying a long history of supposedly impartial jurors being influenced by sexist bias, he continued, "A lot of the jury felt what [Depp] was saying, at the end of the day, was more believable. He just seemed a little more real in terms of how he was responding to questions. His emotional state was very stable throughout."

The court system isn't exempt from critiques of policing and its destructive impacts on sexual violence victims. Earlier in 2022, in a different court in Illinois, a judge overturned the conviction of an eighteen-year-old man who had raped an intoxicated sixteen-year-old girl, because a prison sentence "is not just" for a young man with a bright future. The judge, instead, blamed the victim's parents for allowing "16-year-olds to bring liquor to a party" and "provid[ing] liquor to underage people, and you wonder how these things happen."[3] The year before, a judge in New York decided, "after praying," not to send a twenty-year-old white man from a wealthy family to prison for sexually assaulting four teenage girls. In 2010 an Ohio judge called for four teenage rape victims to be required to undergo polygraph tests, even though their attackers had already been found guilty. And in 2019 a New Jersey judge rejected a petition from a rape victim's family after a sixteen-year-old boy filmed himself raping her while she was intoxicated and unable to consent and sent the video to his friends with the text "When your first time having sex was rape." According to the judge, who praised the teenage rapist's "good family," this was not a "traditional case of rape" because the assailant hadn't held his victim at gunpoint.

All of these are examples of a legal system fundamentally at odds with sexual assault survivors, sympathetic to if not outright supportive of rapists. Before many cases involving sexual violence go to trial, they're handled by police departments. This—cops handling rape cases—is supposed to make us feel safe; copaganda quite literally relies on rape victims as a narrative device, teaching us to understand white-washed notions of safety and justice from a lens of punishment and policing, of abusers and law enforcement as at odds rather than one and the same. We've been taught to understand violence from a uniform, racist, and classist lens, while ignoring institutionalized, white-supremacist state violence that unfolds all around us. We've been taught to understand the criminal legal system as cops keeping rapists and killers off the streets, instead of questioning the vast, overarching intersections between these two supposedly oppositional groups, or why some acts but not others are seen as violent, pending who performs them.

The inherent fragility, even coercive transactionality, of the relationship between the police state and those subjected to gendered violence has been laid bare by police departments' responses to a 2020 letter of support for racial justice and abolition called "The Moment of Truth," written and cosigned by domestic violence advocacy groups and direct services organizations across the country. Some of these organizations had previously received public funding from local governments and had referral partnerships with police departments. After they signed onto the letter, some lost funding, and others said police stopped referring victims to their services.[4] Police and other state actors have long capitalized on the vulnerability of groups like domestic violence victims for power, funding, and even legitimacy. When survivors identified this exploitative dynamic for what it is in their letter and questioned what abuse victims have ever gained from more funding for policing, law enforcement institutions openly, unabashedly retaliated against them.

A HISTORY OF GENDER AND CARCERALITY

In 1985 the Bedford Hills Correctional Facility for women in New York held historic hearings on the devastating links between criminalization and gender-based violence; incarcerated women and their advocates testified about the devastating pipeline between experiencing sexual violence and incarceration. Sisters Inside, an Australian abolitionist group that supports incarcerated and formerly incarcerated women, in 2001 presented the term "state sexual assault" to argue that the state itself is a perpetrator of sexual violence through policing, incarceration, and other carceral methods. State sexual assault is strip searches and cavity searches of incarcerated or arrested people; it's the enabling of rampant sexual assault by police officers and prison guards, the general punitiveness and systemic denial of incarcerated people's bodily autonomy. Sisters Inside organizers who had been incarcerated themselves described how physical and sexual abuse from interpersonal partners and from agents of the state carry many of the same impacts and feel virtually indistinguishable from each other.

Despite the inevitable sexual violence perpetuated by the prison system, mainstream feminist leaders like Gloria Steinem spent the summer of 2022 shilling for the creation of an ostensibly "feminist" women's prison to be built in a shut-down jail in Harlem. It would be called the Women's Center for Justice and incarcerate "women and gender-expansive people." The proposal was immediately shot down by abolitionist feminists, pointing out how prisons are inseparable from white supremacy and are innately sexist and dehumanizing, no matter what they're called.

"Feminist" organizing for the Women's Center for Justice is hardly the first time criminal justice reformers have unveiled supposedly more humane forms of prison, like house arrest, electronic monitoring, or parole. This level of state surveillance amounts to a prison without walls, all around us. In their 2020 book *Prison by Any Other Name*, Maya Schenwar and Victoria Law note that all these ideas raise fundamental questions about the prison system as a whole: "What does it mean to reform—to improve—a system that, at its core, relies on captivity and control? What are the dangers of perfecting a system that was designed to target marginalized people?"[5]

Abolitionist feminists recognize the futility of reforms or collaborations with police to help abuse victims. Abolition entails the end of prisons and policing; it reconstructs society to ensure everyone's needs are met, survival-based "crimes" are no longer necessary or criminalized, and harm is addressed without dehumanizing, carceral resolutions, which are more likely to reproduce and worsen harm than alleviate it. The carceral system, a fundamentally racist web of processes and institutions that criminalize and incarcerate people, has always been deeply tied to our societal crises of domestic and sexual violence—from the hostility and threats of criminalization that many victims of abuse face when they seek help, to the prevalence of sexual abuse and violence carried out by police officers and within prisons.

Lived experience first prompted me to question the norms of how we understand gender and violence from a carceral lens that frames law enforcement as saviors rather than assailants. With time and reflection on my own experiences with sexual assault, I learned the complexity of acts of interpersonal harm, and multilayered paths to personal restoration that are threatened and upended rather than supported by carceral logic. As a teenager, I balked at the idea of talking to people with guns about what had happened to me when I couldn't even talk to my own parents. When your only option to process or seek "justice" for acts of sexual harm is to implicate yourself and someone who's hurt you—someone you may hold complex or even loving feelings toward—into a violent, permanent system, truthfully, you're left with no options at all.

Even then, I think on some level I understood that victims of abuse are not the people that our law enforcement systems and punitive traditions are designed to serve. The police state is built to perpetuate rather than alleviate abuse, to disempower rather than support those who survive violence. The result is a culture in which victims of a wide range of acts of sexual and interpersonal harms are left to fend for themselves or risk incurring additional trauma—even, in no shortage of documented cases, criminalization and incarceration.

Carcerality is incompatible with creating environments in which abuse victims feel safe enough to seek recourse. Overinflated police and prison budgets mean that publicly funded resources for victims are severely lacking if not nonexistent. Yet carceral policy is the governing model of nearly all cities across the country, which rely on it to generate revenue through policing, incarcerating, and exploiting Black and brown people, consequently slashing funding for essential resources.

In the United States, the criminalization of disproportionately poor people of color is motivated by profit. Policies that criminalize substance use, sex work, or poverty-based crimes deliberately target marginalized people and are designed to allow privatized cities to profit off their poverty and pay back the banks that fund these cities. These are often the same banks that target Black and brown communities and profit off redlining, or housing discrimination in neighborhoods of color, and predatory subprime loans. These practices reflect how violence extends far beyond direct physical attacks perpetuated interpersonally by individuals. Violence—the government withholding essential resources, discriminating against, and criminalizing marginalized people—is perpetuated and normalized by the state itself, and the predacious banking systems at the heart of our capitalist economic system.

CARCERAL FEMINISM

All too often, a broader culture of acceptance of state violence permeates even spaces that are sympathetic to marginalized people who are victimized by the state. As Jackie Wang argues in her landmark essay "Against Innocence," victims of police and prison violence, or even victims who are

harmed or killed without "justice" rendered by the state, are always introduced to the public in the context of their criminal behavior, despite the
overarching power dynamics that should make state killings and abuses
of power exponentially more egregious. Writing about media coverage
of the killing of Isaiah Simmons, a Black teenager who was suffocated to
death by five counselors in a juvenile detention center, Wang observes,
"By emphasizing that it was a juvenile offender who died, the [coverage]
immediately flags Simmons as a criminal, signaling to readers that his
death is inconsequential and thus not worthy of sympathy."

Wang points out that Simmons's killing went largely ignored in
mainstream media, while the 2013 killing of Trayvon Martin, also a
seventeen-year-old Black boy, by a white-supremacist, self-appointed
neighborhood watch volunteer, sparked nationwide outcry. Although
right-wing media would eventually find ways to spin and justify Martin's murder, Wang contends the mainstream liberal response comprised
sympathy and outrage because Martin had been "innocent"—he hadn't
attacked the white man who killed him, he was unarmed, he had no
criminal record. "Innocence becomes a necessary precondition for the
launching of mass antiracist political campaigns," Wang writes.[6]

Further, Wang argues that the state actually capitalizes on outrage
against individual killings and acts of violence enacted on "innocent"
victims, because it can publicly perform as an ally when it inflicts criminalization and retribution on the individuals responsible. In this way,
violence and harm are reduced to individual acts rather than products of
a greater framework of harm, and the omnipresence of institutionalized
state violence is further concealed.

In 2007 the sociologist Elizabeth Bernstein defined "carceral feminism" as "the commitment of feminist activists to a law and order agenda
and a drift from the welfare state to the carceral state as the enforcement
apparatus for feminist goals." Carceral feminism also ignores the massive role of the state in *creating* harm and subsequently punishing victims
for the harm that it inflicts on them, across lines of race, class, gender,
immigration status, and other identities—for example, the targeting and
punishment of sex workers, many who are survivors of sexual abuse, for

trying to make an income and survive. Carceral feminism ennobles itself in promises of protection for women and victims through the incarceration of abusers, all while ignoring the devastating impacts that criminalization disproportionately carries for non-white survivors, as well as the ultimate impact of incarceration—perpetuating and reproducing harm, and deepening the reach and impact of state violence.

If we question the state's reliability as a protector of victims of abuse, that requires us to particularly question the effectiveness of the Violence Against Women Act (VAWA). For decades, the VAWA has been celebrated as a feminist victory for the rights of victims of abuse. It first emerged in the 1990s, introduced by then-Senator Joe Biden as he and President Bill Clinton advocated for violently racist criminal justice "reforms" that have terrorized and defunded Black and brown communities and driven the prison-industrial complex for decades. Clinton and Biden were leaders in pioneering "tough-on-crime," "law and order" policies that invested massively in policing and carceral methods, consequently divesting heavily from welfare and community resources that help low-income abuse victims. Thus, it's unsurprising that two-thirds of the funding that the VAWA provides is allocated to policing, and just one-third to victim resources.[7] The VAWA was introduced and enacted during the height of the Clinton-era crackdown on "crime," and the law was the perfect apparatus to further this era's racist policy agenda, ironically under the guise of feminist compassion.

Importantly, on a cultural level, the VAWA has been key to shifting popular understandings of domestic violence *as* acts of violence, and not just easily ignored private affairs. The 1964 murder and rape of Kitty Genovese in New York is told as a cautionary tale of the bystander effect, as none of her fellow tenants intervened to save her life as she was killed, presumably thinking their other neighbors would. But her story is arguably a harrowing reminder of the fatal dangers of a culture of normalized domestic violence, and passive acceptance of it as "private." One neighbor told a reporter he didn't help Genovese, who was not just repeatedly stabbed but also raped, because he thought she was simply being beaten by her husband in a run-of-the-mill "lover's quarrel." In this neighbor's mind, the assault happening right outside his window would have been all well and good if it had been perpetrated by a partner or spouse. Domestic violence was widely normalized precisely by popular thinking like this.

In 2022 Gabby Petito's parents filed a lawsuit against the police department in Moab, Utah, for failing to recognize crucial signs of intimate partner violence when they stopped her and her boyfriend, resulting in Petito later being killed. The lawsuit cited an allegation against one of the officers, Eric Pratt, who pulled over Petito and her boyfriend (and misidentified Petito as the abuser), that Pratt had threatened to kill his then-girlfriend in another town while he served as police chief there. The mayor of that town, who had personally appointed Pratt police chief, told the *Salt Lake Tribune* that this woman had spoken to him about Pratt's conduct and threats to her. The mayor asked her if Pratt had been in uniform or using a police vehicle while making any of the alleged threats. When the woman said no, the mayor told the *Tribune* that he determined her complaints were merely a personal issue that didn't warrant intervention. He also said that he continued to stand by Pratt.[8]

Historically, the push for legislation like the VAWA emerged from benevolent intentions and real need. In the 1970s women from all walks of life began organizing to raise consciousness about the conditions they faced in reporting and seeking resources for sexual violence and intimate partner abuse. The formation of groups like Chicago Women Against Rape in 1970 and the New York Radical Feminists in 1971 spurred gatherings of women in their communities where they discussed blame, shame, and punishment for speaking up about their experiences. A particularly galvanizing moment for the anti-rape movement came in 1974 with the case of Joan Little, a Black woman incarcerated in North Carolina who was raped by a prison guard and faced murder charges when she killed her rapist and escaped. Little was eventually acquitted in a victory for the intertwined movements for survivor and racial justice.

Across the country, activists and community members hosted speakouts and forums and distributed literature to challenge prevailing myths and narratives about rape that resulted in victim-blaming and stigma.

Their demands included rape crisis centers, crisis intervention resources for abused adolescents, support groups for victims, criminal justice reform to support survivors, and comprehensive legislation and funding to make these resources accessible for all.

Even as the anti-rape movement proliferated across the country, barriers remained to reporting and seeking support for victims of sexual violence. These barriers included the requirement for medical verification of reported rapes, despite how different forms of sexual violence have different impacts on the body, and the medical examination itself can be retraumatizing. In courtrooms, rape and sexual violence trials required witnesses, despite how sexual violence is an inherently private act. It was also unsurprisingly common for the defense to weaponize victims' sexual histories against them—following their logic, any woman who had consented to sex once before therefore consented to all other encounters, for the rest of her life. This fundamentally misogynist tactic persists to this day.

But because white women were the most visible faces of the original movement for survivor justice in the mainstream, and because they had the privilege of being able to place greater trust in policing and the state for support, progress for survivor justice was immediately bound to law enforcement and the greater criminal legal system in mainstream consciousness. By the 1980s, police departments were opening special units for victims and becoming the go-to "resource" for victims; by the 1990s, the Violence Against Women Act emerged.

The nuts and bolts of the VAWA are particularly concerning, as the law includes several mandates that place victims at risk of facing criminalization among other punitive threats. For example, the VAWA requires arrests in reported domestic violence cases, including even dual arrests if police deem there is any ambiguity in who is the victim and who is the abuser, which is a common outcome when a victim practices self-defense or otherwise behaves as an "imperfect" victim. Petito, you'll recall, was deemed the abuser in her relationship by police officers who witnessed her fighting back against her abusive boyfriend Brian Laundrie. An officer—again, later accused of threatening to kill his ex-girlfriend—fist-bumped Laundrie, told him he "did nothing wrong," and put him up in a hotel for free. Petito was forced to sleep alone in the van amid a mental health crisis in a city far from her home. Within days of her encounter with law enforcement, Laundrie killed her.

Additionally, the VAWA prohibits victims from dropping charges—a dangerous restriction for victims of color, or undocumented victims, who might reasonably fear unintentional consequences like deportation and other risks that go hand in hand in cooperating with law enforcement. As recently as 2019, the VAWA's Clinton-era, tough-on-crime mandate has led to district attorneys in some jurisdictions subpoenaing and even jailing victims to coerce them to testify against their abusers, even if a domestic conflict or dispute has been resolved without police involvement. In 2012 a seventeen-year-old rape victim in Sacramento, California, was jailed in a juvenile detention facility to coerce her to testify at the trial of her alleged attacker. In 2017 two women in Hawaii, and one in Oregon the year before, were also jailed for not testifying against their assailants.

The requirement of an arrest being made, and certainly the threat of facing jail time, discourages many victims from coming forward. And without the ability to trust and seek support from the state, many have nowhere else to turn. As a result, the VAWA exclusively serves "good," "innocent" victims—middle-class, straight, white women, who are regarded as the face of sexual violence victims, or at least the only faces worth caring about; the law exclusively serves women who have been perceived as sexually demure, compliant with tacit, patriarchal rules governing proper sexual conduct. Those who don't fit this mold are exponentially more likely to be disbelieved, blamed, and criminalized. Research on campus sexual assault reporting has found Black women students who reported assaults were less likely to be believed by peers and authority figures—and also, unsurprisingly, less likely to report their experiences at all.[9] Early on, Black girls are immediately regarded not only as little adults but also potential criminals; they are seen as less innocent, less credible, and consequently punished more harshly, beginning as early as elementary school, feeding directly into the school-to-prison pipeline.

Historically, our law enforcement and criminal legal systems have fixated on fundamentally white-supremacist notions of protecting the virtue and innocence of white women and girls, primarily as justification for enacting horrifying acts of violence upon non-white, non-citizen men. Simultaneously, police and the prison system have always regarded women and girls of color with skepticism and hostility. The VAWA was enacted within a context and legacy of women of color and especially Black and brown women experiencing such prevalent state and police violence in their communities that seeking help from law enforcement isn't an option. In this sense, the law embodies white feminism. As author and activist Rafia Zakaria notes on the very first page of her 2021 book *Against White Feminism*, white feminists aren't defined by their race but by their refusal "to consider the role that whiteness and the racial privilege attached to it have played . . . in universalizing white feminist concerns, agendas and beliefs as being those of all feminists."[10] It's an ideology that universalizes *white* women as *all* women, and consequently harms women and femmes of color through the carceral "solutions" that it asserts will protect (white) women.

Per the 2012 Rights4Girls study "The Sexual Abuse to Prison Pipeline," 76 percent of incarcerated survivors in the Oregon prison system experienced sexual assault by the age of thirteen and are predominantly women and girls of color.[11] The same study found criminalization and incarceration of those who had experienced early sexual traumas often stemmed from being unable to access crucial resources and supports to cope with their trauma. In many communities, lack of resources for victims is a direct result of overinvestment in policing and incarceration.

White women–led survivor justice movements exist in sharp contrast with historically Black women–led reproductive justice advocacy, which has always recognized how criminalization and incarceration are inherently anti-feminist. From policing the pregnancy outcomes and self-managed abortions of women of color, to the prevalence of Black families and families of color being torn apart by the prison system (one in nine Black children has an incarcerated parent, compared with one in twenty-eight white children[12]), abolition is requisite to reproductive justice—and consequently, survivor justice.

In their book *The Feminist and the Sex Offender*, Levine and Meiners highlight how panic and outrage about sex crimes or crimes targeting children are often reserved for white, middle-class child victims, while violence and disappearances of children from poor communities of color are all but erased in media. Violence is normalized and regarded as acceptable when the victims aren't white and their lives and experiences are deemed disposable.

In particular, Levine and Meiners contrast the stories of Etan Patz, a white child who disappeared from his upper-middle class, white neighborhood in 1979, and the disappearances and killings of fifteen children from a predominantly Black neighborhood in Atlanta between July and October the following year in 1980. They highlight the jarring double standards in constant national media coverage and proactive police action to find Patz and his assailant, in contrast with near silence from national media and neglect by law enforcement in response to the fifteen other children. "Because race in America is the foundational arbiter of sexual innocence and guilt, only some children qualify as tenderly incompetent and deserving of protection, or even as children. . . . In white American culture, nonwhite children are not really children; they're small (and potentially 'bad') adults, in need of correction not protection," Levine and Meiners argue.[13]

Nearly four decades later, little has changed. The country that either scorned or ignored the murders of Black youth like twelve-year-old Tamir Rice in 2014, or sixteen-year-old Ma'Khia Bryant in 2021, is the same country that sympathized with, humanized, and even fundraised for seventeen-year-old Kyle Rittenhouse, a white boy who shot and killed two people protesting police brutality in 2020. While internet white supremacists crowdfunded more than $2 million for Rittenhouse to post bail and spend Thanksgiving with his family, a Black woman named Cynthia Green, whose eighteen-year-old son Sincere Pierce had been killed by police, couldn't afford costs for his funeral arrangements.

Double standards in media coverage and public consciousness surrounding sexual violence and abduction cases are rampant. In the summer of 2019, it was reported that at least 5,500 Native American women and girls are missing in the United States. According to US government statistics, Native American and Alaska Native women are more than 2.5 times more likely to be raped or sexually assaulted than other women in the US.[14] Amnesty International reports that many Indigenous women they interviewed said they didn't know anyone in their community who had *not* experienced sexual violence.[15] And notably, non-Native men commit most assaults against Native women and girls, and tribal courts lack the jurisdiction to prosecute non–tribal members for many crimes including sexual assault even if it occurs on tribal land.

Public silence about the epidemic of violence against Native women and girls, again, largely committed by white and non-Native men who enter reservations or sovereign Native lands and face no accountability from the US government, stands in sharp contrast with mass media coverage of rapes and disappearances of middle-class white women and girls. These young women are the subjects of most *Dateline* episodes, documentaries, and social media awareness campaigns; Petito's disappearance trended on all social media platforms for months. Much of this is steeped in both cultural white supremacy and institutionalized white supremacy within bureaucratic procedures—research shows state and local governments often fail to accurately record or track the disappearances of Native girls. They're often misclassified with the wrong racial identification, which can make official searches for them more difficult or altogether impossible due to lack of accurate information about their identities.

The VAWA extends directly from the forces of white supremacy that center white middle-class victims and threaten to criminalize nearly all others. Still, it remains important to differentiate conservative opposition to the VAWA, and especially conservative opposition to newer iterations of the law that include protections for immigrants and LGBTQ people, from abolitionist, non-carceral feminist opposition that protests the VAWA's deep reliance on the criminal legal system. Senate Republicans have repeatedly attempted to defund or not renew the VAWA for decades now, despite sharing common goals with the law, like the expansion of the prison-industrial complex. This, if anything, speaks to how deeply they disdain victims of sexual violence, and particularly queer, trans, and immigrant victims. They don't care whether victims live or die. In contrast, abolitionist opponents of the VAWA *do* care—and they also recognize that many victims *aren't* white, middle-class, cis, straight women, and, thus, stand to be harmed by the law's carceral features.

Survivors need community-based supports—not more policing. Instead, laws like the Violence Against Women Act compound their victimhood, and all too often, feed deeply entrenched cycles of simultaneous state and interpersonal violence.

3

INTIMATE DAMAGE

It sounds inappropriate, even crass to describe sexual and domestic violence—shattering, devastating, traumatizing acts of violation—as "intimate." Yet intimacy is a common thread that connects most acts of sexual violence, which are committed in the confines and privacy of the home, or by a partner or spouse or family member, perhaps a trusted friend, mentor, or supervisor. Research has found that contrary to prevalent narratives and cultural lore, eight out of ten rapes are committed not by a stranger but by someone the victim knows—and often knows intimately.[1] Domestic abuse itself is inherently intimate, rooted in exploiting the trust and power dynamics of an existing relationship. Despite this, the perpetrators of sex crimes are usually portrayed in mainstream media as armed, bestial boogeymen waiting in dark alleys at night, rather than wealthy, white fraternity brothers from old-money families, long-term boyfriends and partners, even family members.

This misconception is no accident; rather, it's intentional victim-blaming and implicitly asserts that if women don't want to be assaulted and raped, they simply shouldn't walk alone at night. The myth of the dark alley sexual predator presents sexual violence as wholly prevent-able, if only the victim were more careful; it reifies conservative, "family values" narratives that home is the safest place for women—when home and intimate relationships can be sites of deep trauma and emotional and physical violence.

In addition to warped societal conceptions of safety and abuse, to the detriment of victims, there's also lack of broad public consciousness about the inherently political nature of domestic violence. Unsurprisingly, neither available scholarship about abuse nor scholarship about voting and elections considers the connections between something as private and intimate as abuse behind closed doors, and something as public as politics and elections. Yet abuse and politics are closely intertwined in a manner that invisibly threatens the very core of so-called American democracy. The politics of patriarchy assumes many forms, including the political and electoral empowerment of white, male patriarchs and abusers in government offices at every level, as well as the operative definitions and collective understandings of sexual and domestic abuse that protect abusers, that erase and obfuscate the full spectrum of what victims endure behind closed doors. We're socialized to understand acts of sexual violence as limited to the grisly murder-rapes that make cable news or are scattered across popular, male-written HBO shows—not the exploitation of power dynamics, like a powerful elected official or executive soliciting "consensual" sexual favors from a subordinate, a suburban husband who exerts total control over his wife's finances—or refuses to let his wife vote.

POLITICAL VIOLENCE BEGINS AT HOME

Many victims may not even see political coercion from their partners as an abusive act. In our conversation, Tawni Maisonneuve, the survivor and advocate I referenced earlier, attributed this in part to the reality that we still "have a hard time believing emotional and mental abuse occurs," let alone recognizing political control over a partner as abusive.

But Maisonneuve experienced abuse in this form firsthand, from multiple abusive partners obstructing her access to political information, and at different points, even controlling her voting. She finally began to understand her partners' political coercion of her as abuse when, in 2013, she joined a program that she called "intense victim recovery therapy."

"In that group, our instructor brought up that sort of behavior. I never really thought of it before as if it was some kind of control," Maisonneuve said of her former abuser's control over her politics. She added that she doesn't think a lot of people talk about "politics in domestic abuse" because "they think, 'oh, yeah, it's an argument anyway' or 'yeah, people don't usually see eye-to-eye" and dismiss the potential of these "disagreements" to yield violent outcomes and disenfranchisement.

Yet in many ways, Maisonneuve believes controlling a partner's vote is one of the most powerful forms of abuse. "When you look at that, if I can control the way you vote even in your community and everything else, I know I really have control of you at home. That's what we dove into in my victim recovery class," she said.

Maisonneuve recounted how her "first marriage was the hardest one when it came to voting." Prior to her abusive marriage, she had worked as a manager in a state senator's office and had deep roots in community activism and political engagement. "It turned into a situation where I didn't even register to vote anymore," Maisonneuve said. Again, her divorce was finalized in 1994, but she says she "didn't even vote after that for the simple fact that I didn't want to run into [her ex-husband] at any polls" or "deal with any of those dynamics."

In her next relationship, Maisonneuve's partner accompanied her to polling places and voted on her behalf. "I felt if I didn't vote the way he did, or I didn't agree with those political views, it would really be a physical issue," she said. "So whenever I would go vote with him, I would need to get things approved before I submitted them. And he would tell the people, 'Oh, she's slow, I gotta walk her through it.' It was those kinds of humiliating things that I dealt with when I went to go vote, when I was in bad relationships."

This might seem like a lot of effort from her ex-partner, all for *one* vote that's hardly likely to sway an election. But according to Maisonneuve, this extent of calculation and control by an abuser isn't at all out of the ordinary. For an abuser, acts of political coercion including controlling a partner's vote aren't necessarily about impacting an election or achieving specific political outcomes, but making their victim feel powerless, denying them agency in the home and in society at large. "It's about complete power and control," she said, "where there's no room for disagreement, no room for your own opinions or even your own thoughts."

Maisonneuve said she also thinks political control within abusive relationships is rarely discussed because of the broad cultural misunderstanding that it's easy for victims to get the resources they need to leave and be autonomous after an abusive relationship. "But we don't even really have victim recovery services, we have battery intervention programs, sure—but unless a victim really, really seeks out some mental health help, it's not even really offered to us," she said. "We're given protection orders, or people think you're at a shelter so everything's fine. But victim recovery services are far in between, just like shelters."

To Maisonneuve's point, victims of emotional and nonphysical abuse are often written off when they seek resources and services for victims. Jennifer Kelly, the Black woman and veteran I interviewed who said her white ex-husband in the Air Force abused both her and their kids, was denied entry to a domestic violence shelter in Alaska because it required that her abusive partner had hit her in the last three days. At the time, her ex-husband had been in rehab for several weeks. Domestic violence victims are also unable to apply for subsidized housing without a job; most can't get a job without child care; and they can't apply for daycare without having a job. They're stuck—and often unable to vote for policy change that could help them.

To protect victims' voting rights, Maisonneuve argues it's critical that polling places educate volunteers and staff on how to ensure voters can vote independently. "It should be a red flag at polling stations if someone comes in and their partner or family member says, 'Oh, they're slow, they're learning.' In response, it should be, 'Well that's OK, we have somebody that can help them. Because the voting right is individual. We'll help them,'" she said. As for absentee ballots, because states don't mail ballots to PO boxes and only to residential addresses, Maisonneuve's political mail has been going to her local domestic abuse shelter for years and will be shipped there indefinitely. "I'm fortunate that our shelter will allow me to still send my mail there, for the rest of my life. That's the kind of stuff you go through, that survivors and victims don't talk about, because people are like, 'Oh, well they got services,'" she said. "Well, no, not enough." Most shelters can't offer this option as a resource. "They don't have that kind of capacity," Maisonneuve said. "It's very hard. I'm very lucky. The whole mailing system—that is a big issue for survivors."

Maisonneuve, who has since founded the Purple Owl Project in Toledo, Ohio, as a resource for victims and survivors to support each other, believes a path to political autonomy "needs to be part of the safety planning conversation," when victims turn to advocates and organizations to create a comprehensive plan to leave an abusive relationship. According to Maisonneuve, starting the Purple Owl Project has shown her what she sees as her own privilege as a survivor. "There are so many people who have no idea how this system works, where to get help—I could rely on my education, on my previous work, to know how to navigate that journey," she said. In the years since leaving her abusive partners, Maisonneuve has become not only politically active and a regular voter once again, but a leader in supporting victims and survivors and advocating for policy change.

Jeff R., a survivor of domestic violence who grew up in a household in Ohio with alcoholic parents and family, works with Maisonneuve at the Purple Owl Project. He told me Maisonneuve was his "savior."

"When you grow up in a household where it's you have to do it this way or that way or get your ass beat, get belittled—you no longer see the value in your own feelings, your own beliefs," he told me. "It would just be, 'Oh, who did you vote for?' and I'd say what I needed to say, or not say anything, to avoid a conflict, avoid belittling or a beating. Even now, I just don't talk about politics with anyone anymore. Even now, I still can't talk about it, let alone engage much in the community."

Voting in particular is a "sore subject" to Jeff, drawing on his own experience with living in a household where his abusive parents and older family members controlled everything for him and his siblings, affecting his conceptions of power and politics. "The way I see it, it's almost like the electoral college, the US Senate—the majority of us will vote or choose certain things, certain representatives, but it's the electoral college or it's these other states that control us anyway," he said. "It's a lot like living in a home where you have no control, the decisions are made for you, the powerlessness."

Like Maisonneuve, Jeff said his access to resources to get to safety were severely limited. His attempts to leave his home started as early as age fifteen; at the height of his parents' violence, he recalls pitching a tent in the nearby woods to escape his home, and at different points, sleeping in his car at rest stops down the road and trying to save money at his job to leave long-term. A turning point came when his father beat his mother especially violently. "And in response to me, she was just like, 'Don't call the police, don't call the police, it will just make everything worse,'" he said. Eventually, when he and his brother were older, they "were able to force our father to leave the home."

Jeff said his experiences showed him the institutional failures of the government to support victims of abuse. "The senators, the representatives we have—they don't care about us, it's just money, it's just power for those people," he said. That is, ultimately, what brought him to the Purple Owl Project in Toledo. "I don't do politics; I don't see what I'm doing as that. Just helping Tawni, helping people like I once was myself, who don't know where to turn to—we have only our communities to turn to."

Heather, who told me she was experiencing domestic abuse at the time of our interview in 2020 and asked for her last name to be withheld, said she relates to Maisonneuve's and Jeff's experiences with intimidation and control in their households leading to the suppression of their political activities. While Heather declined to give specific details about her experience, she speculated that "the reason [political coercion] isn't included" in people's definitions and understandings of domestic violence is that "people think someone isn't being physically harmed, so why bother speaking up?"

Dr. Tonisha Pinckney, who researches and teaches about domestic violence, sexual violence, community engagement, and other issues, is a survivor of domestic violence herself and told me she was once convinced by an abusive partner that she was inherently unworthy and too uneducated to have a political voice. "I'm a Black woman, and when you're a Black woman and dealing with domestic violence, it's such a difficult situation, because there's people who will always treat you like you're completely stupid and unworthy," she told me.

For eight years, her husband, who she married at eighteen, subjected her to emotional and physical abuse and often weaponized their two children and attacks on her self-esteem to deny her political power. "Anytime I tried to use my power at all as a human being, to do anything that would feel empowering to me, that's what my ex-husband tried to take away," Pinckney said. "It wasn't always about the fact he hated voting or politics, it was that he didn't want me to feel as though I could do it, or my voice was loud enough."

Prior to her abusive marriage, she had always been active in her community. Her mother had been a community organizer, and Pinckney had studied political science as an undergraduate. After surviving sexual assault prior to her relationship with her then-husband, she'd also been a vocal advocate for victims' rights. But after marrying him, she said, over time he began to use the family they shared to prevent her from voting or attending political or community events.

"Once I had the kids, it became, 'Oh, you want to go and hear this political speaker? Sure, you can go, but I'm not watching the kids,' and they're young, and we're too poor [for child care] and didn't have a car, so I couldn't go. Or, 'You want to vote? That's stupid, you're just wasting your time,'" Pinckney recounted. "A lot of his barriers were not specifically, 'You can't be involved in political things,' or, 'You can't go vote,' it was, 'I'm not stopping you, but I'm stopping you from doing it in other ways.' It was, 'You can go, I'm not telling you you can't go, I'm just *making* it so you can't go.'"

Her ex-husband would also refuse to let her speak about values and political issues with their children. "With him it was, 'You're not smart enough, so you're just going to teach them to be dumb too.' It was, 'You're trying to put your politics on them, your religion on them.'"

Despite how deeply her abusive marriage had affected her political engagement, Pinckney said our interview was the first conversation she'd had about the impacts of domestic abuse on political autonomy. Why are these connections rarely made? "Some of it plays to the patriarchal system of, 'Why do you need to vote anyway? You're just a woman, you need to stay in your place'—that kind of thing," Pinckney hypothesized. "Those were some of the arguments I'd have, 'You need to be home with the kids,' or, 'Charity starts at home, why are you out there in the streets trying to make the world a better place? You should be here cooking me food.'

"And I think it just doesn't really occur to people, that connection, because you don't vote every day," she added. "So even for victims of domestic abuse, who go through abuse every day, voting and politics isn't something you really consider when you think of your abuse overall."

Looking back on her experience and those of survivors around her, Pinckney is especially concerned with what Black women and women of color who experience domestic abuse may face in trying to vote or participate in public life. She said she often reflects on the roles of white supremacy and the disenfranchisement of Black people and people of color in shaping electoral processes, and whether some men of color might take out their frustrations with these systems of oppression on female partners, by exerting control over *their* politics.

"The political conversation as a whole can sometimes be limited, especially in the Black community, because of a lot of conspiracy theories and lack of feeling empowered as a community," Pinckney said. She recounted stories of other women of color she knew who shared her experience of having a partner insist that they were too ignorant and uneducated to vote or participate in political discourse. "I see this so often, when the woman wants to be political, or do things to make a difference—it's, 'You're overstepping, you're not paying attention to your family, you're not smart enough, you're trying to be the white people's pawn.'"

Pinckney says there are crucial steps we can take to support victims and survivors' ability to vote and participate in political processes. Lack of access to child care, and thus being unable to leave the house and engage in public life, held her back for years; so did lack of information about different options for voting, including absentee ballots, or the full range of forms of civic engagement. "Having some child care supports, having information about how to do mail-in ballots—I didn't even know that existed," Pinckney said. "And part of that is systemic racism, being in a minority community, we just didn't get that information. There was no effort to inform us and encourage our engagement."

Pinckney also believes there's a need for more direct access to voting at shelters; many victims—especially if they've only recently escaped their abuser—don't leave the shelter at all for significant periods of time. "There should be a polling site near shelters, so people can be taken there, and people can go vote if they're in a shelter situation."

Beyond these essential, material resources for victims and survivors, from child care to polling sites near shelters, Pinckney argued we need formal, cultural recognition of the inherently political nature of domestic violence. "The main thing right now is to be vocal that these issues are connected, politics and voting and domestic violence, and this is absolutely a form of abuse and violence," she said.

Pinckney said she hopes the historic nature of living through a simultaneous pandemic and election cycle in 2020 was a wake-up call for people. "People are just now realizing with COVID, that's what it's like when you can't leave the house?" she said. "Imagine being trapped all your life, and not only is the government saying you shouldn't leave, but the person in the house with you is now using COVID to further control you—*and* we're in an election cycle."

The personal is the political. Yet in the context of elections, we've often ignored this reality, overlooking stories like those of Maisonneuve, Jeff, Heather, and Pinckney unfolding all around us behind closed doors.

THROUGH ELECTORAL OUTCOMES, THE STATE BECOMES THE ABUSER

Nearly a decade since the 2016 presidential campaign trail, I still think about Trump supporters at his rallies who would reflexively chant from the rafters "Lock her up!" about Hillary Clinton, despite approximately zero criminal charges brought against her. These were the same people who had the "due process" and "innocent until proven guilty" song and dance down to a T when it came to sexual misconduct allegations against Trump and other men they claimed. They worshipped their alleged serial sexual abuser president all while waxing poetic about the supposed sexual threats that Black incarcerated men and immigrant men, ostensibly flooding the US border, posed to American (more specifically, white) women. Trump, himself accused of several sexual assaults and a vocal sympathizer of numerous high-profile white abusers, in the 1980s paid for a full-page newspaper ad asserting five young Black men—then known as the Central Park Five, today known as the Exonerated Five— were guilty of raping a white woman, despite their proven innocence. He maintains this transparently racist belief to this day.

"Due process," to considerable swaths of conservative voters and politicians, is little more than a racist, sexist dog whistle. It's a buzzword to reinforce an oppressive worldview—they say they want evidence and "innocence until proven guilty." But these are fundamentally unserious claims, salient hollow talking points deployed to frame survivor justice advocates as vile, lying women bent on hurting innocent, good men. They don't offer examples of evidence that could sufficiently prove guilt for the overwhelming majority of victims who aren't wearing body cameras or staffed with around-the-clock witnesses. When it comes to allegations of sexual harm, who is and isn't believed is determined by vastly unequal, identity-based power dynamics, by predictably skewed, race-gendered distributions of credibility; it's not about evidence, especially for such inherently private acts of violence that seldom leave a paper trail—it's about power, who we instinctively empower with collective trust and authority as credible witnesses to their own experiences.

The policies that determine whether victims stay or leave, live or die, are also shaped by who holds power in society and in elections. To state the obvious, legislation is enacted by lawmakers who run and win elections, securing majorities of an electorate that contains a considerable number of victims of domestic abuse, whose votes may be stolen, influenced, or denied by their abusers altogether.

As previously noted, one in three women and one in four men have experienced some form of intimate partner violence. These rates can look vastly different state-by-state, and in combing through the NCADV's 2019 data on incident rates in each state—which defines domestic abuse as intimate partner physical violence, intimate partner sexual violence, and/or intimate partner stalking—I observed a trend of states with higher rates of reported domestic abuse implementing especially harmful policy outcomes for women, pregnant-capable people, and survivors.

States with more liberalized policy landscapes also reported concerning rates of sexual and domestic abuse. But it seems notable that most states that passed and introduced abortion bans, that don't recognize certain acts of marital rape as criminal, and maintain the highest populations of incarcerated people (90 percent of incarcerated women are sexual assault survivors) also have domestic abuse rates that are higher than the national average. Interpreting the extremely limited available data, it's possible that abuse at home—and the voter suppression this yields—could contribute to the election of more conservative lawmakers, who implement policies that are harmful to women and victims and further perpetuate cycles of abuse.

ELECTIONS AND STATE REPRODUCTIVE COERCION

In 2019, the same year that NCADV collected this data, thirteen states passed total or near-total abortion bans, though *Roe v. Wade* was still in place, and these bans were consequently blocked in court at the time. Alabama passed a total ban on abortion without any exceptions; Georgia, Kentucky, Louisiana, Mississippi, and Ohio passed bans on abortion at six weeks—before many people realize they're pregnant; Missouri passed a ban on abortion at eight weeks; Indiana and North Dakota banned the safest method of abortion after the first trimester; Arkansas and Utah banned abortion at eighteen weeks; Montana passed a ban on abortion after twenty-two weeks; Arkansas, Kentucky, Missouri, and Utah passed a ban on abortion based on speculation about the patient's motives (for example, if it's assumed the patient is seeking abortion due to certain fetal anomalies); and Arkansas, Kentucky, Missouri, and Tennessee adopted legislation that would ban abortion if the US Supreme Court overturned *Roe*, known as trigger laws.

This particular rash of abortion bans, three years before the eventual overturning of *Roe*, was ultimately decades in the making. Since *Roe* was decided in 1973, nearly 1,500 state-level laws restricting or banning abortion have been enacted; as previously noted, there have been almost 2,000 cases of pregnancy outcomes including self-induced abortions that have led to criminal charges. The steady erosion of voting rights in the decades since the Voting Rights Act in 1965 has yielded Republican majorities in state legislatures across the country, each frothing at the mouth to ban and criminalize abortion, while Republican presidents have stacked the federal judiciary with anti-abortion judges to uphold these bans.

In 2020 Alabama, Ohio, Arkansas, Louisiana, Texas, Oklahoma, Iowa, and Tennessee attempted to use the pandemic to ban abortion care by identifying it as nonessential health care and banning all nonessential health services. And in the immediate aftermath of *Roe*, thirteen states— Kentucky, Louisiana, South Dakota, Idaho, Tennessee, Texas, Arkansas, Mississippi, Missouri, North Dakota, Oklahoma, Utah, and Wyoming— had readily prepared, built-in trigger laws.

It's critical to understand just how deeply connected abortion bans and domestic abuse are. The pioneering study-turned-book *The Turnaway Study* has shown that people who seek and are denied abortion care are more likely to experience long-term domestic abuse, among other alarming consequences such as poverty and worsened economic outcomes, which make it exponentially more difficult to leave an abusive relationship. If someone can't get the abortion care they seek and can't afford to raise a child on their own, or can't afford the legal resources to separate from an abusive partner, they may be forced to not only stay with their abuser but raise a child with them. All of this underscores the importance of policy change that treats basic needs like income, housing, and health care—including abortion—as human rights, rather than commodities that abusers can leverage to entrap their victims.

And while it's alarming that Alabama and other states' 2019 abortion bans didn't include exceptions for pregnancies caused by rape, rape exceptions to anti-abortion restrictions have historically contributed to counterproductive outcomes for survivors. As Alison Turkos, a reproductive justice activist and survivor, put it when I interviewed her in 2022 for Jezebel, for decades anti-abortion lawmakers were able to pass hundreds of bans and restrictions by "using survivors as a shield while trying to fast-track these bills through the legislature." In other words, lawmakers weaponized surface-level compassion for survivors to pass atrocious forced-birth bills. Few rape victims have been able to even *try* to invoke the exception, because many laws require them to report their rape to law enforcement, an act that can be retraumatizing or overtly dangerous for victims. Rape exceptions to abortion bans perpetuate the myth that it's safe and easy to prove your rape to medical professionals and law enforcement, despite how sexual violence perpetuated by doctors and police officers is rampant, and so too is disbelief and dismissal of survivors.

In the vein of making abortion bans and restrictions socially acceptable, anti-abortion politicians have also relied on stigmatizing and banning abortions based on certain conditions, such as abortion later in pregnancy, or abortion in cases of severe fetal anomalies, or so-called sex- and race-based abortions. Despite their insidious language, these laws have one goal: to ban abortion and create public confusion and hostility toward it. When we enact bans that speculate into the patients' motives for seeking care—for example, that people perceived as being from Asian countries are more likely to have abortions based on a fetus's sex—abortion is misrepresented as racist and ableist. And when later abortion is banned or restricted, this leads to dangerous discourse that equates abortion with murder and "feticide," language that's frequently incited retaliatory violence against abortion providers and patients. Many patients are forced to delay abortion care by myriad restrictions and barriers. They may be forced to seek abortion care later in pregnancy by a variety of extreme, sometimes life-threatening health circumstances. No reason to seek care is more valid than another.

Notably, most states that enacted these anti-abortion laws have disproportionately high rates of reported domestic abuse. Of the eighteen states that attempted to ban abortion in 2019 and 2020, fifteen have rates of domestic abuse that are higher than the national average, which stands at about 33 percent of women and 25 percent of men who have experienced some form of violence by an intimate partner.

In Georgia, 37.4 percent of the state population has reported experiencing domestic abuse; in Kentucky, 35.1 percent of women in the state have reported experiencing domestic abuse. In Mississippi, this number stands at 35.1 percent; in Ohio, 35.6 percent; in Missouri, 36.1 percent; in Arkansas, 37.3 percent; in Utah, 36.9 percent; in Indiana, 40.4 percent; in Montana, 39.2 percent; in Tennessee, 40 percent; in Oklahoma, 49.4 percent; in Texas, 34.5 percent; in Louisiana, 33.4 percent; in South Dakota, 33.7 percent; and in Wyoming, 35.8 percent of women.

There are exceptions to this trend: In some of these states, NCADV reports rates of domestic violence that are lower than the national average.[2] In Alabama, 31 percent of women have reported experiencing domestic abuse. In North Dakota, 25.3 percent of women have, and in Iowa, 31.3 percent of women.

Anti-abortion laws in these states are part of a greater policy landscape that enacts disparate harm on victims and survivors. Of these states, Alabama, Iowa, Oklahoma, Mississippi, Kentucky, Ohio, South Dakota, and Wyoming also maintain laws that don't allow for a spouse to be convicted of "raping a partner who was unconscious, drugged, or otherwise incapacitated," as well as laws that exclude spousal rape from the criminalization of "statutory rape and/or sexual contact between people with a supervisory relationship," per 2019 reporting by *Mother Jones*.[3]

Shortly after *Roe* fell in 2022, Media Matters for America reported a rising trend of right-wing influencers and Republican leaders advocating for the end of no-fault divorce—a policy that allows people to end a marriage without being required to prove wrongdoing by their partner, including adultery, abuse, or desertion.[4] No-fault divorce was first enacted in California in 1969 and has always been a feminist issue. It's allowed domestic abuse victims to leave a bad marriage without onerous barriers, and it certainly empowers women and all people to escape legally binding situations with someone they don't love. But Justice Clarence Thomas's concurring opinion in the Supreme Court's decision overturning *Roe* very clearly opened the door for further rights, particularly around marriage, to be overturned, too. In its 2022 platform, the Texas Republican Party proposes "to rescind unilateral no-fault divorce laws and support covenant marriage and to pass legislation extending the period of time in which a divorce may occur to six months after the date of filing for divorce."[5]

"If you're a woman that comes from meager means, and you want to get wealthy—you've never worked, you didn't get a degree, you have no skill set, but you're good-looking—your best path to victory is simply to marry a man, leave him, and take half. . . . We need to reform divorce laws in this country," conservative influencer Steven Crowder said in 2022. It's tempting to write off Crowder's words as an obvious projection of his own insecurities that no woman would ever marry him for love. Men like Crowder could go to therapy for their anxieties or advocate for economic policies to address the conditions that theoretically make marriage and divorce women's best options. Instead, they see the solution as legally entrapping and holding women hostage. And conservative politicians are steadily growing the electoral power to make this possible.

ABUSE, ELECTORAL OUTCOMES, AND CARCERALITY

Like abortion bans, spousal rape laws, and other innately anti-women legislation, "tough-on-crime" policies that escalate policing and incarceration also further harm victims. People who have survived sexual violence, you'll recall, are disproportionately represented within the prison system. And within the prison system itself, sexual violence is rampant.

Of the top ten states with the highest incarceration rates—Louisiana, with 719 inmates per 100,000 residents; Oklahoma, with 704; Mississippi, with 619; Arkansas, with 598; Arizona, with 529; Texas, with 553; Missouri, with 532; Kentucky, with 527; Georgia, with 506; and Alabama, with 486—all have also banned abortion in some way.[6] And nearly all maintain rates of domestic abuse that are above the national average. This isn't mere coincidence: Domestic violence inevitably affects victims' political power, their ability to vote, advocate, and participate in movements. When their voices aren't heard, our policies—abortion bans, laws that excuse abuse, policing and criminalization that target sexual violence victims—reflect this and enact further harm upon victims.

The state benefits from the political repression of abuse victims: There is a greater profit incentive to maximize the numbers of those imprisoned, to maximize the power and reach of surveillance and policing technologies, than there is to invest in resources and supports for victims. This is the nature of the prison and policing industrial complex, which doesn't just profit from the labor extracted from incarcerated people, but also the multimillion-dollar contracts the government establishes with security companies that rely on imprisonment and surveillance to exist. Victims of sexual and domestic violence who try to escape the power of their abusers are placed in greater proximity to criminalization, as they may be more likely to commit need-based "survival crimes" in the absence of resources and support systems. If they're criminalized and incarcerated, the prison system can then extract their cost-free labor. And because abuse victims are often poor women, girls, and LGBTQ people of color, they're seen as disposable—more valuable to the state for their free labor than for their political expression, votes, and activism that might challenge the existing, oppressive system.

The most vulnerable women and victims of abuse, armed with the least resources, are the most susceptible to criminalization and incarceration. As previously noted, in many documented cases, women who are victims of abuse face more severe punishment, often for acts like "enabling" child abuse or practicing self-defense, than do their abusers. A Texas woman named Melissa Lucio was held on death row for fifteen years after her infant daughter died in a tragic accident in 2007. Lucio, the mother of several other children, had survived years of domestic abuse from family members and partners, and her legal team argued that she had been coerced and manipulated into accepting responsibility for her daughter's death. Advocates and gender-based violence experts said Lucio's "confession" had been the product of aggressive interrogation from law enforcement and a coping mechanism stemming from her life-long history of trauma and domestic abuse.

The incarceration and criminalization of women and victims for harm inflicted on them can also be traced to abortion bans, which open the door for police to investigate, charge, and even jail all pregnant people for the outcomes of their pregnancies. As previously noted, forty states as of 2022 have laws that were written with the explicit intention of protecting pregnant people from domestic violence but have since been hijacked by anti-abortion policymakers, rogue prosecutors, and law enforcement to punish those who experience miscarriage or complete their own abortions. In some cases, these individuals may experience miscarriage from harm caused by their abusers or terminate their pregnancy through self-managed abortion to escape an abusive relationship for their own safety. The criminalization of miscarriage and self-managed abortion has become an especially urgent issue in post-*Roe* America.

The same year Louisiana signed a six-week ban, in 2019, its district attorneys unanimously opposed a bill that would have protected sexual violence victims from being jailed to coerce testimony against their abusers—an outcome we've seen in previously mentioned cases in California, Oregon, Hawaii, and other states. Victims are also criminalized and incarcerated for other victim-blaming reasons: In Tennessee, Cyntoia Brown, a Black woman who was trafficked and repeatedly assaulted as a teenager, received a life sentence for killing her attacker in self-defense. (In 2019 she had her sentence commuted after spending fifteen years in prison.) One unnamed rape survivor in Houston was jailed in 2016 for the great crime of having a mental breakdown at her trial.

Contrary to the claims and fearmongering of carceral feminism, we are placed in existential danger by incarceration, policing, and the policies that fund these programs at the expense of resources for victims. American policing, which traces its origins to slave patrols, is meant to protect property and capital, to empower mass wealth hoarding, and subsequently deny basic, life-saving resources to the poor—including entrapped abuse victims. There's a reason copaganda-entrenched legacy media devotes entire news cycles to panics about looting and property damage. There's a reason protesters can be jailed for vandalism but police officers are almost routinely acquitted for extrajudicial killings and egregious sexual assaults: Abuse is normalized and tolerated within policing; police protect property, not people, and certainly not abuse victims.

The deep connections between policing and enforcement of private property reflect the United States' history of interconnected racial violence and gendered violence. Property rights are associated with freedom and empowerment, but throughout most of history, rape was not viewed as a crime precisely *because of* property rights—that is, women were considered property of men, and therefore, men had unbridled rights and access to women's bodies. Historically, men were socialized to view taking land—and land predominantly occupied by people of color—and taking women from these lands as mere property acquisition.

Notably, throughout English history, the punishment for rape included castration or death for the rapist—but this recourse was reserved exclusively for victims born into the privileged, property-owning classes, who met several rigid requirements. The historian Sidney Painter wrote in his 1953 book *History of the Middle Ages*: "If a member of the feudal class committed his crimes against anyone other than the king or a great lord, he was fairly safe from prosecution, or at least from punishment." In medieval England, a woman had to be a wealthy, propertied virgin to have legal recourse against her rapist. In the colonial United States, early colonies defined rape as "carnal knowledge of a woman ten years or older, forcibly and against her will"[7]—yet, so long as slavery remained legal, rapes and abuse victimizing enslaved Black women were not only permissible but normalized, as Black people were relegated to property. Sexual violence, and certainly safe, legal pursuit of justice for sexual violence, has always been inextricably linked to property, capital, and class; policing and the law function to uphold said inequitable distributions of property, capital, and class.

Even living under the police state we have in place, only about 5 out of 1,000 rapists will ever be incarcerated.[8] Yet we're told all rapists are simply behind bars, that everyone behind bars is a rapist—even as data reveals that police *are* abusers, that they *are* rapists, that they're endangering women and survivors.

The data I've presented about rates of domestic abuse in states that have banned abortion, uphold egregious marital rape laws, or maintain some of the highest prison populations in the nation is insufficient to sweepingly suggest that higher rates of domestic abuse in a state can significantly or definitively impact electoral outcomes and policymaking. States like California and New York, which are known for their more liberalized policies, hold domestic abuse rates below the national average. But Oregon and Washington, which share similar ideological landscapes, hold domestic abuse rates that are actually above the national average. Alaska guarantees the right to abortion and has one of the lowest incarceration rates in the country, while 59 percent of Alaskan women report experiencing domestic abuse. This statistic is alarming and a moral outrage, shaped by Alaska having the highest population of Indigenous people in the nation.

It's hard if not impossible to speculate based on any of this data alone, especially when each state likely has a different climate around reporting, different resources available to victims who come forward, and potentially widely varying rates of unreported domestic abuse, among other factors. Altogether, questions remain unanswered: Why do some states have higher rates of domestic abuse? Do the politics and ideologies of these states impact rates of domestic abuse? Do higher state-level rates of domestic abuse impact voting behaviors and electoral outcomes and legislation? The majority of states that passed abortion bans in recent years and have the highest incarceration rates also have domestic abuse rates that surpass the national average. But there are far more policy areas beyond abortion access that carry disparate impact on survivors, and there's no clear data on the extent to which rates of domestic abuse limit victims' political power and consequently shape electoral outcomes.

It can't be emphasized enough that people in all parts of the country across the political spectrum commit horrendous acts of domestic and sexual violence behind closed doors; in this way, abuse *is* nonpartisan and non-ideological. But the limited data I've reviewed offers hints and reveals patterns and threads that I believe are worth continuing to pull. Far more research remains to be done, and the vastly limited available data and information we have underscore the dismissal and deprioritization of survivors' safety in society broadly. Yet the daunting reality is that the private nature of domestic abuse and voting make comprehensive numbers and answers about this issue impossible.

We're not completely in the dark about the realities that victims of abuse face, or the erasure and suppression of their political voices by abusive partners. There is continual research on the national, state, and in some places even local levels examining the prevalence of domestic violence and the different forms it takes. Nearly all states also run varying forms of programs to assist people who escape abusers or stalkers with safer, more private options for voter registration. Legislators who advocate for abuse victims should introduce legislation to gather data on how many people are seeking these services, and even more urgently, should educate the public about the resources and options available to victims.

We need more research, but more than that, we need more resources and options for victims and survivors so that they can safely tell us what they need, what they've suffered in silence, and how we can restore and protect their political power. And certainly, we need more storytelling, reporting, and power analysis that recognizes the interconnected, inherently political experiences of victims and survivors.

4

REPRODUCING STATE VIOLENCE

Voting isn't easy, even for the most privileged among us, and even for those our voting system steeped in exclusionary racism was designed to serve. In the first election I voted in, in 2016, I wound up casting provisional ballots in both the primary in June and the general in November—I can't quite remember the mix-up, only that as desperately intent as I'd been on voting, I'd somehow messed up my voter registration. In other states, and for communities that face more significant barriers, making time to vote and participate in elections can be nearly impossible.

Between 2010—incidentally, the same year the far-right, insurgent "Tea Party" movement swept Congress and state legislatures across the country—and 2022, thirty-six states have enacted new voter identification requirements at the polls, including seven states with especially strict photo ID laws. These laws are designed with the specific purpose of blocking people of color, Black voters, immigrants, Indigenous voters, low-income people, people with disabilities, trans people, and other marginalized groups from voting. Within months of the 2020 presidential election that saw former President Trump sweepingly write off hundreds of thousands of votes from predominantly Black voters and voters of color in states like Pennsylvania, Georgia, and Michigan, and incite an insurrection on January 6, 2021, nineteen states passed thirty-four laws restricting access to voting, and forty-nine states introduced more than 440 voter suppression bills in total.[1]

Voter suppression laws have always been justified by some variation of the conspiracy theories that drove Trump's lies that the election was stolen from him and voter fraud can easily be committed. Voter fraud accounted for 0.02 percent—two one-hundredths of a percent—in the 2012 presidential election; the Brennan Center found just 30 fraudulent ballots are cast for every 23.5 million.[2] In a handful of documented cases, the fraud was actually committed by Trump administration officials and supporters. Nonetheless, Trump's claims, called the "Big Lie," led to the predominantly women secretaries of state in Michigan, Pennsylvania, Arizona, and other swing states in the 2020 election being subjected to violent threats and intimidation for their role in protecting fair elections in their states.

Before Katie Hobbs was elected Arizona's first Democratic secretary of state since 1995, in 2018, she was a social worker who helped run a domestic violence shelter. Within two years of that election, handfuls of armed pro-Trump protesters would be camped outside her house threatening her life over the outcome of the 2020 presidential election. "Far-right trolls threatened my children, they threatened my husband's job as a therapist at a children's hospital, they called my office saying that I deserve to die and asked, 'What is she wearing today? So she'll be easy to get,'" she told me for a 2022 article in Jezebel. Jocelyn Benson, Michigan's secretary of state at the time, said protesters "were showing up outside my house" and "demanding that I not certify the election because folks didn't like the results."[3]

In the aftermath of 2020, voter suppression laws proliferated in state legislatures; although often written in race- and gender-neutral terms on the surface, they're designed to disenfranchise marginalized people. Language barriers can make casting a ballot inaccessible to people of color and non-English speakers, while voter ID laws disproportionately target Black and Latinx voters, who are less likely to own IDs. Trans voters may face discrimination for not having IDs that match their gender identity. Narrowing early voting and closing voting stations can disproportionately suppress the vote for low-wage workers who struggle to take time off work to go vote.

Twenty-one million people—disproportionately representing Black, Latinx, and immigrant communities and low-income people—don't have identification cards, in no small part because, as the American Civil Liberties Union has argued, ID cards aren't always readily available for everyone: "The ID itself can be costly, and even when IDs are free, applicants must incur other expenses to obtain the underlying documents that are needed to get an ID," the organization says.[4] Required travel is another associated cost and obstacle for people with disabilities, the elderly, and people living in rural areas lacking nearby polling sites. Other states purge hundreds of thousands of voters from voter rolls every year or hold and suspend some people's voter registration without warning for ridiculous reasons, such as not voting in previous elections. Voters of color are unsurprisingly targeted at higher rates.

Voter suppression is coordinated, calculated, and has an explicit purpose: to disempower the most marginalized and entrap them in a position of powerlessness, further empowering their oppressors. Survivors and victims of domestic violence are an especially impacted but overlooked electoral group. The United States' system of voter suppression carries vast impact up and down the ballot, and it accords disproportionate power to candidates and politicians who enact anti-victim, anti-women policies, attacking their bodily autonomy and limiting their access to resources to leave their abusers. Systems of oppression are built to reproduce themselves, and institutionalized voter suppression is one apparatus through which the state subjugates and suppresses the political power of victims and survivors.

In 2021 Georgia Gov. Brian Kemp signed a law that reduces the number of ballot boxes, narrows the window for early voting, creates additional discriminatory ID requirements, and grants state officials greater authority to possibly circumvent county election officials if they don't like the outcomes of their elections. Kemp himself only narrowly won Georgia's 2018 gubernatorial election, at which time he served as secretary of state overseeing that election. He wielded that office to purge more than half a million disproportionately Black voters from the state's voter rolls in 2017 alone, and shut down at least 214 polling places primarily in neighborhoods of color over the course of six years. All of these moves were ostensibly to combat so-called voter fraud. But "voter fraud" has always been a dog whistle to delegitimize and invalidate the political demands and voices of people of color—when you don't see people of color as citizens, even as human beings, of course you see their votes and political activities as fraudulent, as innately illegitimate threats to white-supremacist authoritarianism.

GENDER AND GERRYMANDERING

Mother Jones reported in 2019 that, after relying heavily on voter suppression operations to win a majority in the state legislature, Georgia Republicans used these majorities to enact legislation that would allow them to hold power years to come via gerrymandering:

> *Extreme partisan gerrymandering has helped Republicans establish strangleholds on state legislatures around the country. After winning control of the redistricting process following the 2010 election, Georgia Republicans concentrated black voters into as few districts as possible in order to maximize the number of heavily white Republican seats. In 2018, Kemp narrowly won with 50.2 percent of the vote, but Republicans held nearly 60 percent of state's legislative seats. There are few swing districts left in the state—in 2018, an incumbent was elected with no opposition in 112 of 180 House districts in the state.[5]*

Gerrymandering has been key to states enacting roughly 1,500 abortion restrictions and bans since *Roe v. Wade* was decided in 1973; hundreds were enacted in the decade between 2010 and 2020 alone, per Guttmacher Institute's tracking, all against the will of most voters. Voter suppression paved the way for this legislative trend, ultimately yielding the overturning of *Roe* when Mississippi's fifteen-week ban reached the Supreme Court.

In the 2018 midterm elections, Ohio Republicans won 50 percent of the votes cast but won 63 percent of legislative seats in the state House. In the same election, Missouri Republicans won 57 percent of the votes but won 71 percent of state House seats. The Associated Press reported that in the 2019 legislative session, Indiana, Alabama, and Texas were among other states that won significantly higher numbers of state legislative and Congressional seats than their share of the vote in the 2018 elections; not so coincidentally, Republicans held control of the redistricting process in 2010. Michigan, Pennsylvania, and North Carolina are other states where Democrats won the majority of votes in the 2018 election but Republican legislators maintained majority control of the state houses. Outcomes like this don't happen overnight: Ever since the passage of the Voting Rights Act in 1965, redistricting has yielded partisan fights and conservative pushes to write districts with majority-Black voters and voters of color out of existence. Even with the Voting Rights Act in place, Republicans in the 1970s and 1980s continued to organize in "task forces" to intimidate Black voters and voters of color at polls—Republicans' 1981 "task force" in New Jersey assigned white "officers" to harass and even chase away Black and Latinx inner-city voters in droves; consequently, Republican Tom Kean won the gubernatorial race that year by just 1,800 votes. Racist voter intimidation tactics perpetuated by right-wing militias near polling places in communities of color continue today.

The seizure and disparate allocation of power to conservative ideologies in certain, especially gerrymandered, states are inextricably tied to the plight of victims and survivors. Voter suppression places nearly immeasurable control in the hands of politicians who enact policies and make funding decisions that target and harm communities of color and deny vital resources to survivors and victims of domestic abuse. Look no further than the output of legislation from the state houses of states with some of the highest reported domestic abuse rates—which are, unsurprisingly, also epicenters of voter suppression and gerrymandering. In a particularly jarring example of the impact of gerrymandering on electoral outcomes at the federal level, in 2018 Texas Democrats won 47 percent of the vote statewide but won only thirteen of the state's thirty-six Congressional seats.[6] The policy outcomes for women, abuse victims, and marginalized people in this state are especially egregious: Abortion is banned, doctors can face prison time for offering abortion care to pregnant people who are dying, the state maintains a shockingly high population of incarcerated people (many are survivors), and parents who support trans kids can be investigated for child abuse—all while nothing is done to help actual victims of child abuse or other forms of sexual and domestic abuse.

Institutionalized voter suppression in a variety of forms exists on every level of government. That certainly includes Congressional maps, and also the electoral college itself, which accords disproportionately greater power to Republican candidates who support anti-women and survivor ideologies and policies—since the early 2000s, almost every Supreme Court justice has been appointed by a Republican who lost the popular vote.

Many of the states with the highest rates of reported domestic abuse also have a greater proportion of electoral college representation than their proportion of the US population. For example, Alaska, where 59 percent of women have reported domestic abuse, sends 3 electors out of the total of 538 electors in the electoral college; that—0.56 percent of the electoral college—is more than double its share of the US population, which is 0.22 percent. Similarly, Montana, where more than 39 percent of women report experiencing domestic abuse, also has electoral college representation that's almost double its share of the US population—0.56 percent of electoral college electors, with just 0.3 percent of the US population. A significant portion of these states' populations are inevitably survivors who are denied representation by their abusers.

WEAPONIZING THE EXECUTIVE
BRANCH AGAINST SURVIVORS

The electoral college itself is weaponized as a tool against survivors, as the apparatus through which the president and executive branch are filled. And particularly relevant to matters of survivor justice, at least since the 1970s, the presidency has been instrumental to overseeing Title IX policy, which addresses campus sexual assault and gender equality at publicly funded institutions. Prior to the Obama era, Title IX disputes primarily surrounded funding for gender-segregated sports. Since the Obama years, Title IX itself has become virtually synonymous with rights and protections for victims of campus sexual assault—and presidential administrations have sweeping powers to dictate these policies. Presidential administrations also make rules governing Title X, which provides federal funding for reproductive health care and was enacted in 1970 as part of the Public Health Service Act. Title X, which prioritizes the needs of low-income and uninsured people, is prohibited from covering abortion care due to the Hyde Amendment, a Congressional budget rider that's blocked federal funding for abortion care since 1976, to tremendous consequences for low-income people who rely on Medicaid coverage for health care. Per one study from All* Above All, one in four pregnant people on Medicaid who's sought abortion care has been forced to carry an unwanted pregnancy to term because of Hyde.[7]

Title IX and Title X, ever politicized, have strong bearing on the health and safety of victims and survivors—Title X determines whether they can afford and access the reproductive health care they may need to leave an abusive relationship. And Title IX policies determine whether sexual and domestic violence victims can go to school in safe environments. The Trump administration worked closely with militant men's rights activists to enact policies that included narrowing the parameters of sexual misconduct that schools are required to respond to, allowing schools to not investigate off-campus sexual assaults, and even opening the door for student survivors to be cross-examined in-person by their assailants. Trump's Education Department also reversed the Obama-era guidelines that instructed colleges and universities to investigate reports in a timely manner and lowered the evidentiary standard for reported assaults so that more survivors would be comfortable coming forward. Survivor-supportive Title IX policies are a lifeline: 34 percent of campus sexual survivors are forced to drop out of school,[8] and 90 percent of campus sexual assaults aren't reported at all. Research published by survivor justice group Know Your IX in 2021 found a common trend of student survivors being the ones to be threatened or punished by their schools for behaviors like drinking and substance use prior to being assaulted. Lack of proactive protections for student survivors delineated by Title IX also leaves them vulnerable to intimidation and silencing, primarily through the threat of costly defamation lawsuits from their assailants.

I find myself constantly returning to the statistic that 34 percent of student sexual assault survivors are forced to drop out of university. This statistic inevitably contributes to the disproportionate impact of student debt on survivors, among the many financial ramifications of surviving sexual trauma: Between 2012 and 2017, nearly 40 percent of people who took out student loans didn't complete their education in that time period.[9] Included in that group, surely, are some of the 34 percent of student survivors who were forced to drop out of school; with debilitating debt and without degrees, they are essentially set up for failure.

It's no accident that Black women and women of color are among those most impacted by the student debt crisis—they also experience disproportionately higher rates of intimate partner violence and campus sexual assault.[10] All of this is a reminder of how economic policies contribute to or literally create the optimal conditions for domestic abuse to thrive. In the absence of living wages and universal health care, many women are entrapped in abusive relationships specifically because they rely on their abusive partner for health insurance, shelter, assistance with paying off debt, or money in general. If abuse victims have significant student debt, they could be rendered even more reliant on abusive partnerships and face even greater financial barriers to leaving the relationship. These are the conditions to which we're subjecting young people and survivors when we elect presidents who don't care about them.

FEDERAL JUDGES AS ABUSERS

Arguably the most impactful and long-term power of the presidency is determining judicial appointments—a role that requires the cooperation of the US Senate. While the House of Representatives is oriented to roughly match the population with proportionate representation, the Senate sweepingly assigns two Senate seats per state. California and New York together share almost 20 percent of the US population and have the most diverse populations in the nation, but they're represented by just 4 percent of the US Senate. Much smaller, more white and conservative states have historically capitalized on their disproportionate power over the Senate to confirm extremist Supreme Court justices and federal judges to lifetime seats, where their rulings have national implications for abortion access, survivor justice, immigration, and carceral and economic policies that carry the most harm for women, survivors, and people of color.

In the first three years of Trump's presidency alone, he appointed 30 percent of circuit court judges. At 193 appointments by April 2020, Trump appointed 15 percent more than the average president at that stage and significantly more than his predecessor. Trump's picks displayed a pattern of inexperience, religious extremism, and, to put it mildly, political views that carry disparate harm for women and victims of color. Several of his appointments were deemed unqualified by the nonpartisan American Bar Association, but in an unprecedented trend, they were confirmed anyway due to the Republican-controlled Senate.

Supreme Court Justice appointees like Brett Kavanaugh and Amy Coney Barrett, who had virtually nonexistent experience as a judge and once held a leadership role in a Christian extremist group accused of rampant child sexual abuse, will be remembered as Trump's most consequential and dangerous judicial picks—for good reason. But Trump appointed dozens upon dozens of extremists to other federal courts, too. Judge Neomi Rao on the US Court of Appeals for the District of Columbia Circuit faced backlash for her prior inflammatory writings blaming victims of date rape for their assaults and also blasting the perceived "advantages" of LGBTQ students and students of color. In 1994 Rao, as a student at Yale, wrote in a column about rape culture:

> *It has always seemed self-evident to me that even if I drank a lot, I would still be responsible for my actions. A man who rapes a drunk girl should be prosecuted. At the same time, a good way to avoid a potential date rape is to stay reasonably sober.[11]*

Another example: Trump-appointed Judge John Bush on the US Court of Appeals for the Sixth Circuit compared abortion to slavery, and at one point called for Speaker of the House Nancy Pelosi to be "gagged." Before Trump appointed Barrett to the Supreme Court, he first appointed her to the US Court of Appeals for the Seventh Circuit. In Barrett's earlier speeches, she's called birth control coverage "an assault on religious liberty"; in 2018, while serving as a judge on the US Court of Appeals for the Seventh Circuit, she overturned a jury award to a teenager who was allegedly raped in jail by a guard. Her connections to gender-based violence would later manifest in her support for overturning *Roe* in 2022 and imposing pregnancy and childbirth on pregnant people without their consent.

Judge Kyle Duncan on the US Court of Appeals for the Fifth Circuit, another Trump appointee, rose to legal prominence through the "surgical precision" with which he dismantled voting rights, as Lambda Legal put it. Trump also appointed Judge Wendy Vitter to the US District Court for the Eastern District of Louisiana, despite her numerous previously published writings in which she falsely claimed medication abortions could be reversed and that Planned Parenthood kills "150,000 females every year." Judge Mark Norris on the US District Court for the Western District of Tennessee, another Trump appointee, previously swore by opposing abortion "under any circumstance," and Judge Matthew Kacsmaryk on the US District Court for the Northern District of Texas called being transgender "a delusion."

These are the judges and justices currently deciding cases about everything ranging from whether a fetus is legally a person to whether trans people have rights to health care, whether insurers should cover birth control, whether sexual harassment in the workplace is in fact bad, whether protections for students against campus sexual assault are legal, whether people of color have the right to vote.

Presidents come and go, and senators, too—but a forty-year-old judge could hold power and shape policy for the next decades, literal generations; they hold their offices for life, unless they willingly retire or are miraculously removed by Congress. No amount of progress in any issue area is possible, no matter how many progressive, feminist lawmakers we elect, if their legislation could just as easily be struck down by right-wing hacks in the courts.

Universal health care policies, livable universal basic income, abortion care coverage, housing for all, non-carceral protections and resources for victims of domestic abuse and survivors, and more could all create an entirely new, more just, and equitable world for victims and survivors, or prevent some acts of violation from happening in the first place. But none of these policy changes are sustainable within a hostile, repressive judicial system. And a hostile, repressive judicial system becomes inevitable when the Senate and electoral college accord vastly disparate power to conservative states.

Frankly, the only reasonable solution is to abolish the US Senate, the electoral college, perhaps even the Supreme Court—or at the very least, make compromises like establishing statehood for Washington, DC, which has a substantially larger population than the state of Wyoming and other states that receive two senators. The progressive DC electorate could begin to balance small, majority-white states that wield their disproportionate Senate power to carry out a ruthlessly anti-women and anti-victim policy agenda.

When conservative politicians enact legislation that restricts who's able to vote, they tip electoral scales in their favor, pick up seats in state legislatures, and use these seats to pass harmful legislation that perpetuates violence on the most marginalized—including and especially those who are harmed by domestic violence. With this electoral and legislative power, conservatives also seize control of redistricting processes and can cement their agenda in place for years to come, in state houses, in Congress, in the White House, on the judiciary.

The system continually reproduces itself by design. And women, abuse victims, and marginalized people pay the price.

THE MYTH OF THE COASTAL LIBERAL
AND SOUTHERN BIGOT

In my analysis of electoral and policy outcomes in the South, Midwest, and traditionally "red" states and regions, I would be remiss to not acknowledge my own biases and blind spots as someone who grew up, went to school, and has worked exclusively in famously liberal metropolises. As an adult, I've lived in the Bay Area, Los Angeles, and Washington, DC. Beneath the "Black Lives Matter" murals, rainbow flags, "no one is illegal" street signs, and "the future is female" posters, these cities have led the nation in policy-making that empowers gentrification and dehumanizing unhoused people. The Silicon Valley tech bubble pioneered ballot measures to deny living wages and health care to gig workers like Uber drivers starting in 2020, routinely expands the surveillance state by pioneering products like home Ring cameras, and works closely with law enforcement every step of the way. In 2022 a US Senate investigation revealed Amazon has been sharing customers' Ring camera footage with law enforcement agencies without owners' consent for years.

Big tech's coziness with police has particularly unsettling implications in post-*Roe* America: That same year, Vice News reported that a private firm was selling the location data of people who visited abortion clinics for as cheap as $160 a pop. For years now, search history and location data from Google have contributed to people facing criminal charges for pregnancy loss, while Meta has been sharing the private data of people seeking abortion care with anti-abortion crisis pregnancy centers, as well. Within weeks of the fall of *Roe*, the company shared the text messages of a Nebraska teen who had self-managed an abortion with police, who then arrested and charged her with a felony.

Beyond shilling for police and developing carceral technologies, the Silicon Valley has gone out of its way to harm sexual assault survivors.

Also in 2022 (a truly banner year for tech companies, apparently), Lyft agreed to a $25 million settlement to resolve claims from its shareholders that the company failed to be transparent about "safety problems"—which sure seems like a gentle way to phrase 2019 lawsuits from fourteen women who say they were raped or sexually assaulted by their Lyft drivers. The survivor-plaintiffs suing Lyft—including one woman who was kidnapped by her Lyft driver, held at gunpoint, and gang-raped in 2017—didn't receive a dime.[12]

Put simply, regions viewed as progressive bastions all have their own issues. Meanwhile, activists of color in the South are on the front lines of revolutionary efforts to fund abortion access, support bail funds, and lead transformative movements rooted in mutual aid and community care. In 2022 Alabama and Tennessee became two of the first states in the nation to move to formally ban slavery through forced prison labor in their state constitutions via ballot measure, while nearly every other state—including in coastal, ostensibly liberal regions—continues to allow this. Yet this work is oft erased by mainstream liberal talking points that ignore Southern activism and blame the South (a region that many Black communities and communities of color call home) for Republican policies.

Extremist anti-LGBTQ laws and abortion bans enacted by Southern or traditionally red, heavily voter-suppressed states often prompt unsolicited advice from liberals in blue states on social media. Much of this "advice" calls on those in affected states to just "vote harder"—despite the fact that said abortion bans and anti-LGBTQ laws are widely unpopular and enabled by rampant voter suppression. Blue-state liberals have also called on marginalized people in red, voter-suppressed states to up and move to another state, as if it's *that* easy. Even top liberal politicians from Democratic states have co-opted some of this language. Shortly after Texas moved to criminalize gender-affirming care for trans youth in 2022, California Governor Gavin Newsom tweeted, "To fearful families in Texas right now—California's door is always open to you." The sentiment was echoed by New York City Mayor Eric Adams, who similarly tweeted: "You're welcome in New York City . . . Always."

"It's so insulting to the people that have been on the ground doing this work for decades, trying to ensure access to no avail, to act like you have the answers and we don't," Aimee Arrambide, executive director of the grassroots reproductive justice organization Avow Texas, told me in my reporting for Jezebel in 2022, referring to statements like Newsom's and Adams's.[13] She's spent the last several decades organizing for abortion rights on the ground in her state. Indigenous reproductive justice activist and Indigenous Women Rising executive director Rachael Lorenzo added that, in particular, telling Indigenous people who live in red states to just move has an added dimension of colonialism: "It's another form of saying that your ownership, your ties to your land and communities, are disposable." Instead, both Arrambide and Lorenzo agree that advocates in Democratic states who want to help women, pregnant people, LGBTQ people, people of color, and victims and survivors in red, voter-suppressed states should listen—and certainly donate—to abortion funds, mutual aid groups, and grassroots organizers on the ground.

To politically empower and truly advocate for survivors and marginalized people in these regions, for starters, we can't just erase their existence for political expediency and convenient liberal talking points about red states. Survivor justice requires us to challenge the voter suppression myths and apparatuses that create and maintain conservative majorities in these states. Survivor justice requires us to follow the leadership of Southern activists of color and support their on-the-ground efforts to help victims and survivors in their states, rather than dismiss them. And certainly, survivor justice requires an overhaul of the broader systems of power—the Senate, the electoral college, the Supreme Court—that are at odds with the empowerment and well-being of women, gender-oppressed people, and abuse victims.

5

RAPE CULTURE IN THE CARCERAL CAPITALIST POLICE STATE

In 2022 San Francisco District Attorney Chesa Boudin made a stunning announcement: The city would henceforth no longer use DNA collected from sexual assault victims to investigate them for unrelated crimes. What was stunning about the announcement was its necessity. It came just weeks after the San Francisco Police Department had been exposed for quite literally using a victim's rape kit collected six years prior to charge her with a poverty-based crime in February 2022. Around that same time, it was reported that for the last seven years, SFPD's crime lab had maintained a database of DNA from victims of violent crimes and even child victims, which could be used as evidence in possible future, unrelated criminal cases against them. Boudin, who had earned a reputation as a "progressive" prosecutor (if such a thing exists) seeking to reform the system from within, was removed from office mere months after rolling out this effort to protect victims from state punishment.

Boudin's recall came just two years after a national reckoning with the role of policing in perpetuating white-supremacist violence and racial caste in the US—emblematic of the whiplash-like backlash that almost automatically follows any progress toward social justice. The emergent anti-racist mass movements of the 2020s had, of course, been spurred by several police killings of Black people, including George Floyd and Breonna Taylor, whose deaths sparked nationwide protests. Protests across the country made the devastating, anti-Black violence of the police state we live in increasingly impossible to ignore, and they coincided with mass organizing to demand the release of incarcerated people across the country who were placed at exponentially greater risk of contracting and dying from COVID. It seemed, finally, many people were willing to listen for the first time to discourse on police and prison abolition that once seemed far-fetched in the mainstream.

Seasoned activists and ordinary people across the country marched in the streets, even as the pandemic raged on, and demanded divestment from policing and prisons. After years of tepid police reforms failing to stop the violence, there was a growing understanding that broader, deeper change was needed.

In May 2022 a mass shooting perpetrated by a self-admitted neo-Nazi killed ten people in the beloved grocery store of a Black neighborhood in Buffalo, New York. Mere days later, the Uvalde, Texas, elementary school shooter killed nineteen kids and two teachers at a primarily Latinx elementary school. For forty minutes, Uvalde police officers—whose department swallows up 40 percent of the small town's budget—stood outside as a gunman locked himself in a classroom of fourth graders, because, in their words, "no children were at risk." To say they did nothing is to give law enforcement too much credit; they offered the gunman a defensive line, tackling, beating, assaulting, and handcuffing parents who tried to rush the classroom to save their kids.

Still, Democrats and Republicans both responded by insisting more funding for police was the solution to the very carnage police enable, if not *cause*, by hoarding money and resources that could otherwise be dedicated to actual prevention of violence and crime. How exactly will police, who kill 1,000 people per year with guns, be the ones to stop gun violence?[1] In 2020, at the height of calls for police to be defunded, we were asked, "What about school shootings?" as if—in all cases of crime and violence—police do anything but show up after the fact and brutalize or kill people of color. Uvalde was a devastating, radicalizing moment: Police willfully refuse to save us from the problems they create, and no amount of reform can change this. We need abolition.

REDEFINING VIOLENCE

Abolition is a necessity of anti-racist liberation within a white-supremacist, carceral police state like the US, which has long profited off criminalizing, incarcerating, and exploiting predominantly Black communities. Naturally, abolitionist thought requires imagination that many of us were actively discouraged from developing in a state that maintains its power through exploiting innately racist definitions of criminality and violence. When we hear about a society without police, our minds have been molded and disciplined to immediately picture stereotypical violent crimes, largely because many people sweepingly associate violence with individualized acts: murder, armed robbery, assaults, rape. We're socialized to understand violence exclusively as interpersonal, individual acts, as opposed to institutionalized state violence—the conditions that create poverty, that force people to remain pregnant, that criminalize victims of sexual violence—resulting in more than 2.3 million people imprisoned in the US, often for the great crime of being unable to afford to live in a society that spends more on policing than health care. Violence, following these limited, carceral definitions, could never be understood as incarceration itself, or as police departments, say, using a survivor's rape kit to later charge them with a crime—we're taught it's something perpetuated by individuals, not systems of power.

And when conversations about abolition arise, it never takes long for sexual violence to be invoked to defend and justify the imagined need for policing and incarceration, despite how carceral responses continually reproduce and exacerbate sexual violence rather than protect victims and survivors. Survivors should never be invoked as convenient political talking points—*especially* not to uphold a system in which, as previously noted, nearly half of police officers themselves are known domestic abusers, and victims of sexual violence are almost exponentially more likely to be charged with crimes and imprisoned than their assailants. A quarter of surveyed women have said they were arrested or threatened with arrest when they called 911 to report intimate partner violence. Hundreds of thousands of rape kits sit untested in police departments across the country, despite how police have more than enough funding to process them.[2]

Beyond high rates of sexual and domestic violence perpetrated by police officers, law enforcement has proven untrustworthy and dangerous to victims in other ways. A 1997 study found that half of police officers adhere to victim-blaming myths and ideologies, including believing most rapes are committed by "the man in the bushes" rather than "the date that got carried away," and consequently being skeptical of reported rapes perpetrated by an abuser who the victim knew, which comprise most rapes. About a decade later, their grasp of gender and violence remained alarmingly backward. As previously noted, in 2010 about half of surveyed police officers said they were unlikely to believe a woman who said her husband had raped her, and most surveyed officers believed the majority of rape reports are false; police departments often classify rapes that didn't involve use of a weapon or were between people who used to share a romantic relationship as "false reports." As we've seen, all these biases and misconceptions inform how local police appraise and report rates of supposedly falsely reported rapes to the FBI.

This willful ignorance among officers who wield tremendous state power is fundamentally rooted in white supremacy—law enforcement routinely dismisses or further harms victims, while weaponizing feigned concern for victims' safety to target and enact violence on men of color. Narratives about false rape allegations center wealthy white men almost exclusively, despite research that shows Black men are 3.5 times more likely than white men to be wrongfully convicted of sexual assault. The hyperfixation on wealthy white men as the face of false rape accusations,

Amia Srinivasan writes in her 2021 book *The Right to Sex*, is ultimately rooted in the racist panic that there exists even the slightest chance that white men might be treated like Black men by state apparatuses such as the prison system—the very white-supremacist institutions built by design to protect wealthy white men.

The women and victims who police and their supporters claim to protect are not-so-subtly coded as white, because other victims are more likely to know from experience to not seek help from police in the first place. White women themselves have historically fed this panic about the inherent danger that Black men purportedly pose to their fragile white femininity by calling the police on Black people, including kids, whom they perceive as threatening. A white woman named Amy Cooper broke the internet for calling the police on a Black man who was bird-watching in Central Park in 2020, but this wasn't an isolated or exceptional incident. Within months, a different white woman would be caught trying to frame a Black man for stealing her cell phone and calling the police on him—an act that could easily have cost him his life. Historically, false claims of rape and violence by white women against Black men and even Black children were frequently invoked to galvanize lynch mobs. Angela Davis writes about this phenomenon in *Women, Race and Class*:

> *Whoever challenged the racial hierarchy was marked a potential victim of the mob. The endless roster of the dead came to include every sort of insurgent—from the owners of successful Black businesses and workers pressing for higher wages to those who refused to be called "boy" and the defiant women who resisted white men's sexual abuses. Yet public opinion had been captured, and it was taken for granted that lynching was a just response to the barbarous sexual crimes against white womanhood.*[3]

In contrast, the same societal panics about white women ostensibly being attacked by Black men deliberately ignore the violence endured by women of color, especially Black women. The implicit cultural and political hypersexualization of Black men as subhuman, innately bestial beings reinforces and operates in tandem with the hypersexualization of Black women as similarly subhuman, and culturally and politically unrapeable: In 1859 a Mississippi judge ruled than an enslaved man couldn't be charged for the rape of a ten-year-old enslaved girl because the "crime of rape does not exist in this state between African slaves . . . [because] their intercourse is promiscuous"—in other words, the Black girl had been legally deemed unrapeable. In 1918 Florida's state Supreme Court ruled white women who allege they've been raped should be believed and presumed innately sexually virtuous, but not women of "another race that is largely immoral and constitutes an appreciable part of the population." This ruling evidenced the institutionalized sexualization of all women and victims of color, who are sexualized and, in their own ways, marked unrapeable owing to numerous stereotypes rooted in white supremacy. But the ruling was, inevitably, distinctly targeted at Black women.

White supremacy ensures Black women and survivors are oppressed by not just white men and the state, but by men within their own racial community who harm them. From Supreme Court Justice Clarence Thomas in the 1990s, to R&B singer and convicted rapist R. Kelly in 2022, to former Lieutenant Governor Justin Fairfax of Virginia in 2019, powerful Black men publicly accused of sexual violence have weaponized language about historical lynch mobs and anti-Black oppressions to defend themselves and spin the Black women they harmed as perpetrators of white supremacy. What's ignored, of course, due to historical erasure of racist violence against Black women, is that Black women, too, were victimized by lynchings; they, too, are brutalized by police and the state to this day, despite dehumanizing viral videos of Black, male corpses, slain and mutilated by law enforcement, that have convinced the public that Black men, and not women, are solely victimized by racist state violence.

As recently as 2015, a white Oklahoma police officer was caught abusing his power to sexually assault dozens of Black women with impunity for years.[4] This—police officers exploiting their state power to more easily perpetrate or enable sexual violence, especially inflicted on women of color—is a recurring theme. In many other documented cases, officers have been exposed for abusing information databases to stalk, harass, and target women. Months before the wave of anti-police protests throughout the summer of 2020, a Utah police officer who had denied a woman a restraining order shortly before her stalker killed her was caught sharing explicit photos of her with other officers.[5] In September 2022 a Florida police officer was fired but charged with no crimes for allegedly repeatedly groping a minor in his custody and looking at nude photos of her on her phone, per the *Tampa Bay Times*.[6] Roughly overlapping with the police killing of Sarah Everard in London in 2021—a reminder that policing is a fundamentally violent institution around the world, not just in the US—between 2019 and 2021 officers in Arizona, Georgia, Maryland, Kansas, and other states were fired or put on leave for stalking individual women.[7]

PREGNANCY AND CARCERALITY

The most visible, unsurprisingly white advocates of the MeToo movement inadvertently tied it early on to carceral solutions, celebrating long prison sentences for abusers. But by 2020, public opinion within progressive and intersectional feminist spaces began to veer toward recognition that reliance on policing will always carry the most harm for victims of sexual violence, and particularly those of color. The Violence Against Women Act's mandatory arrest provision for domestic abuse cases that are reported to law enforcement has often enough led to dual arrests, or even coercion of the victim with jail time to compel testimony against their abuser. Victims may also face criminalization for practicing self-defense against an attacker, or "exposing" their children to their abusers, or their immigration status—even the outcome of their pregnancy, if they're suspected to have "endangered" their fetus from substance use struggles, harm from their abuser, or having a self-managed abortion. The reasons victims are policed and criminalized are endless.

Prosecutors and local police departments have virtually unfettered discretion to monitor and punish pregnant people specifically. Shortly after news the Supreme Court would reverse *Roe v. Wade* in the spring of 2022, for my reporting in Jezebel I talked to California's attorney general,

Rob Bonta, who was the first state attorney general to give explicit guidance telling police departments to not prosecute pregnancy loss or self-managed abortion—a guidance that wouldn't be necessary at all were it not for the state violence inherent to policing. As California's top law enforcement official, Bonta led the nation in efforts to prevent the criminalization of pregnancy loss, which he noted "can be deeply personal and traumatic," and to protect people from prosecution for pregnancy outcomes that include miscarriage, stillbirth, or self-managed abortion.

In January 2022 Bonta issued a statewide alert advising law enforcement to not charge people for murder over pregnancy loss, regardless of their behavior—including drug use—before losing the pregnancy. The alert came after two California women had been charged with "fetal murder" in 2017 and 2019 for stillbirths that allegedly involved substance use. Both women, Adora Perez and Chelsea Becker, in that order, have since had their charges dropped with support from Bonta and his office. Perez, who was sentenced in 2017 to eleven years in prison, was finally released in March 2022 after serving four years, isolated from her family and forced to endure the trauma of her pregnancy loss and substance use struggles behind bars.

Bonta said these charges stemmed from misuse of fetal homicide laws on the books in California and most states. The laws have been weaponized by some prosecutors and local police departments to punish and criminalize disproportionately Black, brown, Indigenous, and other people of color for pregnancy loss, which research has shown they experience at higher rates, while also facing over-policing as an extension of the racist War on Drugs.

"The legislature did not intend to include a pregnant person's own actions that might result in a miscarriage or stillbirth—rather, the addition was meant to criminalize violence done to a pregnant person," Bonta said of his directive in a press conference. "The loss of a pregnancy at any stage is traumatic, it is physically traumatic, emotionally traumatic—it's an experience that should be met with an outreached hand, not handcuffs and murder charges."

In Wisconsin, fetal homicide laws are taken a step further by the state's dated Unborn Child Protection Act, or Act 292, which allows Wisconsin to take pregnant people into custody, assign a lawyer for their embryo or fetus (but not the pregnant person), and send the pregnant person to drug treatment, psychiatric hospitals, or even jail if they're suspected of substance use. Act 292, enacted in 1997, is ultimately just one of many ways law enforcement and carceral actors are empowered to insinuate themselves into every aspect of our lives, including pregnancy. Incarcerated pregnant people face similarly bleak, dehumanizing conditions: As of this time of writing, more than a dozen states still permit prisons to shackle pregnant people, even while they give birth, despite the tremendous danger this poses to the pregnant person and their pregnancy. One study from before the overturning of *Roe* found most incarcerated people didn't know they still had the right to abortion. Most prisons require the pregnant person to pay for both the abortion and all associated costs, including gas, transportation fees, and even "officer time" for those who escort them. This is often impossible: In California, for instance, incarcerated people working full-time are paid $0.08 an hour, and at most $3.90 per day.

Notably, prisons have long been plagued with rape and sexual violence, with 60 percent of prison rapes committed by guards. That some incarcerated people could be impregnated by their rapists and denied abortion care only compounds this trauma. A Black, formerly incarcerated woman named Sadie Bell sued New York state in 2022, recounting to the *New York Times* that she had been raped and impregnated by a prison sergeant at Bayview Correctional Facility in Manhattan years ago. When Bell learned she was pregnant, she was moved into solitary confinement for weeks before eventually being transferred to Bedford Hills Correctional Facility. At Bedford, Bell said, she experienced highly painful pregnancy complications before being shackled and rushed to the hospital. She learned she'd had an ectopic pregnancy resulting in a ruptured fallopian tube, loss of five pints of blood, and permanent infertility. Ectopic pregnancies can cause severe complications and even death without abortion, despite how laws in some states prohibit abortions even in cases like Bell's. Bell told the *Times* she never "received treatment for all of this."[8]

Reproductive oppression and coercion are an indelible feature of the carceral system. As recently as 2017, a judge in Tennessee offered to reduce jail time for incarcerated people (who are more likely to be poor people of color) who "willingly" opted to be sterilized.[9] In detention facilities for migrants specifically, reports in 2020 revealed that an ICE doctor had performed hysterectomies on migrant women without their knowledge or consent. The ICE doctor in question reportedly "performed 'excessive, invasive, and often unnecessary gynecological procedures' on dozens of women detained for deportation proceedings" per the 2022 findings of a Senate investigation.[10]

Endemic prison rape exemplifies how the carceral system presents no solutions to societal gender-based violence; instead, it recreates and exacerbates the conditions that breed this violence. Just as the existence of prisons is erroneously justified as a means to protect rape victims, other carceral tools like sex offender registries and criminal policies governing child offenses have, in many cases, carried harm for children. Notably, statutory rape laws that purport to protect children, the most vulnerable members of society, have been wielded by local law enforcement to have the opposite impact, carrying disproportionate harm for young queer people of color. Nonpartisan state and federal sex offender laws across the country are more likely to criminalize minors who engage in sexual behaviors with other minors or young people than to protect children from predation and abuse.[11] This is, of course, all while sexual health education in schools is so lacking that young people can't be expected to know state and local laws about sexual behaviors that could possibly result in their criminalization. Black, brown, and LGBTQ youth face the highest rates of criminalization, even as minors. LGBTQ youth are at greater risk because they're especially marginalized within the carceral state, imprisoned at three times the rate of the general population in no small part because our institutions continue to regard queer sexuality as inherently deviant.

SEX WORK AND CARCERALITY

In the vein of threats to young people's safety, the criminalization of sex work places queer youth and women of color at perpetual risk of punishment, policing, and state violence. Laws like the FOSTA-SESTA Act of

2018 often result in sex workers in street economies being unable to share life-saving information and resources without the possibility of their communications being surveilled, leading to their criminalization. As a result, abusive clients roam free and can harm sex workers with impunity; so long as sex work is criminalized, sex workers who experience sexual violence and assaults have nowhere to turn.

Sex workers can and often do face criminalization and incarceration for self-defense against their abusers. Cyntoia Brown was imprisoned for more than fifteen years for killing a man who assaulted and tried to kill her. In the summer of 2022, nearly sixteen years after Brown was convicted, Pieper Lewis, a seventeen-year-old survivor of trafficking and sexual assault, who's also Black, was ordered by an Iowa judge to pay $150,000 in restitution to the family of her abuser after killing him in self-defense.

Notably, queer and trans youth who are cut off from their families are more likely to become sex workers. So, too, are poor women and girls of color, undocumented people, and people with disabilities, for whom sex work may be their most accessible means to make an income and survive.

While many people are forced into sex work because they don't have other options, others choose sex work from the options they do have—it may pay better and come with more agency and superior working conditions. People can and do experience sexual harassment, abuse, assault, and certainly degradation and exploitation in any job, all while being underpaid and accorded little control over their hours and conditions. No job or line of work is inherently dignified under capitalism, a system that forces all of us to commodify our skills and our bodies for wages. There is no dignity in a system that requires us to either work or die. Revulsion aimed at sex workers—who don't harm anyone—but not, say, investment bankers who actively work to exacerbate wealth inequality, or computer engineers who advance the neo-fascist, surveillance-state agendas of tech companies, is entirely rooted in slut-shaming, sexism, classism, and racism.

The criminal status of sex work also leads to misguided sex-offense charges that can entrap disproportionately queer people of color on sex-offender registries for the rest of their lives, and subsequently lead to them be denied crucial public resources. While sex-offender registries are purportedly meant to protect children from sexual predation, in most states, minors can be registered as sexual offenders themselves for sexual contact and activities with other minors, and certainly for sex work—especially if they're LGBTQ or people of color and immediately regarded as "criminal" by the state.

The "sex offense legal regime," as Judith Levine and Erica R. Meiners call it in *The Feminist and the Sex Offender*, plays a significant role in the expansion of policing and mass incarceration and can lead to lifelong carceral punishments for vulnerable populations. While there are no simple answers to the policy changes required to protect youth from the very real threat of child sexual predation, one way to protect and care for children is to invest in child care, health care, education, housing, and other community resources, rather than policing, imprisonment, and surveillance. Even when abusers and rapists are incarcerated for their crimes (though rapists rarely are), it's worth critically interrogating what survivors gain from this outcome. Prisons and the judicial system do not provide resources or support to those who have been harmed; they only function to reproduce the trauma and violence that victims have already suffered.

ABOLITION

To help make the case for abolition, in June 2020 survivors and advocates took to Twitter en masse to share stories of police who did nothing in response to their reported rapes and assaults. They shared stories of officers telling them they didn't have enough evidence for anything to be done, asking if the incident in question had just been a misunderstanding, even using reported rapes to access victims' contact information and inexplicably flirt with them. There is evidence that police departments downgrade reported offenses, for instance, from assault to harassment, and discourage victims from filing complaints to artificially inflate success rates at reducing crime. One 2020 survey of twenty anti-violence organizations and rape crisis programs that have worked with over 5,000 sexual assault survivors in New York City found most of these groups said the NYPD is failing to meet survivors' needs.[12] The carceral capitalist police state is inherently at odds with the well-being of women and survivors, because interpersonal and state violence are inseparable from one another.

Abolition as opposed to reform is the backbone of survivor justice. And as authors and scholar-activists Angela Davis, Gina Dent, Erica Meiners, and Beth Richie argue in their 2022 book *Abolition. Feminism. Now.*, abolition expands beyond police and prisons to the massive overhaul of social and economic policy that would render crime and criminalization obsolete. Abolition also acknowledges that a wide range of state apparatuses that are less overtly carceral still expand the police state, requiring state surveillance and punishment of marginalized groups. For example: the surveillance of mostly poor parents and families of color seeking welfare services, and the invasive and often punishing methods deployed by social workers. Nearly all government family regulation systems, in general, are structurally designed to shame and control poor communities of color. Further, abolition demands personal interrogation of our own internalized, carceral values and logics, which stymie our ability to imagine and fight for a less cruel world.

Generations of co-opting survivor justice to breathe fire into public support for the carceral police state have convinced many of us that we need police to protect victims and in general make society a safer place. This notion is, again, a result of our racist, classist conceptions of what constitutes and defines "violence" and "crime." These definitions erase how the majority of incarcerated people are imprisoned for so-called survival crimes—they face punishment, policing, and criminalization for growing up in a country where we invest drastically more in prisons and police than in fulfilling basic human needs. To that end, it's not only rape and sexual violence that are used to justify police and prisons—many defenders of the carceral police state also invoke specific, highly racialized crimes such as gang violence. They consequently ignore that gangs often form due to lack of investment into community resources and as a means for members to protect themselves *from* police.

These definitions of crime absolve white, wealth-hoarding capitalists of the daily violence they enact on society with the explicit help of police. This exploitation leads to millions dying each day from being unable to afford health care or housing. Specifically, when they hoard wealth by denying living wages and benefits to workers, and by refusing to pay taxes to support a thriving social safety net, vulnerable, low-income people of color are unable to afford the astronomical costs of living in this country. The result is mass suffering and death. Yet these behaviors from the wealthy are normalized, rather than singled out, identified as criminal and violent, and punished.

When the poor and exploited are unable to care for themselves and afford the resources they need to live, we should collectively recognize this as violent. Capitalism normalizes lethally violent acts that render the country unlivable for poor communities of color. Domestic violence victims are forced to remain in violent living situations by the government's refusal to offer resources meeting our basic needs as a right to each individual. Interpersonal and domestic violence, racist policing, and exploitation by capitalism are ultimately inseparable from each other.

White supremacy and our overarching capitalist system have always been collectively entrusted to define "crime"—they conveniently ignore that nearly every cent that billionaire capitalists reap is from some degree of theft and exploitation, yet Wall Street bankers responsible for the 2008 financial crash that ruined countless lives will never see the inside of a prison. Police actively enact violence not just through physical assaults and killings but also through inherently violent enforcement of capitalist conceptions of private property rights to enable massive wealth inequality and exploitation. Protesters and everyday, exploited workers may be arrested and imprisoned for property damage or stealing goods from massive, multibillion-dollar corporations that exploit them. But in contrast, the rules of our carceral capitalist police state will protect the well-being and property of these same corporations and allow them to steal from workers through starvation wages with impunity. Police are also an indispensable source of revenue for cities amid a mounting trend of municipal privatization. To reimburse massive bank loans to pay for city budgets (which invest disproportionate amounts into policing), cities have relied on over-policing and criminalizing Black and brown communities to generate revenue through fines, asset forfeiture abuse, prison labor exploitation, and other dehumanizing means.[13] Abolishing police and prisons is a necessity to dismantle racial capitalism.

As legal expert and journalist Dave McKenna wrote in 2020, invoking the ongoing, racist crisis of poisoned water in Flint, Michigan, "Poison a person, go to jail, they call you a felon for life. Poison a city resulting in dozens of deaths and thousands with brain damage, get a teaching fellowship at Harvard, they call you ex-Governor of Michigan Rick Snyder."[14] He also highlighted how wage theft by employers and capitalists is the most prevalent form of theft—far more common than the burglaries and robberies that are frequently cited by those who defend the police state. Similarly, in *Are Prisons Obsolete?*, Angela Davis argues the existence of prisons allows the state to conveniently tuck away these harrowing truths and inequities behind bars, far from public observation and critique. In reality, the state itself creates the crimes for which it prosecutes marginalized people.

Abolition requires us to consider and address the roots of all "crime." It requires bold changes that could prevent many if not most "crimes," a dramatic transformation of what we understand as criminal, what we understand as the solutions to criminality. Certainly, where crimes of sexual violence are concerned, mass incarceration has failed to make any of us safer from rapists—the prison population continues to swell each day, yet gender-based violence persists. In contrast, comprehensive, required education about consent to prevent rapes could go infinitely further toward addressing this.

The crisis of our police state requires abolition, as it extends far and away beyond good vs. bad individual cops, a few concerning bad apples, to an incurably violent system. As activist Abbas Muntaqim wrote in 2017, "Policing is not a question of individualism." Policing, he noted, "evolved from the slave patrol system." During this time, the role of police was to protect the "property" of white slave-owning landowners. When slavery was technically abolished, Muntaqim noted, the Thirteenth Amendment "institutionalized slavery through the federal government," and specifically the US prison system. "The police transformed into the gatekeepers of the prison slavery industry. . . . The more bodies in prison the more potential for exploited labor and disenfranchisement," he wrote. "The police also serve as a neo-colonial paramilitary force that protects and promotes the white capitalists' interests." Further:

> To suggest that there are good cops is like saying there's good slave patrols or good colonizers. It acts as if policing is an individual act that isn't a product of racial capitalism. A cop might have "good intentions," but these good intentions don't change the fact that they are a part of a system that is rooted in anti-Blackness. These "good intentions" don't change the fact that the system they work for criminalizes the whole Black community. . . . The police must be abolished if police brutality is to end. There's no such thing as reforming a system of policing that was founded on slave-catching.[15]

To Muntaqim's point, calls for police reform are also innocuous and ultimately counterproductive because they'll inevitably lead to *more* funding for police, diverted from investments in vital community resources that actually prevent crimes or meaningfully support marginalized people and victims of abuse. Police budgets are already unjustifiably high—they bleed cities dry, from Los Angeles (which allocated 44 percent— $3 billion—of its budget to policing in 2020) to my suburban hometown of Fremont, California (which allocates 42 percent—$93.3 million— to policing), and result in the defunding of literally everything else, like, say, shelters for domestic violence victims, or resources for schools.

This is precisely why survivor justice advocates have long been critical of the Violence Against Women law for investing more funding into policing. While the law has been helpful in collectively recognizing the crisis of domestic and sexual violence and offers some funding to hotlines, shelters, resources, and public education to support victims, its role in funding and legitimizing policing inflicts only greater harm on victims and communities of color.

2020 was transformative in greatly expanding the public imagination. But because 2020 was an election year, many people who organized in liberal electoral politics responded to mass anti-racist protests and discontent with oversimplified calls to vote. Of course, one in thirteen Black Americans has lost their right to vote through criminalization and the racist, long-term consequences of felonization.[16] Framing voting as the sole solution to police and state violence will always be misguided, even counterproductive, at least until more Democratic politicians—especially at the local level—take meaningful steps to support divestment from police and disempower police forces and police unions, or challenge policing in other meaningful ways. Cities and localities with the most violent police responses to protests, such as Los Angeles, Oakland, and New York City, are all governed by Democratic mayors.

Fixation on reform and elections as a cure-all to the crises we face can breed passivity and a false sense of resolution, even when nothing fundamentally changes. Police departments may adopt feckless reforms to pacify liberal protesters, and ostensibly progressive candidates may win their elections—but when police continue to receive exorbitant amounts of funding, we continue to see the same outcomes. After all, if police aren't following existing rules (hence the killings and brutality we are constantly protesting), why do we have any reason to believe they'd follow new ones?

SURVIVOR JUSTICE BEYOND THE PRISON SYSTEM

In my early advocacy for survivor justice as a teenager, many of the writings I was exposed to convinced me that locking up as many rapists as possible was the lone solution to our rape culture, the lone path to achieving justice. Of course, almost ironically, this was despite my own refusal to see a former friend who had assaulted me in a criminal light, and the fact that I'd never even dreamt of confronting him on a personal level let alone seeking any sort of legal recourse.

I know now that much of this stemmed from fear on some level—fear of disbelief, fear of blame, fear of punishment and judgment and scrutiny, even fear of sympathy; fear that all I would ever be was a victim. But it was more than that: It was also deep, personal acceptance that punishment was not going to move either of us forward. That's not to say that those who commit harm, those who rape and assault, should not face accountability and consequences, especially to protect others from being victimized. But victims of harm, not adversarial systems designed to dole out winner-take-all punitive outcomes, know best what they need to move forward, what they need to heal. And many of us know that bargaining with and begging a patriarchal, white-supremacist institution like our criminal legal system to recognize our humanity would only subject us to additional trauma and prolonged suffering.

Much of our misunderstandings of sexual violence and its relation to the carceral capitalist police state emerges from fundamental misunderstanding about what most rapes and sexual and domestic violence cases entail, and who the perpetrators are. Most rapists are not bestially violent strangers waiting in alleys; far more often than not, they're friends and family members, they're "normal" guys who know their victims; they're boyfriends, partners, co-workers. Many if not most of us have been friends with people who have committed acts of sexual harm without our knowledge, friends with other people who are friends with assailants. In many social circles, men brag to their male friends about acts that constitute rape and sexual assault and are often even praised and socially rewarded for it.

We're surrounded by sexual violence, whether we witness it or not, and the carceral state does nothing to alleviate or address this reality. And what makes these known statistics even more jarring is that they're skewed by vast underreporting. An estimated one in five women has experienced sexual assault, with even higher rates for women of color and LGBTQ people—nearly 80 percent of sexual assaults are unreported to law enforcement. Among different communities, and certainly communities of color, rates of unreported assaults are even higher, as victims of color have greater reason to fear for their safety in coming forward. According to a 2015 report by American University's National Immigrant Women's Advocacy (NIWA), for example, immigrant women are less likely to report rapes and assaults due to fear of a whole host of consequences, like deportation, family separation, or loss of employment and income if their abuser is their employer.[17] NIWA's research found one of the most significant factors impacting migrant women's decision to report abuse is their immigration status, as well as language barriers that could impede their communication with law enforcement.

The fundamentally problematic nature of the state as an arbiter of justice and protection for gender-based violence survivors extends beyond even the insidious systems of prison, policing, and immigration in the US. In the military, sexual violence is endemic and options for recourse are limited. Jennifer Kelly, the Black woman veteran I interviewed and referenced in the introduction of this book, alleges that her white ex-husband in the Air Force subjected her to years of emotional and physical abuse, including sexual assault, and was also violent toward her kids. Kelly claims he subjected her to a string of miscarriages between 2017 and 2020, but her reports about his abuse to his superiors and local police near the Alaska military base on which her family lived were steamrolled. She filed for divorce and ran away to Washington state to keep her kids safe—only for a judge to rule that her ex-husband should have sole custody of her three kids (including one she had from a previous relationship), resulting in Kelly being arrested and jailed for a month, while her kids were returned to her abusive ex in Alaska. The judge also issued a restraining order barring her from contacting her kids and ruled that she owes her ex $1,200 per month in child support payments, yet she's been barred from receiving VA benefits or food stamps because of the ongoing criminal charges against her in Alaska.

"I knew I meant nothing to [the military], I knew my daughters meant nothing to them," Kelly told me in 2022. "I tried to kill myself at different points. I had nothing."

Per the latest internal report released in September 2022, 8.4 percent of female service members and 1.5 percent of male service members experience unwanted sexual contact. Reporting of military spousal abuse is notoriously suppressed. Per some figures, incidents of spousal abuse in the military affect 1.1 percent of military spouses, according to Defense

Department data from 2019—more than twice that of the national population. Kelly's story is an ominous, almost viscerally violent portrait of how local law enforcement, the court system, and the US military systematically punish victims of intimate partner violence—especially those like Kelly, a Black woman who says she tried to defend herself and her kids from her ex-husband, and broke the law by taking her kids and running away from him.

With the current system in place, most sexual assailants and abusers are walking free—some even working as police officers or in the US military. Racial and economic privilege largely determine who is among those 5 out of every 1,000 rapists who are incarcerated. Our cultural imagination misrepresents most people behind bars as rapists and abusers, and most rapists and abusers as being behind bars, when in reality, neither is true.

None of this is to say it's wrong or unnatural to be instinctively outraged by, say, Brock Turner, the Stanford rapist, serving only three months in county jail in 2016; by the Illinois judge who in 2022 overturned the conviction of an eighteen-year-old white man who had raped an intoxicated sixteen-year-old girl, because a prison sentence "is not just" for a young man; the New Jersey judge who in 2019 rejected a petition from a rape victim's family after a sixteen-year-old white boy filmed himself raping her while she was intoxicated because he came from a "nice family."[18] But more of that outrage should lie with the underlying white privilege and white supremacy that produced Turner's minimal sentence and the victims' dismissal, more so than the lack of prison sentences and carceral punishments for the assailants. When we demand our carceral society to be harsher, it's more likely Black people and people of color will shoulder the brunt of these harsher outcomes than their white counterparts.

As Chanel Miller writes in *Know My Name*, Turner serving jail time isn't what brought her healing, and many survivors have the same experience. Justice isn't selectively locking up a rapist here and there but not others. In fact, the process that's required to charge and imprison rapists often comes at great cost to the survivor, while failing to provide them with resources and supports they need to heal. Prison sentences for rapists aren't a substitute for material resources, counseling, and other supports for survivors—carceral processes only reproduce the violence survivors have already suffered; they only match trauma with trauma.

No one can speak for all survivors, and many may conceive of justice in different ways. But justice certainly isn't wielding those who have experienced sexual violence as a go-to, politically convenient shield to defend police and prisons. For non-white victims, what may be more effective and appealing is restorative justice—a response to harm that gathers all affected by conflict to collectively decide how to repair harm and how to respond to harm without creating more by involving punitive state systems. Alexandra Brodsky, a co-founder of the survivor justice advocacy organization Know Your IX and civil rights lawyer, writes at length in her 2021 book *Sexual Justice: Supporting Victims, Ensuring Due Process, and Resisting the Conservative Backlash* on the importance and effectiveness of institutions and communities like schools, churches, employers, and other organizations internally handling allegations of interpersonal harm, including sexual harm. These entities typically provide more support and protections for victims and community members, and in a more timely manner, than police departments and the legal system. The false understanding of acts of sexual harm as uniquely criminal matters, rather than civil rights violations or community matters, perpetuates prevalent rape myths about those who report sexual violence, framing them as vengeful liars trying to punish innocent men, when many victims are simply looking for support, repair, or some sort of compensation for the harms they've experienced.

If the government were adequately performing its moral and practical function of redistributing wealth, fulfilling basic needs, and investing in humanity, many people and institutions wouldn't exist—billionaires, charities, privatized philanthropy, and perhaps above all, prisons. Many if not most "crimes" would likely cease to exist, because most are survival crimes committed out of necessity. Many acts of interpersonal violence mirror the institutionalized violence of the carceral capitalist police state or take their cues from a government and culture that do not recognize and respect the dignity of women, survivors, LGBTQ people, and other marginalized people.

Eliminating policing and prisons should be a shared human goal. In the short term, it's critical that we support bail funds and grassroots criminal justice efforts in our communities, that we support groups—like the organization Survived and Punished—that are dedicated to liberating criminalized survivors. For a long time, I believed decriminalizing nonviolent and victimless crimes and liberating individual "nonviolent" incarcerated people was enough, and I had concerns about what prison abolition could mean for "violent" offenders. It's innately human to crave safety, to fear what we've been socialized to perceive as the only legitimate forms of violence. But when we rely on arbitrary definitions to differentiate between violent and nonviolent crimes and what those offenders deserve, we're allowing this to distract from a greater system of racist, classist, colonialist oppression. We reduce this system of oppression to individual acts, without consideration of the social and economic inequalities that may predispose some communities to commit survival crimes, or skew public perceptions of who deserves punishment and public sympathy.

At the core of our infinite debates about violent vs. nonviolent crimes is a fundamental question of who is and isn't worthy of dignity and humanity. The only moral answer to this question—the only answer that does not regard endless cycles of retraumatization as a valid solution—is that *every* human being is worthy.

6

SEIZING THE MEANS OF REPRODUCTION

My upbringing in the public school system of my hometown of Fremont, California, was an unremarkable experience. And yet my life has been indelibly shaped by the abysmal sexual health education that my peers and I received. It was at least a couple notches better than the curriculum doled out by *Mean Girls*' Coach Carr—the instructor who told his fictional class of horny teens in 2004, "If you have sex, you will die." It was certainly better than the utter lack of sex ed that friends of mine hailing from public schools in states like Texas and Florida received. Nonetheless, it wasn't great, and as a young person, I suffered the predictable consequences of this.

A few years after I graduated high school, teachers at the public schools I'd attended moved to adopt LGBTQ-inclusive sexual health education. In response, outraged parents in our predominantly Asian American suburb flooded city council meetings, applying pressure to our already conservative mayor and city council members, eventually overhauling school sex ed programs in the district, and banning several books with LGBTQ themes and references as well. Parents in a suburban, ostensibly liberal Bay Area town literally beat Florida Republicans to the punch.

What many of these parents failed to understand or simply chose not to consider is that sexual health education is about more than sex. Sex ed is foremost about safety—safety from not just sexually transmitted infections and unintended teen pregnancy but also jarringly high rates of youth sexual violence, if we properly teach young people about consent. Young people are also safer when they understand that sex is about pleasure, expression, and enjoyment, which we can't experience when we're pressured and coerced into disempowering situations, an issue we can't even address when young people who experience sexual violence are shamed into silence about our experiences.

I can say as an adult who's since spent the bulk of my career reporting on sexual and reproductive health, gender, violence, and identity that the course of my life might have been different if my ninth grade health class had taught us about more than just a house-of-horrors catalog of the different kinds of STIs. Nothing we learned even vaguely challenged the reality that I and all teenage girls had been socialized to attach our self-worth to pleasing others, to make male figures in our lives happy no matter the cost to us, and to regard our own happiness, certainly our own pleasure, as an afterthought. Hyperfocused demand for better, accurate, and wide-ranging sex ed programs in public schools is, inevitably, an oversimplified solution that ignores how not all sex ed is good or even accurate. Rather, bad sex ed and puritanical policing are passed between generations—and who is going to intervene to teach sex ed teachers to teach better sex ed?

The consequences of bad sex ed impact the trajectory of a young person's life. Shortly after being forced into a sexual encounter at sixteen that I would come to understand in my adult life as a sexual assault, I continued to partake in—on my end—deeply unenthusiastic sexual relationships. As if the discomforts and general awfulness of bad sex weren't punitive enough, eventually, inevitably, the situation spiraled out of my control. I can still vividly remember being belittled by drugstore clerks on multiple occasions, first when I pooled together savings from my after-school job to buy emergency contraception locked away behind counters, and later when I purchased a pregnancy test. A doctor berated me after I disclosed that I had been having unprotected sex, asking if I were purposefully trying to become pregnant and "throw my life away," and prompting me to conceal pretty important truths from medical professionals for years out of fear of being similarly shamed.

None of that, of course, even compared to the harassment and verbal assault I had to endure, eventually, just to walk into a reproductive health clinic all by myself amid a medical emergency. It was there that I learned I was losing a very much unplanned pregnancy that I hadn't even known about, causing heavy bleeding and intense pain, which I was able to take medication abortion pills to safely end. Save for the support I received inside the clinic, I was alone throughout this terrifying experience, and mostly alone throughout processing the uncomfortable and at times coercive unprotected sexual encounters that had led to it. I didn't know how to talk about any of this—frankly, as an adult, I still don't really. It was a minefield that nothing in my life or public school education had prepared me to walk through.

Anna, a young, Asian American organizer with Jane's Due Process, works with the Texas-based abortion fund in its mission to help primarily minors and young people navigate the state's restrictive laws to reproductive care. She began organizing for reproductive justice after repeatedly facing barriers and harassment trying to get birth control pills and then Plan B, eventually seeking Jane's Due Process's help to get an abortion when she was seventeen and forced to navigate the state's tricky restrictions for minors—back when abortion was still legal in the state at all. Anna told me in January 2022, amid my reporting for Jezebel, that she had been struck by how "all the adults that had the power to help me used it against me and put me in a position where I would be forced to become a mother."

"My abortion saved the life I want for myself. It let me control my own body, it proved to me I'm not just a government baby-making machine. . . .

Young people of color are the future, and we should be leading the way on this," she said. More than any of the adults who had mistreated her, Anna knew what was best for her life.

The right sexual health education could and should make consensual sexual activity a more open and communicable topic for young people. It could and should encourage safe and pleasurable sex for anyone who seeks it, and strive toward preventing sexual violence by dismantling a culture that shames and punishes survivors. Eventually, as I grew up, I came to recognize the shaming and harassment I faced—from drugstore clerks, peers, a doctor—as an extension of broader forces of patriarchal, even capitalistic violence beyond my individual experience. Explicitly stated or not, the goal of this stigma and systematic harassment and mistreatment is to teach women, girls, and all pregnant-capable people that sex and sexual acts are not for or even about us, but either the satisfaction of men or the fulfillment of our reproductive potential in an economic system that subsists on exploited labor, an economic system that relies on an endless supply of needy, desperate, and replaceable workers.

It's quite a leap from childhood stories of being slut-shamed for teenage sexual proclivities and harassed outside an abortion clinic, to broad assertions about capitalist exploitation. But in a society that treats women and survivors as state-controlled ovens, as bodies to be used and abused, all these realities are inseparable and inextricably connected.

THE MEANS OF REPRODUCTION

Within days of overturning *Roe v. Wade* in 2022 and essentially fulfilling the crown jewel of their political agenda for the last fifty years, Republican legislators still somehow, almost admirably, found a way to blame everything—and I mean *everything*—on abortion. After years of gutting the social safety net, Republicans on the House Ways and Means Committee managed to attribute this country's utterly depleted Social Security and Medicare systems to abortion. Rep. Kevin Hern, a Republican from Oklahoma, claimed at a committee meeting in June 2022 that we have abortion rights to thank for the reality that none of us will ever be able to retire, claiming *Roe* took away the "supply"—a pretty shocking way to refer to "unborn babies" you presumably care about—of workers who could collectively fund Social Security. "If you think about 70 million people being aborted over the last 49 years, assuming half and half men and women . . . 70 million not in the workforce, assuming they have a child, two children, we've got somewhere between 100, 140 million people that have not worked, that are not with us because of the *Roe v. Wade* issue," he managed to say with a straight face. "And so, we've taken away the very workforce that was needed to supply both Social Security and Medicare." As of 2022, House Republicans' website further contends that "abortion shrinks the labor force" because "if all of these aborted babies had been otherwise carried to term and survived until today, they would add nearly 20 percent to the current US population, and nearly 45 million would be of working age (18 to 64)."[1] Their website also claims that in 2019 alone, abortion rights had "cost the US roughly $6.9 trillion, or 32 percent of GDP" by causing "the loss of nearly 630,000 unborn lives."

I cannot emphasize enough that the "lives" in question were literal fertilized eggs and fetuses. In other words, Hern and his fellow Republicans blamed pregnant people for preventing their embryos and fetuses from clocking in to their 9–5 desk jobs, consequently destroying the social safety net. It would be comical if this weren't an entirely serious and terrifyingly consequential political ideology: Reproductive oppression is a central tenet of capitalism, because forced pregnancy and birth guarantee new, future generations of workers to exploit—an endless "supply," if you will, created through unthinkable state violence.

House Republicans' math (I use that word very loosely) in making these claims did not even add up on a practical level, because many people wouldn't have the children they now have, had they not been able to have an abortion at some point in their life. Abortion has allowed unsaid numbers of women, pregnant people, and their partners to remain in the workforce and fund Social Security through their labor. But reproductive oppression isn't about math or funding public resources, which could easily be achieved through even a modest wealth tax and other redistributive policies that House Republicans diametrically oppose—reproductive oppression is a tactic of state control and abuse.

Even prior to the end of *Roe*, laws like the Hyde Amendment, which prohibits federal funding from paying for most abortions, deliberately targeted disproportionately poor people of color with the goal of keeping them poor. As years of research have shown, being denied abortion care often pushes the pregnant person and their children even deeper into poverty, left to fend for themselves without a social safety net thanks to the policies of lawmakers like Hern. Forced pregnancy and birth ensure there will always be families in such dire economic situations that they'll be forced to rely on low-wage jobs, all while Hern can maintain his $61 million net worth and attack abortion patients as the reason for everything wrong with this country.

Incidentally, nearly all states still permit some form of forced sterilizations: According to a 2021 study from the National Women's Law Center and Autistic Women and Nonbinary Network, thirty-one states and the District of Columbia allow nonconsensual sterilizations, particularly targeting disabled and incarcerated people and migrants.[2] At the height of the eugenics movement between 1909 and 1979, there were an estimated 20,000 forced sterilizations in California alone. During roughly this same period, at least 70,000 people in thirty-two states were subjected to involuntary sterilizations, primarily targeting Black, Indigenous, Latinx, and disabled people. Reports surfaced in 2020 about an ICE doctor performing unwanted hysterectomies on migrant women. People with or perceived to have disabilities can be legally assigned a conservator or guardian and lose many of their basic rights and bodily autonomy—and be legally subject to state-sanctioned reproductive coercion—in the process. Despite the popularization of the term "marriage equality," disabled people under conservatorships can lose their right to marry (and vote, and care for their own children, for that matter). Disabled people who do get married can lose government support and other life-saving benefits, which can render them financially dependent on abusive partners. According to the US Centers for Disease Control, disabled people are up to ten times more likely than nondisabled people to face domestic abuse.

Still, forced sterilizations remain misunderstood as a relic of the past despite persisting to this day. Forced sterilizations and forced pregnancy through abortion bans are two sides of the same coin. Just as Hern and House Republicans ban abortion to add to an expansive labor force to exploit under capitalism, they also see "undesirable" populations—people with disabilities, people of color, people with criminal convictions—as an economic liability. Like historical eugenicists, they implicitly subscribe to racist and ableist notions about who is more likely to seek help from the social safety net, and they craft their policy agendas based on these notions.

Republicans' own words backing up Rep. Hern's claims speak for themselves: "Abortion shrinks the labor force," their aforementioned webpage reads—this isn't about babies, or families, or even God; it's about money. It's about blaming anything, even fetuses that have never touched grass, instead of the shameful state of social programs that Republicans have spent decades attacking while lining their own pockets. Anti-abortion politicians don't see the "unborn" as precious children; they see them as cogs in a machine, as literal dollar signs. In contrast, reproductive justice—the framework created by Black women that asserts that each of us should be able to parent or not parent in safe, healthy communities—is incompatible with capitalism. Reproductive justice demands bodily autonomy and thriving families; anti-abortion politics, as Hern has so shamelessly outlined, demands generations of exploitable labor.

In the final months of *Roe* in the summer of 2021, the House of Representatives passed a historic budget that didn't include Hyde as a budget rider. But celebrations were unsurprisingly premature, and the Senate adopted an amendment to restore Hyde to the budget by August, ushering in yet another year of abortion care being all but banned for those on Medicaid.

The repercussions of Hyde for the last roughly five decades have proven devastating, particularly for low-income victims and survivors of domestic violence. Among pregnant people on Medicaid who are unable to afford an abortion, Hyde forces one in four to carry an unwanted pregnancy to term. Notably, 31 percent of Black women and pregnant people and 27 percent of Hispanic women and pregnant people aged fifteen to forty-four were enrolled in Medicaid in 2015, compared with 16 percent of white women and pregnant people. Despite persistent erasure of Asian women and pregnant people who have abortions, Hyde also carries disparate harm for women and pregnant people of different Asian ethnicities: 32 percent of Vietnamese Americans, 26 percent of Filipino Americans, 27 percent of Chinese Americans, and 26 percent of women and pregnant people across all Asian ethnicities rely on Medicaid or other public health coverage.[3] Hyde also harms Indigenous women and pregnant people who rely on federally funded Indian Health Services for health coverage.

And as the well-known findings uncovered by the Turnaway Study have shown, there are long-term consequences for people who are unable to get the abortion care they seek: People denied abortion are four times more likely to be pushed into poverty and at greater risk of being entrapped in an abusive relationship. The same study found around 10 percent of those who seek abortion care do so specifically because their partners are abusive, and people experiencing domestic abuse are more likely to remain in violent situations if they carry their pregnancy to term. Diana Greene Foster, the author of the Turnaway Study, told Salon in 2014 that "being unable to have the abortion tethered women to violent men, while women who have the abortion were more able to escape abusive relationships."[4]

"Pregnancy is one of the riskiest times for pregnancy-capable people," an abortion provider who's offered abortion care to victims in abusive relationships told Jezebel in 2022, noting that intimate partner violence can either worsen or emerge for the first time during pregnancy. In post-*Roe* America, she added that it's "definitely a concern that people will be forced to continue pregnancies that put them at risk of escalating violence or will continue to be forced to be tied to that person."

As if pregnancy and pregnancy-related complications weren't dangerous enough—especially for Black pregnant people and pregnant people of color, who are more likely to be mistreated and die from complications—homicide is a leading cause of death for pregnant people.

Yet homicide targeting pregnant people isn't even counted in the CDC's tracking of maternal deaths.

The absence of *Roe* and lack of rape exceptions in states' abortion bans necessarily means an increase in pregnancies and even births conceived from rape. But as of the time of this writing, almost half of states lack laws that terminate the parental rights of rapists, while many states require a criminal conviction for this. According to the CDC, almost three million women in the US have experienced a rape-related pregnancy. One woman, Analyn Megison, nearly lost her daughter to her rapist who sued for custody in 2010.

Megison, you'll recall, chose to give birth after being impregnated by rape in 2003. Five years later, she was forced to fight her rapist in court in Florida to keep custody of her daughter. Over the course of the years-long legal battle, she told me she was repeatedly "retraumatized" by being forced to see her rapist in court until 2012, when a judge denied his petition and awarded her sole custody of her little girl. Years later, another judge would cite Megison's continued activism to stop rapists from claiming parental rights to their victims' children as justification for granting custody of Megison's oldest son to her abusive ex-husband. She claims the judge said her work would cause her son to "think negatively about fatherhood." To this day, Megison, now an Arizona resident, continues to make child support payments to a man who she claims once beat her so severely while she was pregnant that she miscarried.

The shaky ground around rapists' parental rights is just one way that pregnancy is weaponized as a means for rapists and abusers to exert long-term control and violence over their victims, sometimes for decades. When Megison was fighting her rapist in court, she noted that there were zero legal protections in place for people like her whose rapists had not been criminally convicted. This motivated her to advocate for legislation to shift the burden of proof required by a mother who accuses her child's father of rape in custody trials from the "beyond a reasonable doubt" standard applied in criminal cases to the "clear and convincing evidence" standard used in all other civil cases. A bill changing this standard passed out of Florida's legislature in 2013; the federal Rape Survivor

Child Custody Act passed in 2015. Today thirty-two other states now use the "clear and convincing evidence" legal standard that Megison says helped her win her custody case—but this means nearly half of all states still require criminal convictions for rapists' parental rights to be automatically terminated.

Stories like Megison's aren't as rare as you might think. You'll recall that Darcy Benoit has endured a similar situation and has been forced to co-parent with her rapist for more than a decade because the child's father hadn't been convicted of rape. For months after the 2011 assault that impregnated her, Benoit repeatedly tried to report it to police but was turned away each time, she said. In 2012 police finally agreed to investigate her case—but only after Benoit had taken drastic action. "I went to the attorney general's office, and they contacted my police department and said, 'If you're not going to take her report, we are,'" she told me. It was only after this intervention, Benoit said, that local police accepted her report and told the attorney general's office they'd always been willing to investigate it, and Benoit had simply "misunderstood."

The investigation that Benoit fought so hard for brought her neither safety nor peace. She recalled being interrogated for hours over the course of two days; she said police interrogated her rapist for thirty minutes. "At the end of it, the officer looked me in the eye, and he told me, 'I believe you *think* you were raped,'" Benoit said. There was no conviction, which Benoit suspected was because she had been dating the man when she said he raped her. "They did not treat me like a victim. I still think about what they said to me all those years ago. These are the people that are supposed to help protect me." Recall the 2010 study that showed police don't believe that marital rape is possible.[5]

In the span of seven years of co-parenting with her rapist between 2012 and 2019—the year that a judge's emergency order briefly stripped her rapist of custody until the order was vacated in the summer of 2022—she received protective orders against him each year, but his stalking and harassment never stopped, she told me. She's been forced to move houses three times to protect herself and her child, despite being part of Arizona's Address Confidentiality Program, which bars her rapist from knowing where she lives. In court documents she shared with me, Benoit said she moved "strictly due to [my rapist] locating us by putting a tracker on our son" and that moving "is not an inexpensive thing," given the housing market.

Benoit's rapist's treatment of her son has been jarring, too. She shared photos with me revealing severe property damage he inflicted on the child's belongings, backing the child's allegations of physical and emotional abuse that he first made in 2019, resulting in the aforementioned emergency order. When her rapist returned her son to her for the holiday on July 4, 2019, the child was missing "chunks [of hair] from the back of his head," court documents filed by Benoit claim. Benoit's son has endured such "severe trauma," she told me, that it's left him "years behind in school." Around the spring of 2021, Benoit's rapist filed an appeal against the emergency order, and as custody trials resumed, at one point, for the first time in the decade since Benoit says she was raped, her rapist all but confessed to the assault on the record to a court advisor, when he said Benoit had "tried to push me off" during the nonconsensual encounter, but he'd resisted because he "was ready to orgasm." Yet nothing came of the confession. Following a June 2022 appeals court ruling reversing the previous one, Benoit's rapist had a path to shared custody once again, and police declined Benoit's requests to reopen her case.

Laurel, a first-generation immigrant, told Prism in 2022 that after she was impregnated by rape and gave birth to twins, she moved across the country—anything to "get as far away from that person having legal access to you as possible." She was forced to "work three jobs to support herself and her twins," eventually landing her in the hospital due to stress-related illness, and she continues to live in fear of retaliation from her rapist. From the moment she conceived, Laurel said she was forced to fend for herself. "I was guilted by practically everyone, including the medical establishment, to keep a pregnancy that was not in my best interest."

Anti-abortion laws empower abuse and inflict gendered violence upon women and pregnant people, who are often already victims of gender-based violence. In Missouri and other states, judges can rule to prevent women and people with uteruses from getting divorced if they're pregnant, requiring them to wait until the baby is born to navigate custody rights. Intimate partner abuse and abortion bans extend from the same well of rampant gender-based violence. When state lawmakers, and certainly Supreme Court justices, exert control over the bodies and reproductive health options of pregnant people, their actions normalize these behaviors and encourage abusers to replicate these behaviors in their relationships. One 2010 study found 15 percent of women who report experiencing physical violence from a male partner also report birth control sabotage—for example, tampering with a partner's birth control to force them to become pregnant against their will.[6]

"Reproductive coercion is typically not the only type of abuse experienced in a relationship in which intimate partner violence is present, and it can be challenging to reveal," Jane Stoever, a law professor and director of the University of California, Irvine, Domestic Violence Clinic and the university's Initiative to End Family Violence, told me in 2021 as she advocated for a California bill to include reproductive coercion in civil definitions of domestic violence, which has since been signed into law. "Naming a problem is often the first step in addressing it. Naming the behavior enables and empowers survivors to identify what they have experienced as abuse."

In September 2022, when a federal judge in Arizona allowed the state's archaic, pre-*Roe* law banning abortion to take effect, a family planning clinic in Phoenix was waist-deep in a legal fight with a man who had created an estate for his wife's aborted embryo and was suing the clinic. The dehumanization of pregnant people in legal and medical systems in favor of embryos and fetuses isn't new—but the overturning of *Roe* created exponentially greater risk. "I could see a universe in which an ex-partner, in an attempt to harass or terrorize or create fear in the pregnant person, would try to bring a wrongful death lawsuit against the pregnant person herself, in addition to the provider," Pregnancy Justice deputy director Dana Sussman told *Rolling Stone* at the time.[7]

As previously noted, states allow judges to hold or delay a divorce while someone is pregnant. Over the last twenty years, separated couples who created embryos together have been pulled into a legal gray area further complicated by the end of *Roe*, as this yielded more state abortion bans that include "life begins at conception" language, treating frozen embryos as children. Between 2000 and 2018, states like Massachusetts, California, Illinois, Pennsylvania, and most recently, Arizona, saw divorced couples drawn into custody battles over embryos, that could potentially force someone to become biological co-parents with an abusive ex.[8]

Yet we don't hear about the ties between state and interpersonal reproductive violence in mainstream media and policy debates. Why would we? There's little reason for people and institutions that hold power to be concerned with seemingly private, intimate realities like acts of domestic abuse, including reproductive coercion that compels unwanted pregnancy because it violently guarantees future generations of workers to exploit. Private as such acts of pregnancy coercion and domestic violence might seem, they're conjoined with the state's greater public agenda of owning and controlling the means of reproduction—and with it, the means of production itself.

Vulnerability to both sexual violence and wide-ranging barriers to reproductive care isn't identity-neutral. By targeting Medicaid, the Hyde Amendment specifically reveals how socioeconomic status and poverty are weaponized to control and coerce the reproduction of low-income people. And consequently, Hyde shows how the state has made poverty and race become risk factors for gender-based interpersonal violence. In the 1970s, Rep. Henry Hyde, the namesake of the notorious budget rider, proudly walked us through his diabolical plan to design a bill that would specifically ban abortion for poor people and people of color. "I would certainly like to prevent, if I could legally, anybody having an abortion, a rich woman, a middle-class woman, or a poor woman. Unfortunately, the only vehicle available is [the Hyde Amendment]," he said of his policy.[9] Congress's renewal of the unapologetic white supremacist's amendment each year since speaks volumes about how little has changed for pregnant people and survivors of color in the last fifty years—except, frankly, to get worse.

STATE RETRAUMATIZATION OF ABUSE VICTIMS

Abortion bans and restrictions are, by nature, an insidious violation of consent, all the more so for those who have experienced some form of sexual harm or coercion beforehand. Forced pregnancy and birth amount to traumatic violations of someone's body, not unlike being subjected to sexual violence. The historical existence of rape exceptions attached to some abortion bans and restrictions in the US has erroneously, problematically implied consent to sex equals consent to pregnancy.

For decades anti-abortion politicians wielded rape exceptions to have it both ways, to claim to simultaneously care about women and also be "pro-life"—two fundamentally incompatible positions. In 2021 and 2022, in the months leading up to the end of *Roe*, this dynamic began to shift, paving the way for nearly all trigger laws banning abortion post-*Roe* to lack such exceptions. Months before *Roe* fell, in February Florida's state legislature voted to reject adding an exception for rape to its fifteen-week abortion ban, which one lawmaker called "generous." Lawmakers in Arizona and West Virginia similarly declined to add exceptions for rape to their own fifteen-week bans. Texas's 2021 abortion ban, SB 8, banned abortion without exceptions for rape. By the summer of 2022, within days of *Roe* being overturned, a ten-year-old rape victim from Ohio was forced to travel to Indiana to access abortion because Ohio's six-week ban lacked a rape exception. By the fall of 2022, an affidavit filed by health care providers in Ohio included testimony from several doctors that, in addition to the aforementioned child, several other underage rape survivors who sought abortion care from them were forced to travel out of state for the procedure.

Around the same time, Planned Parenthood of South, East, and North Florida confirmed that a fifteen-year-old incest victim had been denied abortion care because they were past fifteen weeks pregnant. A northern Florida OB-GYN claimed many of the patients who were denied care by the ban were young or experiencing intimate partner violence: "We are seeing this restriction have profound and terrible effects for some families in the most desperate of situations," Dr. Shelly Tien said at a press conference.[10]

Before this period, anti-abortion politicians who opposed rape exceptions were likely to be very publicly disavowed by the rest of the party. In 2012 Missouri Senate candidate Todd Akin tanked his campaign by asserting that we don't need rape exceptions because "legitimate rape" can't lead to pregnancy. Indiana candidate Richard Mourdock also sank his bid for Senate that same year for saying that when someone becomes pregnant from rape, "God intended" for this to happen. A decade later, Republican state lawmakers proudly went on the record making similar or more offensive comments, to thunderous applause from their base. One Utah Republican claimed women and pregnant people can "control when they allow a man to ejaculate inside of them and to control that intake of semen," shortly after *Roe* was overturned.[11] Months before that, a Michigan Republican state House candidate said he'd told his daughters, "If rape is inevitable, you should just lie back and enjoy it,"[12] and an Ohio Republican in the state legislature called pregnancy from rape "an opportunity."[13] Days before the midterm elections in 2022, a Republican candidate for the North Carolina state House said victims of rape and incest should "be allowed to get an abortion on a case-by-case basis through a community-level review process outside the jurisdiction of the federal government."[14] Surely a community convening to determine if a woman was, indeed, raped and "deserves" abortion is going to end well!

Despite the undeniable ickiness of their comments, they were merely saying the quiet part out loud. The inclusion of rape exceptions to abortion bans functioned almost solely to make the agendas of anti-abortion politicians appear more humane, all while there's little evidence that people have invoked this exception to successfully access care. On a cultural level, rape exemptions helped feed the misconception that rape is easy for victims to "prove" to law enforcement or other authorities, brushing away the exhausting, retraumatizing process of reporting rape as a mere footnote in a survivor's path to getting an abortion.

In reality, that path is harrowing, to say the least. Cazembe Murphy Jackson, a Black trans man, shared his story of being raped by a group of four men in a small town in Texas in 2019 prior to his transition. He learned he was pregnant six weeks later and told NBC at the time that he was able to "scrape together the funds" to have the abortion, and he'd reported his rape to the police, although he recalled feeling "dismissed" by them. Jackson noted that rape exceptions with reporting requirements fail to support "those of us who don't call the police, because the police are often not helpful, particularly to survivors from communities of color." In many cases, rape exceptions amount to a dangerous form of mandatory reporting—a legal requirement for abuse to be reported to authorities—so victims can obtain abortion care, denying survivors agency in the process. This can force pregnant survivors to become involved in the criminal legal system against their will and at risk to their safety.

Shortly after *Roe* fell, anti-abortion lawmakers in Tennessee moved to directly criminally implicate rape victims seeking abortion care. They introduced a bill to add a rape exception to the state's abortion ban that threatened those who "lied" about being raped with up to three years in prison, and require rape victims who receive abortion care to submit embryonic remains to the state government for possible criminal investigation. The bill would allow victims ages twelve or under to receive abortion care up to 10 weeks into their pregnancies, and adultified these child victims by referring to them as "women."

Even abortion bans that don't have rape exceptions are still weaponized by lawmakers to prop up prisons and policing: In 2021 Texas Gov. Greg Abbott promised to simply "end rape" in defense of SB 8, and claimed he'd do so by "getting rapists off the street" despite how most cases of sexual violence are perpetrated in our own homes by intimate partners, not strangers. His promise underscored the inseparability of carceral policy, the anti-abortion movement, and state-perpetuated cycles of gender-based violence. The only way to prevent survivors from being forced to carry their rapists' babies, or be further retraumatized by law enforcement, is to just not ban or restrict abortion at all.

Abortion bans have always contributed to the sexual-assault-to-prison pipeline through the criminalization of self-induced abortion and pregnancy loss, sometimes after individuals have been raped—hardly an unlikely outcome, given the CDC's findings about the prevalence of rape-induced pregnancies. Years before *Roe* was overturned, pregnancy criminalization was already on the rise: Recall that Pregnancy Justice found there were 413 cases of people facing criminalization for pregnancy outcomes including miscarriage and self-managed abortion between 1973 and 2005, compared with 1,254 between 2006 and 2020.

The punishment and neglect of pregnant people and survivors of sexual violence, and especially those who are people of color, are ultimately mirrored in the gendered cruelties of our capitalist health system. The US maintains the highest maternal death rate in the industrialized world, with significantly higher rates in states with more restrictions on reproductive care, and particularly high rates for pregnant people of color. Black pregnant people are three to four times more likely than white people to die from pregnancy-related complications. These outcomes have inevitably worsened in the absence of *Roe*. As Susan Rinkunas wrote in Jezebel in July 2022, contrary to pervasive language about how the overturning of *Roe* meant a return to back-alley, coat-hanger abortions, the crises we face today are different from pre-*Roe* days:

> Unsafe, illegal abortions will—tragically, horribly—still happen, but thanks to safe and effective abortion pills, people will be less likely to seek them out than they were before 1973. The more pressing concern . . . is that women and pregnant people in the US will die from homicide, the physical toll of pregnancy, and being denied emergency care in hospitals—the factors that were already killing pregnant people, only now, more people will be forced to stay pregnant.[15]

Because of ongoing conflict over when exceptions to abortion bans to save the pregnant person's life are applicable—and in some states, over whether doctors who offer life-saving abortion care should face prison time—pregnancy-related care for patients with extreme health conditions has become exponentially more complicated. One abortion provider recalled offering an abortion to her patient who developed a rare form of cancer so the patient could start chemotherapy and maximize her survival, some time before *Roe* was overturned. "If that patient couldn't get her chemotherapy because she's forced to continue her pregnancy, she's not going to die in that moment, but she probably will die much sooner. Maybe significantly sooner, decades sooner," the doctor told Rinkunas. Without *Roe*, it's unclear whether providing an abortion to a cancer patient would still be legal in some states. The aforementioned affidavit from Ohio-based doctors challenging the state's abortion ban in 2022 included testimony about two cases of pregnant cancer patients who had to pause their chemotherapy treatments to travel out of state for abortion care that they'd been denied under the state's then-active abortion ban. It's not just cancer treatments—Rinkunas noted that we could also see pregnant people denied life-saving antidepressants because the drugs could impact the fetus: "It's just another example of how fetal personhood prioritizes potential life over the existence of the person carrying that potential life. If she dies, so what?" In October 2022 there were multiple reported cases of teenage girls denied life-saving medications for chronic conditions because the medications could induce miscarriage, and the girls were of childbearing age.[16]

The issue of pregnant or pregnant-capable individuals being denied vital medical treatments isn't hypothetical. I reported in September 2022 on a New York woman who said she was denied highly effective medication for a chronic, painful condition that's caused her to contemplate suicide, because her neurologist told her she could become pregnant, and the medication might cause birth defects— even though she never plans to have children due to her condition. In audio that the woman, Tara Rule, recorded from her conversation with the neurologist, she asks if the issue preventing her from getting the medication is solely that she's of "childbearing age" and "if I were through menopause, would this be effective for cluster headaches?" When the doctor says yes, Rule asks, "So the only thing that's kind of stopping this is the fact that at some point in my life, I could get pregnant?" In response, he appears to change the subject and asks, "How's your sleep?"

"I think doctors often, in my experience, bank on the fact that people don't know their patients' rights," Rule told me. "We need policy change to reprimand any physician or insurance company that chooses to prioritize a hypothetical life that does not exist over the well-being of a suffering human being who actually exists."

As noted in the introduction of this book, within mere days of *Roe* being overturned, a wave of "trigger laws" took effect and banned abortion. Amid an ongoing legal battle to block Louisiana's ban from taking effect, one woman was forced to endure a painful, hours-long delivery to birth a dead fetus—on top of grappling with the potential trauma of learning that her pregnancy wasn't viable—because the ban had temporarily gone into effect while she was in the hospital, barring her doctor from providing a simple, fifteen-minute abortion procedure. According to an affidavit filed by the woman's doctor, Valerie Williams, against Louisiana's ban, throughout the delivery Williams's patient was "screaming—not from pain, but from the emotional trauma she was experiencing." Following the delivery, it took hours for Williams's patient's placenta to deliver, causing her to hemorrhage nearly a liter of blood before Williams was able to stop the bleeding, the affidavit claims. "There was no way for the pregnancy to continue without putting the patient's health at risk, as the fetus was already starting to deliver," Williams wrote. She added, "Going back into that hospital room and telling the patient that she would have to be induced and push out the fetus was one of the hardest conversations I've ever had."

The ban in question in Louisiana at this time of writing threatens doctors with ten-to-fifteen-year jail terms. It includes an exception for threats to the pregnant person's life, but "how close to death must a patient be?" an attorney for the abortion providers in the state asked in court documents, adding, "Doctors are unsure what counts as a 'medically futile' pregnancy." What about cases like Williams's patient, whose fetus wasn't viable? Given the extreme time-sensitivity of pregnancy-related care, navigating whether an abortion is legal or can land you or your doctor in prison on any given day, at any given hour, simply isn't tenable.

"The trigger bans have turned a hospital room and medical procedure into a legal consultation, all while patients' health and safety are at risk," Williams said. She called this "a travesty," and specified that this incident was "the first time in my fifteen-year career that I could not give a patient the care they needed." A Louisiana doctor said in July 2022 that they feared they "could go to prison just for handling a miscarriage as I always have."[17]

Had Williams's patient not begun to deliver the unviable fetus, it's likely Louisiana's then-active trigger law would have forced her to remain pregnant with it, which can lead to sepsis and other life-threatening infections. In January 2022 a Polish woman named Agnieszka died after being forced to carry a dead fetus for a week due to the country's abortion ban, even though the law technically has an exception if someone's life is at risk. The hospital claimed it had "taken all possible and required actions to save the lives of the children and the patient"—of course, referring to Agnieszka's fetuses and not her three living children—and that "doctors' behaviour was not influenced by anything else other than medical considerations."[18]

On top of these crises, in the day-to-day, health providers can fail to provide trauma-informed options for essential, life-saving reproductive care services, including pelvic exams and Pap smears to pregnant-capable patients; these services can be highly triggering for survivors of sexual harm. Even receiving an ultrasound—a requirement to get an abortion in many states, if abortion is legal at all—is innately, intensely invasive, often requiring someone to be penetrated by a medical wand. The lack of trauma-informed options available to victims, or even cultural awareness that survivors may need special medical care, speaks to the intersecting ways survivors and pregnant-capable people are harmed by the health system. In many if not most cases, patients who have experienced sexual trauma aren't even asked about their levels of comfort with these health services, or what would help them feel safer in receiving them. Like the aforementioned life-threatening health outcomes that pregnant people face in the post-*Roe* medical system, the lack of even basic consideration of the fact that survivors exist and may need certain accommodations from health providers stems from broader societal failure to connect issues of gender-based violence with reproductive health care accessibility.

In chapter 1 I referenced a 2022 study that found nearly a fifth of sexual assault survivors who sought emergency care after their assaults faced bills averaging close to $4,000. Samuel Dickman, one of the researchers and an abortion provider who's frequently worked with patients who have survived sexual violence, told me that a high medical bill in itself can be retraumatizing for survivors: "They're victimized when they're assaulted, and then, essentially, by being asked to pay these bills, they're being told they're responsible for what happened, when they're not."[19]

Some of this is the product of unsurprising shortcomings in the Violence Against Women Act. The law mandates that victims can't be charged for the evidence-gathering portion of their medical care after an assault—for example, putting together a rape kit—but it still allows hospitals to bill victims for a range of health services commonly received after sexual violence, like diagnostic testing, laceration repair, counseling, prevention of sexually transmitted infections, and even emergency contraception, which has become increasingly inaccessible after the fall of *Roe*, in no small part due to its inaccurate conflation with abortion. In June 2022 the Kansas City, Missouri, city health system briefly paused providing Plan B to sexual assault survivors, fearing legal ramifications, the *Kansas City Star* reported.

Abortion can be an essential health service victims seek after their rape, especially given the commonness of rape-related pregnancies. The rapid spread of state abortion bans—most of which lack rape exceptions—means abortion and all the associated cost and logistical barriers to access it are more expensive than ever. That's on top of Dickman's research showing pregnant sexual assault victims already faced uniquely high charges for emergency care ($4,553) back in 2019, years before *Roe* was overturned. Forced pregnancy and costly medical bills for seeking care after an assault go hand in hand: In both cases, the state is an abuser that systematically punishes victims for *being* victims.

Dickman's research was ultimately limited to victims who sought emergency care in the first place. "There's an uncountable number of people who know they would be hit with large medical bills if they go to the emergency room after an assault, and so they just don't go," he said. "And that's even worse."

It doesn't help that in the immediate aftermath of the overturning of *Roe*, some leading national anti-rape and domestic violence organizations like RAINN and the National Sexual Violence Resource Center were conspicuously quiet about survivors' rapidly eroding reproductive rights: no statements responding to the leaked opinion in May, action plans detailing steps they would take to protect survivors' abortion access, social media posts acknowledging this seismic threat to victims' fundamental human rights. Most notably, in the months before *Roe* was overturned, RAINN, the most visible and well-funded organization advocating for victims of sexual abuse, faced allegations that it had pressured an employee who was a survivor herself to complete a work assignment as she bled from a medication abortion.[20] Even some of the most prominent leaders in advocating for victims and survivors have not drawn the connections between their movement and reproductive justice.

PREGNANCY, STATE VIOLENCE, AND THE CARCERAL SYSTEM

Growing up, before I even knew what *Roe v. Wade* was, I knew the story of a great-aunt in the Philippines who had experienced intimate partner violence from her husband that led to a miscarriage. On top of recovering from the traumas of both abuse and pregnancy loss, she had also confided in my mother about her fear of being investigated or found criminally liable for the miscarriage if it was deemed a self-induced abortion.

Her story would not be an anomaly in the US—particularly as an Asian woman, here in a country in which Asian women and pregnant people have been disproportionately targeted and placed at risk of criminalization for their pregnancies. So-called sex- and race-selective abortion bans, which pre-date the fall of *Roe* and were created to interrogate and police the reasons someone might seek abortion, contribute to this. These bans make it illegal for a doctor to offer an abortion if they suspect their patient wants to end the pregnancy due to preference for the sex of the fetus. They're rooted in anti-Asian, anti-immigrant stereotypes that falsely suggest Asian women end pregnancies because they prefer sons, and weaponize racist, fearmongering narratives about immigrants and people of color bringing "backward" values from their homelands to the United States.

Sex- and race-selective bans, which are currently in effect in a handful of states—although some are superseded by total bans since *Roe* was overturned—can require doctors, nurses, and health care workers who even suspect a patient may be seeking abortion due to the race or sex of the fetus to report them to law enforcement. Two of the most high-profile cases of people being criminalized and prosecuted for self-managed abortions or pregnancy loss in recent history both involve Asian women: Purvi Patel, initially sentenced to twenty years in prison for allegedly taking a medication abortion and having a stillbirth in 2013, and Bei Bei Shuai, who lost a pregnancy after attempting to take her own life in 2011.

Bizarre, punishing cases of pregnancy criminalization happen often: In 2019 Brooke Skylar Richardson of Ohio was charged with aggravated murder, involuntary manslaughter, child endangering, and gross abuse of a corpse after giving birth to a stillborn fetus and burying it in her yard in 2017, when she was an eighteen-year-old high school student. She was acquitted of all charges after an eight-day trial in September 2019. That, of course, was the same year that Marshae Jones faced charges for manslaughter in Alabama after being shot in the stomach and experiencing a miscarriage. Police said they pressed charges because Jones had allegedly started the fight that led to her injuries, in yet another example of how victims of violence and abuse can potentially be punished for self-defense—especially if they're pregnant.

In 2016 Katherine Dellis, a twenty-six-year-old Virginia woman, was convicted and briefly jailed for concealing a dead body after she, too, experienced a stillbirth. In 2011 Jennie Linn McCormack of Idaho, a mother of three who had her first child at age fourteen, was arrested for terminating her pregnancy with an abortion pill she purchased online. McCormack was charged under a 1973 state law, Idaho Code Section 18-606, which treats self-managed abortion as a felony punishable by up to five years in prison. In 2007 Amber Abreu, an eighteen-year-old Latinx woman in New York, was criminally charged for "procuring a miscarriage."

Jessica Tebow and her husband were eagerly awaiting the birth of their first child in 2009, when an unexpected miscarriage and the threat of a possibly fatal infection—which could also potentially cause infertility— forced her to have an emergency abortion. Tebow, who detailed the experience in a 2022 op-ed, said she and her husband saved the miscarried embryo as they wanted to have a small, private ceremony to mourn. But when her husband called the nearest funeral home to seek a cremation process, she says they were told they needed a death certificate, to check with the local fire department, and to contact a coroner. Upon doing so, the two were promptly investigated by police in Glendale, California. Still reeling from the trauma of losing a wanted pregnancy, Tebow was questioned by police about "the baby I had put in the freezer," prompting her to realize police had broken into and searched her home. They'd also restrained her husband, threatened to arrest him, and confiscated their frozen, miscarried embryo.[21]

In 2022 it was reported that Etowah County in Alabama had jailed dozens of women—without trials or convictions—for indefinite amounts of time because they were pregnant or postpartum and alleged to have used substances. In one case, a woman with a high-risk pregnancy was forced to sleep on a jail floor for weeks—over allegedly smoking pot. Her lawyers said state investigators pressured her to "admit" to a drug addiction she didn't have so she could access rehab, pay the $10,000 cash bond for allegedly exposing her fetus to drugs, and leave jail. Other women had just given birth and were separated from their newborn infants for months—again, all without any trial. Per Pregnancy Justice, the county had previously required $10,000 bond and in-patient drug treatment for charges of "chemical endangerment of a child," often resulting in pregnant or postpartum people being jailed indefinitely due to lack of availability of beds in treatment centers. The policy eventually changed to $2,500 bond and mandatory, near-daily drug testing for pregnant people—still an inaccessible, needlessly punishing mandate. Once arrested, charged, or imprisoned for a pregnancy outcome, even upon release or having their charges cleared, those who are criminalized for a miscarriage or ending a pregnancy with a self-managed abortion can consequently face a lifetime of being denied housing, jobs, and economic autonomy.

Of the more than 1,700 pregnancy-related criminalization cases Pregnancy Justice has tracked between 1973 and 2020, Alabama led the nation with over 600 cases. Further, just 2 percent of Alabama's population lives in Etowah County, yet the county represents more than 20 percent of pregnancy-related prosecutions in Alabama. In September 2022 five women who were either postpartum or pregnant and had been jailed over substance use charges were released, but their physical freedom from jail didn't mean their state-inflicted suffering was over. Because their criminal cases remained ongoing, they would still struggle to regain custody of their children who have been separated from them amid the Department of Human Resources' (Alabama's "child welfare" agency) investigations of the women. Pregnancy Justice attorney Emma Roth told me at the time that the "irony" of the situation is that "criminal prosecutors say this is all for the best interests of the children, but this is wreaking havoc upon families, and family reunification would go so far toward protecting the well-being of children."

Abortion bans inevitably worsen the crisis of pregnancy criminalization—especially as medication abortion can't be medically distinguished from miscarriage, effectively rendering miscarriage a crime in states that criminalize abortion. Without *Roe*, all pregnancies are possible crime scenes. "The underlying theory behind these charges is the exact same theory that motivates abortion bans or other restrictions on bodily autonomy during pregnancy—it's the notion that when somebody becomes pregnant, their rights no longer matter, their liberty no longer matters," Roth said. "If the only concern of state actors is protecting the health and well-being of 'unborn children,' they feel entitled to trample the rights and liberty of pregnant people in the process."

Some of the aforementioned women faced criminal charges after they say they had a miscarriage or stillbirth—experiences that can be traumatic on their own. "You have a living, breathing pregnant person who's had a loss and is now being treated as a criminal," Dr. Monica McLemore, an associate professor in the Family Health Care Nursing Department at the University of California, San Francisco, and a clinician-scientist at Advancing New Standards in Reproductive Health (ANSIRH), told me in the fall of 2019, amid my reporting on Jones's trial. Dr. McLemore said the criminalization of miscarriage emerges from a culture that insists pregnant people are exclusively responsible for the outcomes of their pregnancies. "We act like they don't live in environments that contribute to those outcomes," she explained. "And as a result, we see criminalization and punitive measures meant to control women and pregnant people, instead of an appropriate, compassionate public health response."

The criminalization of pregnancy and abortion is inseparable from the greater national and global crises of gender-based violence. For the outcomes of their pregnancies, pregnant people can become entangled within the criminal justice system, and, as a result of latent white supremacy in both the criminal-legal and medical systems, those who are targeted are often poor people of color. In the weeks before *Roe* was overturned, a Latinx woman in Texas named Lizelle Herrera was jailed and charged with homicide for allegedly self-managing an abortion after her own doctor reported her to law enforcement. In 2010 an Iowa woman named Christine Taylor, then a mother of two, was charged with attempted feticide after she fell down the stairs, miscarried, and doctors reported her to police when they misidentified her pregnancy as being in the third trimester—an Iowa statute defines termination of pregnancy in the third trimester as illegal. In 2004 in Utah, when Melissa Rowland gave birth to twins and one was stillborn, she was arrested for fetal homicide for not going to the hospital to get help sooner.

Per If/When/How's previously mentioned report, 39 percent of cases of self-managed abortion that come to law enforcement's attention were reported by health care providers, 6 percent by social workers, and 26 percent were reported to police by acquaintances the pregnant person had shared information with, including friends, parents, and intimate partners. A "homicide consideration" was twice as likely in cases involving pregnant people of color. Laura Huss, a senior researcher at If/When/How and co-author of the report, told me in 2022 for an article in Jezebel that when patients know health care providers are policing them, "this can only make people more afraid to get the care they need." New data published within months of the fall of *Roe* showed that people are three times more likely to die during pregnancy in states that ban abortion.[22] These numbers underscore the dangers for people who seek health care in states that humanize fetuses over pregnant people.

Many advocates and Democratic lawmakers have placed an emphasis on reining in digital surveillance and data collection of pregnant people to protect them from criminalization. But these pressure campaigns, ramped up since the fall of *Roe*, have notably been unsuccessful, yielding few changes in the invasive behaviors of data brokers and tech companies. Nonetheless, digital surveillance plays an important role in gathering evidence and building criminal cases against pregnant people for their pregnancy outcomes or abortions—more on this shortly. Interpersonal and digital surveillance are two features of a broader system of punishing and controlling pregnant people in the US.

COLONIZATION AND THE POLICING OF INDIGENOUS PREGNANCIES AND FAMILIES

Black and Indigenous people who struggle with substance dependency and are denied access to quality health care in our for-profit health system are disproportionately vulnerable to criminalization. In the fall of 2021, a twenty-one-year-old Oklahoma woman was convicted of first-degree manslaughter after losing a pregnancy in her second trimester. Brittney Poolaw, who's Native American and a member of the Wichita and Affiliated Tribes, experienced a miscarriage and stillbirth in January 2020 and was sentenced in October 2021 to four years in prison. Poolaw's sentencing came after a medical examiner confirmed that her fifteen-to-seventeen-week fetus had congenital abnormalities and had tested positive for methamphetamine. Her story reflects a years-long trend of increasing cases of pregnancy criminalization—especially in Oklahoma, which has the second-highest population of Indigenous people in the country.

In 2017 Oklahoma's district attorney announced heightened measures to prosecute pregnant people who are alleged to have used criminalized drugs, misusing and weaponizing the state's felony child-neglect laws against struggling pregnant people. And just as data shows non-white people experience higher rates of stillbirths, miscarriage, and pregnancy complications than white people, state surveillance and criminalization of these outcomes—especially if substance use is believed to be a factor—isn't race-neutral, either. People of color and especially Indigenous people like Poolaw have historically faced higher rates of pregnancy- and drug-related criminalization, often stemming from particularly cruel use of feticide and child abuse laws by prosecutors. The reproductive oppression inflicted on Indigenous pregnant people and families is multipronged: Throughout the twentieth century, at the height of the eugenics movement, Indigenous people were disproportionately targeted with forced sterilization efforts by the US government. Prior to the Indian Child Welfare Act of 1978, between 25 and 35 percent of Native American youth were separated from their families and placed in the custody of the state or in foster care,[23] as a transparent extension of the United States' decades-long attempts at cultural genocide through kidnapping and violently forcing assimilation onto Indigenous children.

Nicole Martin, who is Laguna Pueblo and Navajo and a co-founder of the reproductive justice group Indigenous Women Rising, told me that outcomes like this amount to modern colonization. "All of the United States infrastructure was founded on stolen land, the genocide of Native people, the enslavement of Black people. And those are two of the groups who face the highest rates of criminalization, maternal mortality, infant mortality—that's the way that the system was intended to work."[24]

According to Martin, pregnancy criminalization, particularly around substance use, builds on a persistent history of white-supremacist standards for "good parents" and "bad parents" being used to isolate Indigenous pregnant people from their communities. "There's always been a history of Indigenous people being criminalized for not being fit parents, if you look at the Indian Child Welfare Act, separating youth from their families and putting them in non-Indigenous households to overturn tribal sovereignty and culture," Martin said. "Brittney Poolaw, all of this, this is part of that—it's taking people away from their communities with criminalization."

As of 2022, twenty-three states and the District of Columbia have laws that equate drug exposure during pregnancy with child abuse. Twenty-five states and DC require health professionals to report suspected prenatal drug use, according to the Guttmacher Institute. In about forty states "fetal homicide" and assault laws exist and can be abused by law enforcement to grant embryos and fetuses personhood rights, as the potential victims of the person who's pregnant with them, based on their behaviors.

When seemingly benevolent laws are interpreted as conferring personhood upon embryos and fetuses (like, say, a child tax credit for unborn fetuses proposed in Congress in February 2022, or later that year, after the fall of *Roe*, a bill to require men to make child support payments within a month into their partner's pregnancy), the result is the pregnant person's dehumanization, and often enough, incarceration. Pregnant people who miscarry, need emergency abortion care to not die, seek certain medications, or even lose a pregnancy after being physically attacked can all become murder suspects. IVF, which requires routine disposal of unused embryos, becomes a crime—an outcome some Texas Republican leaders and Georgia's Republican governor, Brian Kemp, have overtly advocated for.[25] In November 2022 ProPublica obtained audio of Tennessee lawmakers meeting with top anti-abortion activists in the state to determine the right time to begin restricting and policing IVF.[26] A pregnant person traveling across state lines without their partner's consent becomes kidnapping—Pregnancy Justice's Dana Sussman told me in 2022 that we've already seen this happen. Substance use or certain behaviors before a child is even born become "child abuse."

Native American pregnant people are more likely to be impacted by misuse of fetal homicide laws, as their communities struggle with disproportionately high rates of addiction and severely strained access to health care, resources, and support. One 2012 report found about 2.5 percent of American adults in addiction treatment are Native American,[27] though Native American people account for about 1 percent of the total US population. A different study of 342 Native American patients at a hospital near the Great Lakes region found 34.5 percent of their pregnancies were "substance-exposed."[28]

Insidious policies that criminalize substance use during pregnancy can also be traced to the anti-Black War on Drugs. The myths and propaganda perpetuated by the fundamentally racist 1980s public health panic known as the crack epidemic saw Black pregnant people routinely subjected to mandated drug testing, with positive drug tests treated as proof of child neglect and grounds to separate parents from their newborns or criminalize rather than offer help to struggling pregnant people. "Addiction or substance use doesn't mean [someone is] disposable, or they should be denied dignity or humanity. The hardest thing to witness right is when others have internalized this, and will use this as a reason to punish or deny rather than give people actual care," Martin said.

Again, criminal charges for miscarriages, stillbirths, and all pregnancy outcomes including self-managed abortion have tripled in recent years. Pregnant Indigenous people remain exposed to greater risk of criminalization across the country, as they're more likely to use state-sponsored public health and social services programs, most of which have mandated reporting policies for suspected drug use. Different tribes across the US have their own legal approaches and policies to address substance use during pregnancy, and a 2020 review of available tribal laws from the *AMA Journal of Ethics* found that substance use during pregnancy is criminalized in most tribes, to varying responses and penalties.[29] Tribes like the Navajo Nation and White Earth Nation mandate substance use treatment programs, while tribes like the Little River Band of Ottawa Indians and Standing Rock Sioux Tribe penalize substance use during pregnancy as child abuse.

Consequently, pregnant people who may have used substances or are struggling with addiction are discouraged from seeking any kind of prenatal health care out of fear of possible prosecution and jail time. According to Martin, many pregnant Indigenous people already choose home births, due to concerns about drug testing but also fear of persistent mistreatment in the health system. Indigenous people are twice as likely to die from pregnancy-related causes as white people, according to federal statistics from the CDC.

In contrast with these racist and colonialist systems of pregnancy policing, some Indigenous spaces and pregnancy and maternal care providers have chosen to model compassionate approaches that support rather than criminalize people who may be struggling. Melissa Rose, an Akwesasne Mohawk midwife who works with Indigenous Women Rising's birthing fund to provide care to Native American pregnant people across New Mexico, told me in 2021 that she became a midwife after her own experiences with racism from white health care providers: "So many times I've been told, 'Oh, Native Americans are predisposed to addiction and substance-abuse disorders.' I've been disrespected and had assumptions made about me that have delayed care and led to misdiagnosed illnesses. I've flat-out been told by a doctor that [alcoholism] it's genetic, and I'm predisposed because of my heritage to have a struggle with alcohol," Rose said. She told me that when she asked her doctor to point to "the gene that causes this," her question "led to a whole conversation, and me advocating for my own humane treatment with someone I depended on for medical care."

Rose continued, "It was an unsafe situation because of the power dynamics involved, and it happens over and over again when I and other Native people attempt to access medical, mental health, and substance use services. I didn't drink because I'm Native. I drank to survive colonialism. I learned coping mechanisms to all the layers of experienced and inherited trauma from my family." She also recounted being "dismissed and disrespected" when she gave birth at sixteen years old in a military hospital in Oklahoma, at one point having her newborn taken away from her for hours. "The lack of a culturally matched provider, whether in reproductive health care choices, medical care, mental health, or substance use treatment, really contributes to adverse health outcomes, and constant retraumatization."

Rose has previously met with members of Congress about issues like the inaccessibility of prenatal care and especially midwifery services for Indigenous pregnant people, overly long wait times for pregnancy-related appointments with the Indian Health Service, and the Hyde Amendment, which prohibits coverage of most abortion services by IHS. But in addition to these important demands, Rose emphasizes the powerful potential of "culturally matched providers of care" for Indigenous pregnant people, which can make "a drastic difference" in pregnancy outcomes.

"Your client doesn't need to have the language to explain all of the histories and traumas that they're having to navigate, because it's in our bones," she said. When it comes to meeting the needs of her clients who may struggle with substance use, Rose stresses the importance of ensuring the care she provides "is trauma-informed, tailored towards the most vulnerable, which probably would be Indigenous people struggling with different forms of trauma or substance use." It's her goal to ensure her clients "can feel safe" coming to her for care, no matter what conditions they may be struggling with.

In Blackfeet Nation in Browning, Montana, one of the largest reservations in the US, Blackfeet Community Hospital is also determined to put care over criminality, Dr. Kendall Flint, director of the hospital's Women's Health Center, told Rewire in 2018. Dr. Flint noted that "urine drug screening doesn't improve or positively affect patient outcome," and his hospital's decision to reject universal drug screening was guided by input from their patients. "Our patients told us repeatedly that they don't come and their friends don't come for prenatal care, because of their belief that we would do urine drug screening on them, and would share that information with law enforcement, and become part of a punitive rather than a caregiving team," he said. One of the primary goals at the Women's Health Center is to raise awareness that it doesn't practice universal, nonconsensual drug testing, to encourage pregnant patients to seek prenatal care before giving birth, and consequently improve maternal health outcomes. "The relationship we have with our patients is among the most important interventions we can work with," Flint explained.[30]

By the spring of 2022, tribal lands like Blackfeet Nation would suddenly be propelled to the center of the fight for abortion access when white, liberal advocates began turning to Indigenous land and communities, imploring them to become havens for non-Indigenous people to get abortion care. This conversation was sparked by Oklahoma Gov. Kevin Stitt declaring in May 2022 that he would ban abortion on tribal land after *Roe* fell, in clear violation of Indigenous sovereignty. "Our lands are not just places to skirt laws," Rachael Lorenzo, executive director of IWR and a co-founder with Martin, told me at the time. "I get how well-meaning people are desperate to protect access, but we're failing to acknowledge whether or not tribes have the power and resources to be sued."[31] They added that opening tribal land to non-Indigenous people for abortion access is a matter that tribes should talk about internally "as sovereign nations."

Lorenzo also noted that there are a number of risks involved with increased presence of non-Indigenous people on tribal land, like violence against Indigenous women: "One of the factors that contributes to the many, many missing and murdered Indigenous women and girls is that many of our abusers and predators are non-Native people, who know and take advantage of how tribes often don't have the legal standing to charge them or to prosecute them."

The sudden centering of tribal land in the fight for abortion access by liberal, non-Indigenous activists—in tandem with the extensive state violence and policing Indigenous people already face around pregnancy and health care—was a reminder of the shortcomings of white, non-Indigenous-led reproductive rights activism, and the importance of following the leadership of Indigenous activists and pregnant people. As the threat of pregnancy and abortion criminalization rises for all people, Rose stressed to me that Indigenous people will always be disproportionately impacted. Indigenous communities, she said, are safer when they "have access to all the different variations of sovereignty, like food sovereignty, land sovereignty, cultural reclamation, body sovereignty." She added, "We need access to our sacred sites, to our plant medicines, to our cultural teachings around pregnancy. This is about sovereignty."

SURVEILLING THE WOMB

Shortly after Texas enacted SB 8 in 2021, Texas Right to Life launched what could really only be called a snitch hotline, calling on the nosiest of neighbors to submit "tips" about people they suspected to be seeking or helping people seek abortions. Things didn't go as planned for the hotline, once online teens and other social media users joined forces to inundate the hotline with false tips, Shrek memes, furry porn, and other generally ludicrous submissions, rendering the tip line useless for anyone but particularly committed Shrek fans. The hotline—which would have inevitably been weaponized by abusive ex-partners or anti-abortion activists seeking an easy $10,000 by suing people who help others have abortions—was almost immediately dropped by several hosting services.

But despite the hotline's defeat, the threat of digital platforms being used to surveil and threaten anyone who seeks, provides, or helps someone obtain an abortion ultimately remains larger than ever. For years, anti-abortion groups have benefited tremendously from digital surveillance, online crisis pregnancy centers, and help from leading social platforms and search engines to police pregnant people.

Cynthia Conti-Cook, technology fellow at the Ford Foundation focusing on gender, racial, and ethnic justice and author of the paper "Surveilling the Digital Abortion Diary," told me in 2021 that it isn't just the blatantly ridiculous and often ineffective snitch lines that should concern us. Stunts like that are "often used as an organizing tool to excite the base, whip people up, and get them involved," she said—but there are much less obvious and more threatening forms of pregnancy surveillance happening right under our noses.

Anti-abortion groups are already taking advantage of digital platforms to spy on people: They're funding and partnering with fertility apps that track people's periods—surveillance titan Peter Thiel, founder of the highly secretive software company Palantir (which has played a significant role in helping the National Security Agency spy on citizens), in 2022 invested over $3 million in a period tracking app called "28." The app was founded by the conservative women's magazine *Evie*. Anti-abortion groups also take advantage of mobile geofencing technology to bombard patients at or en route to abortion clinics with targeted anti-abortion propaganda ads.[32] According to Conti-Cook, this practice has also increasingly been adopted by law enforcement agencies using what are called "reverse geofence warrants." Cops, Conti-Cook said, "can ask Google for everyone within the radius of a specific location, at a specific time, based on their phones." They can create a lineup from this data to investigate crimes in a specific location and generate possible leads. This is a practice that can notably be applied in both criminal and civil cases, with reverse geofencing to provide location data that places individuals at abortion clinics or even substance use disorder treatment centers—a significant legal risk if someone loses their pregnancy and is suspected of drug use. According to internal data Google shared with the public in 2020, one quarter of the law enforcement orders the company receives each year are for location data. It received 11,554 geofence warrants that year alone. In July 2022 Politico reported most law enforcement warrants for users' location data that Google received that year came from states that had since banned abortion.

In several documented cases, search histories for medication abortion and options for self-managing abortion have been used as evidence to land people like Latice Fisher, a Black mother of three in Mississippi, in jail. In 2018 Fisher experienced a stillbirth that prosecutors tried to prove had been a live birth. They successfully argued that Fisher had killed her own baby, citing her previous online searches for abortion pills as evidence of her "motive." She was briefly incarcerated, though charges against her were dropped shortly thereafter.

Before Fisher, as previously noted, Purvi Patel was jailed and charged with feticide in 2015 for allegedly inducing an abortion after her online purchase of abortion pills was used as evidence against her. The prosecution also invoked Patel's private text messages with a friend in whom she had confided that she was pregnant and searching for medication abortion online. Just after the overturning of *Roe*, in 2022, criminal charges lodged against a Nebraska teen and her mother for the teen's self-managed abortion relied heavily on digital surveillance. While the teen was first reported to police by a friend, police relied on Facebook text communications handed over to them by Meta in which the teen discussed using abortion pills.

As prosecutors weaponize and misuse "feticide" and child endangerment laws to target people who experience miscarriage or self-manage their own abortions, digital footprints of searching for abortion pills, or even text conversations with friends and family members about pregnancies, are increasingly being wielded as key evidence against pregnant people in criminal trials. In criminal cases like these, Conti-Cook said law enforcement has usually obtained this information through individuals "voluntarily handing their phones in," believing they don't have the option to say no, or through search warrants for individuals' phones. As a result, the very digital platforms that many people rely on to access or learn about reproductive health care like abortion pills could be used to surveil and penalize them through discovery processes in civil cases.

Without *Roe*, in states that ban abortion, all abortions, miscarriages, and pregnancies in general are surveilled and miscarriages treated with criminal suspicion, as people can always be suspected of inducing their miscarriages with abortion pills. The proportion of people who end their pregnancies using medication abortion pills continues to rise, especially amid widespread clinic shutdowns—exponentially increasing online searches for the medication that can now serve as evidence to sue or prosecute people.

It's not just law enforcement agencies acting alone. Anti-abortion politicians and organizations have never exactly been keen on privacy. In 2019 the director of Missouri's health department was outed for tracking state Planned Parenthood patients' menstrual cycles on a spreadsheet. Forty-six states and DC require some form of reporting abortions to the state, while states with fetal burial laws (laws that require people to pay to have fetal tissue from their abortions buried or cremated) typically require people to get death certificates for aborted fetuses, entering their abortions into the public record. In 2022 a Vice News report exposed Meta for sharing the private data of abortion seekers with anti-abortion crisis pregnancy centers. "Crisis pregnancy centers," or CPCs—anti-abortion organizations that lure primarily poor people of color with unwanted pregnancies to their facilities by pretending to offer abortion services, then aggressively try to dissuade them from having abortions—play an especially concerning role in the surveillance of pregnant people, all while receiving massive amounts of state funding to do so.

Some of these "clinics" even have contracts with state governments to help collect data from callers seeking abortion care, in a conjoined effort to stalk, possibly criminalize, and force people to give birth. In 2022 Oklahoma became the latest state to pass legislation requiring that pregnant people seeking abortion care consult with a CPC or anti-abortion "care agent." The bill would assign abortion seekers a "unique identifying number" that must be added to their medical record and tracked in a database maintained by the state. A law like this passed Arkansas's legislature in 2021. Similarly, an Iowa bill introduced that same year would give CPCs funding specifically to target pregnant people online.

The ratio of crisis pregnancy centers to abortion-providing clinics in the US notably stands at 3 to 1, with even higher disparities in states that fund CPCs, like Pennsylvania (where the ratio is 9 to 1), and Minnesota (11 to 1), as of 2022.[33] One 2022 report by the Center for Countering Digital Hate found nearly 40 percent of search results for "abortion" on Google Maps direct people in abortion-hostile states to crisis pregnancy centers instead of real clinics.[34] And because, in most cases, CPCs provide no actual health care, they aren't subject to the patient privacy standards set by HIPAA. As a result, fake clinics' websites have become the key to the anti-abortion movement's surveillance and data-collection operations in recent years. Heartbeat International, a leading network of crisis pregnancy centers, has historically flooded Facebook and Google with targeted ads. A similar anti-abortion crisis pregnancy center organization, Obria Group, notably received $150,000 of free ads from Google in 2019. Heartbeat International uses a chat system called Option Line for "abortion-minded" users who must identify themselves and their locations, and it has shared Option Line with thousands of CPCs and anti-abortion groups across the country to use on their websites, a representative for the women's rights organization Legal Voice told me in 2022.

Per Heartbeat International's own terms of use, "all remarks" sent through Option Line can be used by the organization "for any and all purposes . . . appropriate to the mission and vision of Option Line." In promotions for its data collection practices, Heartbeat International has said, "Big data is revolutionizing all sorts of industries. Why shouldn't it do the same for a critical ministry like ours?"

Moreover, what happens in real life inside fake clinics—and to their victims long after they leave—is just as invasive. One victim has testified to the Expose Fake Clinics campaign that after she left a CPC, one of its workers "began calling her almost daily and telling her aggressively that she would die, or end up in hell, or get very sick if she were to go through with the abortion." Others who had been targeted by crisis pregnancy centers told the campaign they were forced to sign contracts pledging to not have an abortion before being able to leave the clinic. Anna, the youth abortion access organizer mentioned earlier in this chapter, told me about anti-abortion clinics that increasingly rely on "feminist" branding to attract and prey on abortion seekers. This, she said, is a tactic to "confuse people long enough that they might just miss the cutoff and can't have an abortion."

"The consequence of their tactics is it delays people, it causes people to wait on something as time-sensitive as abortion, when they could find actual resources, and could miss the window for an abortion," she said. It's not lost on Anna, who got her abortion in 2018 at six weeks and one day into her pregnancy, that a matter of days can make the difference between whether or not someone is forced to give birth. Within years of her abortion, Texas would ban abortions at the six-week cutoff in 2021, before ultimately banning all abortions after *Roe* fell the following summer.

Fake clinics are given free rein to advertise their websites on Google and Meta's varying social platforms and surveil pregnant people and abortion seekers who are lured there. In contrast, medically accurate information about abortion and reproductive care is often censored from the internet. Kara Mailman, senior research analyst at the grassroots reproductive justice organization Reproaction, told me in 2021 that their research has found that social posts that include keywords like "misoprostol" and "mifepristone" (FDA-approved, highly safe abortion-inducing medications) are monitored and disproportionately restricted by Facebook and Instagram. For example, a cursory search for misoprostol on Instagram often yields the warning label "Recent posts for #misoprostol are hidden because some posts may not follow Instagram's Community Guidelines." In November 2022 when one user shared basic information about how to use medication abortions on Twitter, her posts were flagged, removed, and her account penalized for "promoting self-harm."[35]

There's a blatant double standard in how abortion-related content is monitored and moderated online, and anti-abortion activists benefit from it. Their paid ads and other content about "abortion pill reversal," a medically unproven and unsafe approach that activists claim can stop a medication abortion that's underway, have remained widely available on these same platforms, often without the same flags and restrictions. Yet Facebook on multiple occasions removed Reproaction's medically accurate posts about self-managing abortions with pills, Mailman told me. "They gave us no explanation other than the posts allegedly violated community guidelines and won't give us recourse to put them back up. But anti-abortion groups like Live Action can continue to post misleading ads about abortion pill reversal, sometimes spending thousands on targeted ads per week."

In 2018 when Sen. Marsha Blackburn (R-Tenn.) ran campaign ads about Planned Parenthood selling baby parts—rhetoric that Mailman notes "was word-for-word used by the Colorado Springs Planned Parenthood shooter in 2015"—Facebook briefly removed the ads, only to restore them and apologize to Blackburn in the face of anti-abortion pushback. "The ad was still inflammatory and inciting violence—the reasons it had been taken down—but was reinstated," Mailman said. "Meanwhile, [Reproaction] still can't buy ads for having posted about medication abortion."

As in-clinic abortion access dwindles in most states, it's becoming more necessary for abortion providers and advocates to amplify information about how people can safely and legally get and use abortion pills at home. But they're being censored and penalized for sharing information about the FDA-approved medication. Elisa Wells, co-founder and co-director of Plan C Pills, which helps people get information about and access to abortion pills online, told me in 2021 that in addition to the organization's posts on abortion pills being flagged and removed "a number of times," the organization's Facebook page has "mysteriously shut down" before, too. "Each time we'd just get the generic message that we're in violation of their policies or whatever, but we don't know what we're 'in violation of,' because we provide research-based information—we don't sell products, we don't provide medical care."

If people with unwanted pregnancies can't get information about their options for abortion care, Wells said, some could be forced to either carry pregnancies to term or suffer long-term health and economic consequences as a result. "It's the economic costs, but the emotional, mental health costs, too, of waiting, worrying, and stigma," she said. "If you want to terminate a pregnancy, and you're not able to, that's the ultimate cost."

And where platforms like Google have, again, offered thousands of dollars in free ads to groups like Heartbeat International, and Facebook has publicly apologized to Senator Blackburn, abortion providers and advocates have long been subject to digital threats and even cybercrimes from anti-abortion activists—often translating into real-life violence—with little protection online. The militant anti-abortion group Operation Rescue, which has been linked to the assassination of an abortion provider in 2009, is known to keep an online database that catalogs the names, addresses, photos, and videos of abortion providers across the country. Recent digital attacks on abortion access have ranged from a massive, coordinated hack on the National Network of Abortion Funds' annual bowl-a-thon fundraiser in 2016, which leaked funders and organizers' personal information and subjected them to a barrage of pro-Nazi messages, to the rampant anti-abortion ads and misinformation people are forced to sift through on a daily basis just to find an abortion provider or online resources for abortion care.

When it comes to pregnancy and digital safety, Conti-Cook told me we've largely been left to fend for ourselves—which she noted is possible, for example, with use of encrypted messaging apps like Signal, encrypted email like Proton Mail, and virtual private networks, or VPNs. But it's also important that we demand more from those who serve us. "Lawmakers have to seriously contend with how much data is being collected, and then turned around and sold, including being sold to law enforcement."

Conti-Cook said she hopes providers and advocates aren't intimidated into giving up their vital and often online work, and she believes solidarity within the reproductive justice movement will be essential to keeping each other safe. "When we're thinking about what digital routines we're willing to incorporate in our own lives for our safety, we should think about not just how this issue impacts us, but how it impacts the person in our networks who's most vulnerable," she said. "When you're thinking, 'Do I go through the trouble of getting on Signal or Wire?'—we should be thinking about the person who might be most vulnerable to prosecution, or some SB 8 litigation." In other words, think about the safety of abuse victims, people of color, low-income people, and those who are already over-policed by law enforcement and marginalized within the health system.

ANTI-ABORTION VIOLENCE AIDS STATE VIOLENCE

At the same time that pregnant people and abortion providers have become increasingly vulnerable to criminalization and legal action, they've also faced an increase in "vandalism, assault and battery, death threats/threats of harm, stalking, and hoax devices/suspicious packages," per an annual report the National Abortion Federation (NAF) published at the end of 2021.[36] Most alarmingly, providers reported a 125 percent increase in assaults and altercations instigated by anti-abortion protesters, including "shoving, pushing, tripping, and spitting on clinic escorts, staff, and others outside of clinics."

Violence is an everyday facet of abortion providers' lives—it has been for decades now. The Feminist Majority Foundation reported that between 2018 and 2019 half of surveyed clinics had experienced at least one incident of severe violence or severe harassment, such as break-ins, robberies, and vandalism. Overall, NAF reported 8,812 incidents of violence targeting clinics between 1977 and 2017. Other jarring statistics: Since 1977 there have been at least eleven documented murders and twenty-six attempted murders of abortion providers, on top of hundreds of incidents of arson and bombings targeting providers and all the routine assaults, stalking, doxing, and threats, including a kidnapping attempt on an Indiana abortion provider's young child that came to light in January 2022.

In addition to wielding the carceral system to punish people who are unable to complete their pregnancies, or people who induce their own abortions, anti-abortion activists also rely on acts of interpersonal violence to push their agenda of forced pregnancy. NAF's 2021 report specified that between 2019 and 2020, death threats and threats of harm to clinic staff more than doubled, from 92 to 200. Clinics reported twenty-seven cases of receiving suspicious packages last year, up from just two in 2019, as well as double the cases of stalking clinic staff. There were four reported cases of arson in 2020 compared with none the year before, and internet harassment against providers increased by about 10 percent, too.

"We expected an escalation in anti-abortion activities in 2020 and 2021 due to the political climate, the election, and the increase in hate incidents throughout the country," Melissa Fowler, chief program officer of NAF, told me at the time the report came out. According to Fowler, "some of the people at the January 6 [Capitol] insurrection are the same people who have been targeting abortion providers and protesting at clinics in their communities."

She continued, "The people who threaten clinic workers and harass individuals seeking abortion care are often the same people who participate in other violent and extremist activities that are rooted in racism, white supremacy, and misogyny, and are deeply harmful." Since 2021 NAF's members "continue to report an escalation in aggressive anti-abortion activity," as well as anti-abortion activists being "emboldened by . . . recent Supreme Court activity concerning abortion cases" to target clinics, revealing a disturbing correlation between the anti-abortion movement's political successes and violent acts by anti-abortion activists.

Of course, some anti-abortion politicians have attempted to distance themselves from more overt anti-abortion violence against providers and patients, as we saw in the immediate aftermath of the 2015 mass shooting at a Planned Parenthood clinic in Colorado by Robert Deer, a white man who later said he "killed three and saved 3,000 babies." Anti-abortion politicians including Republican presidential candidates Mike Huckabee and Sen. Ted Cruz all very publicly and immediately denounced the attack, despite their own roles in creating the culture that inspired it. However "pro-life" politicians may claim to be, when they equate a health service ending an unwanted pregnancy to literally killing a baby, they're all but inviting violence against people who give and have abortions—they know this and politically benefit from it.

On the state level, Oklahoma, Georgia, Texas, Alabama, and others have introduced bills in recent years that would make abortion a felony punishable by the death penalty. Post-*Roe*, nearly all states that have banned abortion threaten to investigate or imprison abortion providers or patients, and in South Carolina, even people who merely educate others about medication abortion. Leading politicians like Cruz have worked closely and boasted about their relationships with members of Operation Rescue, the militant anti-abortion group connected to the murder of the abortion provider George Tiller in Kansas in 2009.[37] Surprising no one, numerous protesters present at the January 6 insurrection at the Capitol in 2021 were well-known anti-abortion activists who deployed the violent tactics they use outside clinics at the Capitol. The common thread is masculine violence: Outside clinics, they harass and sometimes dox women and pregnant people, threatening to expose patients who may be domestic violence victims to their abusers by posting their photos online. They took this same energy to the events of January 6, in an attempt to reinstall a virulently anti-abortion, anti-women president.

NAF's report on anti-abortion violence from 2021 remains a disturbing reminder that coordinated violence, intimidation, and dehumanization are instrumental to the anti-abortion movement's day-to-day operations. They might call themselves "pro-life," but their actions speak infinitely louder than their words. The violence of anti-abortion activists, anti-abortion politicians, and their cruelly designed policies is an intentional feature of capitalism, a weapon to guarantee a continued, overinflated supply of generations of exploitable and expendable work-ers through compelling pregnancies, and punishing those who try to resist, or who have or provide abortions.

Yet this violence—abortion bans, invasive protests outside abortion clinics, assaults and attacks on abortion providers—is seldom regarded as violence, at least by those in positions of power. Throughout 2022, before and after overturning *Roe*, conservative Supreme Court justices made a very public fuss about being victimized by protesters who made them feel uncomfortable at their homes and places of work—as if abor-tion bans don't enact violence upon every aspect of pregnant-capable people's lives, as if abortion providers aren't endangered every day they go to work because the court struck down their right to establish buffer zones blocking violent anti-abortion protesters from entering clinics back in 2014. Violent acts that enforce the state's agenda are rarely regarded as violent—in contrast, acts of resistance are.

Days after a preacher showed up with a semiautomatic assault rifle to then-Texas Democratic gubernatorial candidate Beto O'Rourke's town hall in August 2022 to confront the candidate about abortion, FBI Direc-tor Christopher Wray told the Senate that his bureau had opened "a number" of investigations into abortion-related violent crime incidents from "both" abortion opponents and abortion rights supporters, which he claimed had surged since the overturning of *Roe*; the Department of Homeland Security had issued a similar warning months earlier. Back in 2019 Jezebel reported on a briefing the FBI sent to law enforcement agen-cies that warned them about the threat of "pro-abortion extremists."[38] Again, per NAF's research, between that year and 2020, reported physical violence targeting abortion providers surged by 125 percent. False narra-tives perpetuated by state institutions aren't just obscuring the violence abortion providers face, all while they and their patients—rather than increasingly violent anti-abortion activists—face the ongoing threat of criminalization. Abortion providers and their supporters are also being misrepresented as the perpetrators of violence.

The FBI's position is not surprising or out of character. Police and law enforcement agencies are, as their name suggests, the enforcers of abortion bans, a role they've enthusiastically stepped into. In February 2022 the city of Louisville, Kentucky, paid a police officer $75,000 in settlement fees almost a year after the officer was suspended—with pay—for protesting outside a local abortion clinic while armed and in uniform. Abortion clinic volunteers have often raised that police officers either ignore their calls about violent anti-abortion protesters or, in some cases, blame the clinics. Lauren Rankin, a clinic volunteer and author of *Bodies on the Line*, a 2022 book about the work of clinic volunteers, told me for an article in Jezebel that she's heard from other volunteers, "They're told [by police], 'this is what you signed up for,' as a provider or volunteer." For some escorts and clinic staff, she added, calling the police isn't even an option, as police presence is inherently "unsafe for a lot of people of color, particularly undocumented immigrants," and "can place Black people's lives at risk."

But no matter what anti-abortion activists do—assassinate abortion providers, create online registries doxing clinic staff and volunteers, conspire to kidnap abortion providers' children, and, as for those in government, violently compel unwanted pregnancy and birth—abortion advocates and patients will always be the ones on law enforcement's radar.

NO SAVIORS IN THIS FIGHT

Four years after the election of President Trump, in the fall of 2020 the worst fears of reproductive rights advocates were seemingly realized with the confirmation of Amy Coney Barrett to the Supreme Court, cementing a 6–3 anti-abortion majority to gut access to reproductive care and criminalize abortion. Barrett's vote was pivotal to the overturning of *Roe*, and "pro-life feminists" made her the face of their movement. She was perfect for the role: the final "girlboss" to put the nail in the coffin of *Roe*.

Much of Barrett's Senate confirmation hearings in 2020 revolved around her identity as a mother of seven children who managed to excel in her professional career anyway. The implicit message of this not-so-humble brag was that if she could do it, then all the selfish people who have had abortions because of their careers or economic circumstances could have done it, too. Barrett's supporters even weaponize her children (she has two Black children and one child with a disability) to deny accusations of racist politics, or possibly justify support for so-called race-, sex-, and disability-selective abortion bans should they reach the Supreme Court, and deny pregnant people autonomy rather than help born, living disabled people. Barrett was added to the Supreme Court with the explicit purpose of hurling women, pregnant people, and all marginalized people backward, while wielding her gender and motherhood as a cudgel to deflect against accusations of sexism.

Barrett immediately raised eyebrows with her questions and commentary during oral arguments for *Dobbs v. Jackson Women's Health* (the case that resulted in the fall of *Roe*) in 2021, as she told reproductive rights lawyers for Jackson Women's Health that "safe haven" laws allow for people to give up newborn babies within forty-eight hours of giving birth. Following Barrett's logic, this disproved advocates' arguments that Mississippi's ban would lead to, in her words, "forced parenting and forced motherhood" and "hinder women's access to the workplace and to equal opportunities." Because apparently it needs to be said, maybe adoption can be an alternative for forced parenting—but not forced pregnancy and birth, which are dangerous, costly, and physically and mentally brutal. Callous invocations of adoption gloss over the staggering physical and emotional toll of forced pregnancy and birth, which inevitably contribute to more death via higher maternal mortality rates. They also ignore the racist, imperialist foundations of our current adoption system. As Melissa Guida-Richards, author of the 2021 book *What White Parents Should Know about Transracial Adoption: An Adoptee's Perspective on Its History, Nuances, and Practices,* has written:

> *While many think of adoption as a beautiful sacrifice with a happy ending for everyone involved, the truth is much more complicated. And while adoption is often used as the solution in pro-life arguments, it's important to listen to the voices of those who have actually been affected by it. Adoption, particularly international adoption, is a very lucrative business where it's not unusual for adoptive parents to pay between $20,000 and*

$50,000 per child. And while adoption agencies preach of saving children in need, they often make millions of dollars while birth mothers like mine are dumped like recycled bottles, unwanted until they can be used again.[39]

Anti-abortion lawmakers have no real interest in addressing the problems they know they're creating, no matter how often they trot out adoption as a cure-all solution—they aren't going to overhaul the harmful adoption system or enact universal child care. Their movement is rooted in white supremacy and classism; their bans purposefully target poor people and keep them poor.

Nonetheless, despite Barrett's condescending line of questioning on adoption, right-wing narratives have enshrined her as a symbol of women's empowerment. She is perhaps empowering in the same way white mothers who leveraged their whiteness, femininity, and motherhood to advocate for school segregation and "protect" their children throughout the 1960s were empowering. Like her predecessors, Barrett has weaponized her identity, and even her children, to consolidate power and advance an inherently white-supremacist outcome of policing and coercing the reproduction of disproportionately pregnant people of color. It can't be ignored that as a white mother of seven, Barrett is celebrated by the same people who shame and police mothers of color for the families they build.

Naturally, Barrett's appointment to the Supreme Court in 2020 and the overturning of *Roe* two years later were both followed by reinvigorated calls for voting as the sole solution to the crisis we now face. Voting can serve as critical damage control and harm reduction. Yet there has been little recognition that normalized state reproductive oppression is a byproduct of a capitalist, patriarchal nation and the limitations and failures of electoral solutions under these circumstances. Capitalism urgently necessitates reproduction of the most marginalized sectors of the workforce to continue to extract wealth through generational labor exploitation and controlling the means of reproduction by limiting reproductive freedom.

Just as state reproductive oppression has always existed, solutions beyond the ballot box have, too—from abortion funds to legal defense funds for criminalized pregnant people, to broader mutual aid networks-for abuse victims seeking health care and safety—due to the work of people who have long felt their communities are left behind by elected officials. Across the country, mutual aid networks called abortion funds move money, bridge gaps in access, and fund logistical arrangements for people to afford abortion care and contraception, as well as transportation, lodging, and child care to travel across state lines and reach these resources. In a country where abortion is widely banned and there are no clinics in most counties, even in states where it remains legal, abortion funds have created vital infrastructure for low-income people across the country to get care. Some funds, like Kentucky Health Justice Network, have created special resources for trans people who face added barriers to reach abortion and other sexual and reproductive health care; Texas's Jane's Due Process offers legal support and other resources for minors and young people in the state who face added restrictions to get care. The Mariposa Fund specializes in helping undocumented people, who face even greater risks in crossing state lines to get abortion care due to checkpoints scattered across certain states like Texas. Indigenous Women Rising funds abortion and reproductive care for Indigenous people.

Abortion funds across the country supported 56,155 people seeking care from 2019 to 2020,[40] all amid a backdrop of then-unprecedented state-level abortion bans and restrictions being passed. Several funds in different states reported collaborating with each other to help people travel across state lines to get care. Some funds reported that the majority of the clients they served were people of color. Yet companies like Meta, Disney, Amazon, Lyft, Yelp, Citibank, Tesla, and others took it upon themselves to announce insurance plans covering the costs of abortion and abortion-related travel for certain employees—notably, in most cases, those who were high-paid, worked full-time, and covered by company insurance, rather than low-wage, part-time, or uninsured employees who were more likely to struggle to afford abortion-related costs. There were no details about how the companies would protect the privacy of employees who needed to travel for abortion, nor any acknowledgment of how the companies' years of substantial political donations to anti-abortion

Republicans had brought about the very problem they were taking credit for ostensibly solving. In reality, they could have just donated to abortion funds. The hollow gesture from these companies was a reminder that privatized "solutions" are never really solutions, and often exclusionary by nature.

Also following the fall of *Roe,* many social media users shared plans to hoard emergency contraception and birth control pills or start crowdfunding for others' abortions and travel across state lines, as well as legal fees if needed. But rather than personally try to reinvent the wheel and divert attention and resources from people who have long been collectively organizing to do this work, we should instead listen to the expertise of abortion funds and community advocates—who will probably tell you not to hoard basic resources like Plan B, which can already be costly and inaccessible and become even more so in scarcity.

Participating in elections, particularly at the state and local levels, will always be critical to the fate of democracy and the human rights of the most marginalized members of society—after all, elections and voter suppression are what brought us to this point of reckoning in the first place. With the Supreme Court poised to significantly worsen American life seemingly every other day, voting by itself might fix some things—but it just can't fix everything. Investing our money and effort into community care can go further than merely relying on elections and institutions that have always upheld a status quo of capitalist, white-supremacist, and patriarchal oppression. None of us can do everything, or singlehandedly ensure everyone gets the care they need—but we can all find and contact our local abortion funds, learn about ways to volunteer at abortion clinics, pool our resources to support our communities, and bridge the ever-widening gaps in care created by the state.

We have to do more than place all our faith in a capitalist system that's working as it was designed to marginalize women, people of color, and queer and trans people. Reproductive justice demands that we recognize the transformative power and potential of mutual aid and direct action starting in our own communities. And reproductive justice, which asserts that each of us should have the resources and supports we need to parent or not parent in safe and healthy communities, also asserts that all of us—yes, including deeply confused teenagers being deprived of accurate and inclusive sex ed in their public schools like yours truly, once upon a time—have the fundamental rights to experience sexual pleasure, to use substances while pregnant without criminalization, to know that we are fully human and more than just our wombs.

7

AGAINST SAVIORS

In the summer of 2021, I was disappointed but not especially shocked that Rep. Alexandria Ocasio-Cortez had voted "present" instead of "nay" on a bill to give funding to Israel, a colonizing force that has displaced and oppressed Palestinian people for decades. Chronically online leftists, on the other hand, seemed shell-shocked by the news. I don't have any interest in defending Ocasio-Cortez or other politicians, whose literal job is to be challenged and confronted by voters and constituents at all times. But I do question why anyone had a strong reaction to her vote among other disappointing actions from progressive-leaning politicians. What has convinced so many people that individual politicians are our saviors? At best, politicians are semi-decent collaborators in movement work; at worst, they're fixated solely on reelection, vanity projects, and going viral on social media while the world burns and the maternal mortality rate soars. They should be challenged at every turn, and we should also temper our expectations of them as saintly figures, as superheroes who are going to save us. Sometimes it seems like superhero movies—which I greatly enjoy as the wholly fictional spectacle they are—have implicitly encouraged us to buy into comforting, feel-good, neoliberal mythology and propaganda that encourages us to sit back, do nothing, and believe in exceptional, individual heroes who will do the work and save us.

These heroes don't exist.

The perception of individual saviors as the solutions to systemic crises isn't just misguided—it's actively harmful. So is the perception of systemic crises as merely the workings of evil individuals. Growing up as a young person in the Obama era, I perceived our charming and charismatic Democratic president as the lone savior of our country's massive economic crisis and involvement in endless, colonialist wars. It took adulthood and years of listening, learning, and unlearning to recognize that the former president I had been raised to see as a superhero-like figure had fallen vastly short in devastating ways. Life in the Trump era in many uncomfortable ways mirrored life during the Obama era: President Trump was understood as the sole arbiter of racism, misogyny, and all oppression in our country—rather than a symptom, a symbol of generations of violence and hatred that long pre-dated him, and would long outlast him. Even throughout the Biden administration, liberal activists have remained fixated on blaming everything they can on the former president, instead of interrogating the origins of and systems of power that belie these problems. Whether we're discussing Obama or Trump, or Ocasio-Cortez and US-Israel relations, we have to recognize that the crises we face transcend any individual.

The varying writings and speeches of Angela Davis through the years are perennially timely. Her work has been especially indispensable to contextualizing state violence, resistance, and the importance of demanding more of our government no matter who's in power. In one of many emails and correspondence published in Davis's 2016 book *Freedom Is a Constant Struggle*, Davis recalls a reporter asking her if she "approved of violence" at anti-racist and anti-imperialist protests, to which Davis responded, "Ask *me*? If I approve of violence!? This does not make any sense." She continued: "I was attempting to point out that questions about the validity of violence should have been directed to the institutions that held and continue to hold a monopoly on violence: the police, the prisons, the military . . . At the time, I was in jail, having been falsely charged with murder, kidnapping and conspiracy, and turned into a target of institutional violence, and I was the one being asked whether I agreed with violence."[1]

All too often, people in power and uncritical media will question or fault those with the least power—Davis, I cannot emphasize this enough, *served time in jail* for her activism—with societal problems or perceived violence. In the aftermath of the fall of *Roe*, top Democrats chided terrified pregnant people and abortion rights supporters for not voting and asked us what our plans to vote in the next election were. This isn't the 1960s—"ask not what your country can do for you, ask what you can do for your country" no longer holds any relevance. It's time to question, challenge, and hold powerful politicians accountable; it's time to ask them what *their* plan is to serve *us*.

Amid the anti-racist, pro-abolition uprising of the summer of 2020, Davis's teachings became especially relevant as many liberals and people with privilege sought easy solutions to endemic white supremacy and state violence in the US. Some prescribed that we all just "vote." Conveniently enough, they ignored that one out of thirteen Black Americans is unable to vote due to the same racist criminal legal system that many people were protesting in the first place. Domestic violence survivors are often unable to independently vote, too. A colonialist and patriarchal state is built to reproduce itself.

But the main problem with casual invocation of voting in any election as a cure-all is the suggestion that one individual—and specific to 2020, Joe Biden, author of the 1994 crime bill—can sweepingly save us from generations of homegrown all-American racism. The myth of the individual savior is propaganda meant to fuel complacency. It is meant to convince us that because someone is coming to save us, it's unnecessary to organize and mobilize and engage in collective action. In reality, of course, collective action, not individual charismatic leaders, is the only way to bring meaningful, lasting change at all.

In reference to the story of civil rights icon Martin Luther King Jr. and the erasure of Black women who first organized boycotts and protests of segregation before King's involvement, Davis said in a 2013 speech at Birkbeck University: "How can we counteract the representation of historical agents as powerful individuals, powerful *male* individuals, in order to reveal the part played by, for example, Black women domestic workers in the Black freedom movement?" In a speech at Davidson College that same year, Davis elaborated further: "We think individualistically, and we assume that only heroic individuals can make history. That is why we like to think of Dr. Martin Luther King, who was a great man, but in my opinion his greatness resided precisely in the fact that he learned from a collective movement. He transformed in his relationship with that movement. He did not see himself as an individual who was going to bring freedom to the oppressed masses."[2]

Our persistent failure to recognize that "heroic individuals" are not the sole agents of change has been especially problematic in electoral politics—and in particular, presidential electoral politics. When it comes to advocating survivor justice, presidential electoral politics has proven time and again to be an unreliable and even dangerous place to invest our hopes and efforts. We can't build movements around individuals alone, especially not when the patriarchal nature of electoral politics means too many charismatic leaders are either abusers themselves or complicit in covering up and enabling abuse.

Several presidents and presidential candidates in recent memory have been accused of a range of sexual misconduct, from rape, in the cases of Donald Trump, Bill Clinton, and Democratic presidential nominee Joe Biden, to groping multiple women, in the cases of George H. W. Bush and former Democratic presidential nominee Al Gore, to general creepiness and predation from Lyndon B. Johnson. Sexual harassment complaints at the State Department doubled under the Obama administration, during Hillary Clinton and John Kerry's tenures as secretary of state, per a 2015 report from the conservative *Washington Times*.[3] And this is all, of course, just what we know of. It wasn't until the 1990s, amid the fallout of the testimony of Anita Hill regarding her experience being harassed by Supreme Court Justice Clarence Thomas, that "sexual harassment" even became a publicly known term.

All too often, when candidates are alleged sexual abusers, they rely on tired rape culture tropes and rape apologism that harm and demonize women and survivors broadly. Elections that involve candidates who are publicly accused of abuse are a primer in why women don't report their experiences, and subsequently find themselves accused of having a political agenda or seeking fame and wealth.

Following several allegations of sexual harassment and misconduct against New York Gov. Andrew Cuomo in 2021, Cuomo "apologized" if his words and actions had "been misinterpreted as an unwanted flirtation." To be precise, he said, "To the extent anyone felt that way, I am truly sorry about that." His phrasing embodied the same, exhausting gaslighting we've seen from nearly every powerful man accused of harassing and harming women in recent years. Over and over, men like Cuomo have "apologized" if a woman they allegedly harassed or harmed "felt" or "interpreted" their words and actions in a certain way. Put less delicately, the abuse was all in the woman's head, and the powerful male figure who stands accused doesn't bear responsibility for the power dynamics that implicitly drive their every interaction with female subordinates.

Any statement that "apologizes" but claims a woman misinterpreted the exchange is simply blaming, even mocking, the victim for *choosing* to be offended or upset. This defense against allegations of sexist misconduct is fundamentally infantilizing, treating adult women as if they lack the maturity, experience, or worldliness to know how to properly read a situation, and denying them credibility when it comes to their own lived experience.

The allegations against Cuomo primarily came from women who worked for him. A former top Cuomo aide, Lindsey Boylan, was the first woman to offer a detailed allegation against him in the spring of 2021, recounting that in 2016 her boss told her Cuomo had a "crush" on her. Boylan said that in 2017 the governor suggested they play strip poker, and in 2018 he gave her an unwanted kiss on the lips. Another former aide, Charlotte Bennett, said that when she was twenty-five, the governor asked her several invasive questions about her personal life, including whether she had been with older men, and told her he was open to a relationship with a woman in her twenties. By the summer of 2021, as more women came forward, Cuomo was ousted from office—but not before releasing a victim-blaming internal report smearing the women who said he harmed them.

Years before the Cuomo scandal, in the weeks leading up to the 2016 presidential election, in the notorious hot-mic tape from 2004, you can hear Donald Trump brag about how he can "grab 'em by the pussy," referring to women, of course, because "when you're a star, they let you do it." Since the release of the video, more than twenty-five women have credibly accused the president of sexual misconduct ranging from harassment and predation to rape, dating back decades. In the immediate aftermath of the tape and several women coming forward, Trump offered a tepid, politicized apology, in which he focused almost entirely on emphasizing how much better his administration would be for American (read: wealthy, white) women than his opponent Hillary Clinton's. In the coming days, he doubled down, insisting that he didn't even know many of these women, and calling on his supporters to "look at [her]," suggesting some of the women who had accused him weren't even attractive enough for him to want to assault and harass them, as if sexual violence is about attraction and sex rather than power and abuse. When, in 2019, writer E. Jean Carroll said Trump had raped her in a changing room in 1995, the allegation was hardly even a blip in a chaotic news cycle, as then-President Trump broke one law after another with impunity on a daily basis. The former president nonetheless responded to this allegation with the same rebuttal he had for many of the others, insisting Carroll wasn't even attractive enough to be rapeable.

In 2017 when reporters asked press secretary Sarah Huckabee Sanders why Americans should believe allegations of sexual misconduct against Democratic senator and vocal Trump critic Al Franken but not allegations against Trump, Huckabee's answer was simple: because Franken had confessed to allegations against him—Trump had not. The resounding message here is that victims are only to be believed if their abuser confesses, which doesn't often happen; perpetrators of violence are even less likely to own up to their behavior, and try to correct it in any way, if they know they can go to prison for doing so—another consequence of carceral policymaking. Nonetheless, the Trump administration had weaponized the office of the presidency itself to assert that victims were only to be believed if their abuser confessed; otherwise, when it's their voice versus their assailant's, they simply won't be heard. Huckabee Sanders's comments weren't an outlier within the Trump administration; the former president had stacked his administration with known alleged abusers, ranging from his campaign manager Corey Lewandowski to speechwriter David Sorensen and, in the judiciary, Supreme Court Justice Brett Kavanaugh.

During Kavanaugh's confirmation process in the fall of 2018, Trump memorably claimed it was a "scary time for young men," about a year into MeToo's entrance into the mainstream. The violent, reactionary backlash that Trump proudly fed has had consequences that long survived his presidency, lionizing "canceled" male abusers as the real victims. At the height of the Kavanaugh circus, as Trump and other top Republicans dedicated their national platforms to calling Dr. Christine Blasey Ford—the woman who said Kavanaugh had assaulted her—a liar, the *New York Times* reported that Dr. Ford was subjected to numerous terrifying, credible death threats, and had to evacuate her home and request security for herself and her family. Yet in contrast with Kavanaugh's jarring displays and outbursts of rage while testifying in his own defense before the Senate, Dr. Ford simply didn't have the option to express emotion during her testimony. Women are taught early on the consequences of expressions of anger—we're called too "emotional" to be trusted; we're denied credibility to speak on our own lived experiences. When women's words come from a place of emotion, we're immediately dismissed for being too hysterical to be objective. In contrast, when men speak from a place of emotion, they're often lauded as real, authentic, perhaps even more believable.

Kavanaugh's anger and profound sense of loss and injustice highlighted the abject rarity of women's voices being heard in any capacity. That Dr. Ford had even been allowed to testify, to speak up for herself and survivors and challenge the inevitability of a powerful white man, was perceived as a shocking threat to male power and hegemony by Kavanaugh and his supporters. Part of this anger certainly stemmed from their awareness that the ground is shifting underneath them, and that women and our refusal to be mistreated will increasingly stand in the way of abusive men getting what they want. Dr. Ford's testimony was about infinitely more than herself and Kavanaugh as individuals—it held up a mirror to patriarchal authority and mounting resistance.

Within two years of Kavanaugh's confirmation to the Supreme Court, in March 2020, Tara Reade alleged Biden had raped her in 1993. After attempting to ignore the allegation for weeks, the Biden campaign eventually vehemently denied it the following month. Biden initially responded by sharing the following "talking points" with campaign surrogates to disseminate, Buzzfeed News reported at the time:

> *"Biden believes that all women have the right to be heard and to have their claims thoroughly reviewed," the talking points read, according to a copy sent to two Democratic operatives. "In this case, a thorough review by the New York Times has led to the truth: this incident did not happen."*
>
> *"Here's the bottom line," they read. "Vice President Joe Biden has spent over 40 years in public life: 36 years in the Senate; 7 Senate campaigns, 2 previous presidential runs, two vice presidential campaigns, and 8 years in the White House. There has never been a complaint, allegation, hint or rumor of any impropriety or inappropriate conduct like this regarding him—ever."*[4]

There is . . . a lot to unpack here.

The *New York Times* article in question was criticized at the time by some journalists and feminist media, who called it a problematic work of journalism that dismissed the allegation despite including testimony from Reade and Biden's former Senate staff who corroborated her claims. Nonetheless, despite Reade being one of several women who have accused Biden of sexual misconduct in some capacity, the *Times* said point-blank that Biden had not demonstrated a "pattern of sexual misconduct." Such a claim was illogical at best, pure gaslighting at worst. The talking points pushed out by Biden's campaign took full advantage of this dubious and misogynist conclusion from the *Times*, shrugging off Reade and all the other women as liars.

It's also notable that the talking points directed surrogates to pivot to Biden's policy record, which includes introducing the Violence Against Women Act—a piece of legislation that notably, counterproductively invests heavily in policing—as if someone's public policies render it impossible that they could be privately abusive.

Trump, Kavanaugh, and Biden's paths to power all involved steamrolling and discrediting women who said these men had harmed them. There are certainly vital differences between mainstream Democrats and Republicans, but sexual violence and the repression of survivors happen across the political spectrum, and survivors deserve better than what electoral politics and its deifying of individual politicians have to offer.

And of course, it's not just male political leaders who hold up rape culture and prop up systems of patriarchal violence—Hillary Clinton played an active role in discrediting some of the women who alleged Bill Clinton harmed them. It's naturally frustrating that women but not men are expected to be the only ones who know and care about rape culture, and the only ones expected to truly answer for it. In the summer of 2018, during a promotional stop for his new book, Bill was asked whether he would extend an apology to Monica Lewinsky. His answer was simple: no. But what made the moment so memorable was his visible shock— like most men in politics, he was likely accustomed to sexual abuse being regarded solely as a women's issue, a question reserved for women, a question beneath his dignity as a man. While Hillary had been fielding questions about Bill's behavior for years, he'd mostly been left unscathed.

This gendered expectation in who is tasked with answering for or speaking about gender-based violence is fundamentally sexist; so, too, is media coverage that fixates solely on the perspectives of women who are protective of male loved ones accused of abuse, prioritizing their voices over the voices of the women who say they were harmed. A man, after all, does not need to have harmed every woman in his life to be an abuser, and women who come to alleged abusers' defense can't possibly know who they are at all times. Yet contrary to some women's claims that Hillary shouldn't have been asked about her husband's behavior on the campaign trail, this line of questioning is perfectly fair game for anyone who maintains ties to alleged abusers, especially if they're vying for the highest office in the country. Regardless of gender, political party, or any other facet of an individual's identity, we can't rely on any single politician to be survivors' savior—nor should we ever absolve them of responsibility to do better.

HISTORICAL RESISTANCE THROUGH THE LENS OF RESPECTABILITY POLITICS

That political candidates are often hiding or denying heinous records of abuse is just part of why elections—particularly federal elections—can't bring the revolutionary change we need. Candidates are required to filter themselves through a lens of respectability politics to have broad appeal in a fundamentally racist, colonialist state founded upon patriarchal oppression. Historically, the figures we choose to celebrate and lionize are oft misrepresented in the popular imagination, bound to white-washed, diluted versions of their legacies that can be neatly reconfigured to allow privileged white people to feel comfortable. (For what it's worth, respectability politics has also always played a pivotal role in which victims are deemed credible and worthy of compassion, and which victims—often "imperfect" victims who fought back, who are sex workers, struggle with mental illness, or are otherwise marginalized—aren't.)

Rosa Parks, the civil rights icon most famous for refusing to give up her seat at the front of a bus as a Black woman, is a prime example of the white-washing of activists' legacies. Parks's story is often told without the context of her extensive prior background as an activist and organizer for racial and economic justice. Her bus protest had been extensively preplanned and supported by other Black women activists, nearly all of whom have been erased from history books. Most notably, Parks's devotion to civil rights and racial justice can be traced to her organizing in support of Recy Taylor, a Black sharecropper and mother of four from Alabama who was attacked and raped by six white men in 1944. Despite the white, male perpetrators' own confessions, two grand juries declined to indict them, deeming Taylor, as a Black woman, unrapeable. The erasure of Parks's anti-rape organizing and support for Taylor from mainstream political consciousness not only serves to individualize, isolate, and exceptionalize her famous bus protest in 1955, but it also obscures the historic leadership of Black women in feminist and survivor justice movements. Parks's now famous refusal on the bus is portrayed as a solo act, as this innately diminishes the role of organizing and solidarity in fighting for social change—and, certainly, makes Parks come off as less calculating and strategic, and therefore more traditionally feminine, sympathetic, and worthy of martyrdom.

Mainstream depictions of Parks portray her as quiet, tame, and polite. These representations of Parks are deliberate, as they allow her character to neatly bypass persistent, racist tropes of the "angry Black woman" and come off as likable and nonthreatening in mainstream, white American consciousness. Many stories of women like Parks similarly exclude key details about their lives and work that aren't as digestible for general audiences that are presumed to be white by default. The realities of tone-policing and selective memory are hardly unique to Parks's story. Plenty of critically important female historical figures in American and global history are often nearly erased from the record altogether, based on race, sexual orientation, and any other facet of their identity, or their approach to activism and radical criticisms of dominant power structures. Petra Herrera, a cross-dressing Mexican Revolution freedom fighter, led her own all-women, nearly 1,000-strong brigade against the dictator Porfirio Díaz's armies in 1910—a violent struggle that would culminate in the fall of a thirty-year dictatorship and installation of a republic. Herrera was eventually awarded the rank of captain in the rebel army, and even given a brigade of 200 men to command. She's remembered as a vicious fighter, and her story lacked a classically tidy, happy Hollywood ending: Herrera was murdered in a bar in 1917.

Kathleen Cleaver, the first woman to join the Black Panther Party's decision-making cabinet, survived several attacks from law enforcement, including injuries from being shot. During her time as the Black Panther

Party's press secretary, she led initiatives to feed community members, provided medical care to poor families, took families to see loved ones in prison, and worked to free incarcerated Black Panthers, all while focusing on uplifting Black women who had survived violence. Lyda Conley was the first Native American attorney to launch a legal challenge to the US federal government to protect sacred Indigenous land, as well as the first woman admitted to the Kansas Bar Association. In 1906 Conley filed a permanent injunction against the US Secretary of the Interior and Indian Commissioners in US District Court to prevent the sale of the Huron Indian Cemetery, even building a physical fort to block trespassers from the cemetery. Her lawsuit was eventually defeated, and Conley was arrested multiple times for her activism; she would eventually be murdered in 1946 and is buried in the Huron Indian Cemetery today.

Despite these women's accomplishments, groundbreaking social justice advocacy, and revolutionary activism, they're just a few examples of less-than-palatable women who are today relegated to the margins of history. Their legacies are either upsetting or simply unrelatable to white liberal audiences seeking feel-good stories about docile, peaceful advocates of color, who never returned state violence with violence of their own and complacently settled into their victimhood.

Respectability politics still, obviously, shapes the women leaders and icons we choose to recognize. However much the late Supreme Court Justice Ruth Bader Ginsburg's record as an attorney and judge has positively altered the course of history for many women and marginalized people in this country, there are fair criticisms of the unchecked lionization of her legacy. In particular, Ginsburg's advocacy for ladylike, "decent" behavior; her since-redacted criticisms of Colin Kaepernick's protests of police brutality; harmful rulings on Indigenous people's rights and sovereignty; and her repeated praises and defenses of extremists like Justices Brett Kavanaugh and Neil Gorsuch are just a few examples of her shortcomings that deserve consideration from her passionate, feminist fan base.

For all the discrimination and oppressions Ginsburg overcame as a woman who rose to power in an unrepentantly sexist time, she simultaneously enjoyed the privileges that are accorded along lines of both whiteness and class. Ginsburg is as good a reminder as any that we all experience privileges and oppressions simultaneously, that all women and people in power should be challenged and held accountable rather than idolized and iconized.

Today, in a post-*Roe* America, Ginsburg's proscriptions for ladylike behavior and peaceful, respectful protest against a fundamentally very-not-peaceful, violent state have aged frustratingly poorly. Protest of oppression of any kind is policed by conservatives and liberals alike, as they selectively oppose violence and incivility when perpetrated by those who hold no state power, but not by state systems that are killing marginalized people. And when it comes to protests of gender-based violence and reproductive oppression, women, femmes, and allies who are on the frontlines of these struggles are disproportionately policed for ostensibly overreacting or being overly emotional; naturally they're perceived as especially threatening if they're Black women and women of color. In May 2022, shortly after news leaked that the Supreme Court planned to overturn *Roe* that summer, the Biden administration joined Republicans in denouncing mostly women protesters who gathered outside anti-abortion Supreme Court justices' houses. Congress expeditiously passed legislation—signed by Biden—to fund additional security measures for the justices, all while reproductive rights legislation and other policies to address gender-based violence stalled, as they often do. The civility police argued that no matter how many people the justices sentenced to death with their decision-making, they deserved privacy, civility, and respect from those of us who quite literally live at their mercy.

The argument that anti-abortion justices deserved the very protections from protesters that they had denied to abortion providers and patients (who are actually endangered, harassed, and physically harmed by protesters on a daily basis) in the 2014 decision *McCullen v. Coakley* was nothing if not ironic. In *McCullen* the court struck down clinics' right to maintain buffer zones to protect from anti-abortion protesters; since 1977, there have been at least eleven murders and twenty-six attempted murders of abortion providers, and hundreds of incidents of bombings targeting clinics and homes, arson, assaults, stalking, doxing, and other threats to providers. But the real problem, Congress concluded, was a handful of noisy women waving signs on Kavanaugh's lawn.

The bipartisan chiding of protesters by those in power, mere weeks before the fall of *Roe* would serve as a death sentence for many pregnant people's rights and safety, is emblematic of double standards in what is and isn't seen as violent, and who is and isn't held accountable. While liberals and conservatives in power demand privacy for millionaire Supreme Court justices, the Republicans with whom these justices collude are taking all possible steps to reduce pregnant people to state-controlled incubators. The end of *Roe* means the door is fully open for the end of same-sex marriage, even the literal policing of sex positions, a measure that some Texas officials have supported.[5] Dated sections of Michigan's constitution continue to felonize same-sex relationships and sex positions.

The Supreme Court is literally inside our bedrooms and uteruses; yet we're told the real problem is that people have made Kavanaugh, accused of sexual assault by several women, uncomfortable by protesting *outside* his house. The real problem, we were told in May 2022, is that someone violated the Supreme Court's privacy in leaking a draft opinion of the overturning of *Roe*. *That* is the crime the FBI was directed to investigate, not the violent relegation of women and pregnant-capable people to second-class citizens. The real safety concern, they said, was that security had to build barricades around the Supreme Court because anti-abortion justices who regard women and pregnant people as less deserving of rights than our fetuses were afraid to be confronted about this.

All these reactions, from people in power and the ordinary citizens who shill for them, fundamentally misunderstand violence and power. Violence is children going to bed hungry in a country that refuses to tax billionaires. Violence is a higher education system so wildly unaffordable that disproportionately poor people of color have no other options but to enlist in the US military, an institution the US pours trillions into while poor and uninsured people die because they can't afford to call an ambulance. And violence is certainly holding the highest maternal mortality rate among wealthy nations—with higher maternal mortality rates in states with more abortion restrictions, owing to an utterly stymied, depleted, and over-policed reproductive health system.

Today the work and voices of women who resist this oppression by unladylike means, who come off as angry, calculating, ambitious, self-assured, and passionate—or "too emotional"—are written off; we're told to calm down and be civil while men and wealthy elites in our government refuse us abortion care even when our lives depend on it. This has always been the struggle of women whose activism makes powerful people uncomfortable, who are consequently erased from white-washed, deradicalized historical accounts.

Simultaneously, gender and marginalization shouldn't be co-opted or weaponized by capitalists to ennoble diverse oppressors or align them with progressive movements. The term "girlboss" was first popularized by Sophia Amoruso, founder and "she-EO" of the clothing brand Nasty Gal, in the early 2010s. Amoruso, who sold the world on a narrative of herself as a plucky feminist heroine, was later called out by numerous employees who accused her and the brand of fostering a toxic work environment. In recent years the girlboss has become synonymous with someone who weaponizes their gender to excuse or even righteously justify harming others— particularly women and marginalized employees with less power.

In 2022 Kim Kardashian tried to shut down undeniably sexist narratives that she owes her business success exclusively to her 2000s sex tape, by advising less privileged women in business to "get your ass up and work." She inexplicably further claimed "no one wants to work these days." The sentiment embodied just how misaligned feminist empowerment is with capitalist values: Ironically enough, at the time, Kardashian was being sued by seven people for withholding pay and denying them overtime and legally required breaks when they worked for her.

Scholar-activists Cinzia Arruzza, Tithi Bhattacharya, and Nancy Fraser wrote in their 2019 manifesto, *Feminism for the 99%,* about the destructiveness of the corporate, "lean-in" feminism espoused by women like former Meta executive Sheryl Sandberg, author of the corporate "feminist" manifesto *Lean In*:

*On the one hand, Sandberg and her ilk see feminism as a handmaiden of
capitalism. They want a world where the task of managing exploitation in
the workplace and oppression in the social whole is shared equally by rul-
ing-class men and women. This is a remarkable vision of equal opportunity domination: one that asks ordinary people, in the name of feminism,
to be grateful that it is a woman, not a man, who busts their union, orders
a drone to kill their parent, or locks their child in a cage at the border.[6]*

Elevating individual women to prominent positions of power won't effectively tear down patriarchal oppressions, as women can and often do
reproduce the violent structures that target and harm women with less
privilege.

Within the same economic system that's enabled she-EOs and mul-
timillionaire girlbosses, non-white working-class women remain wildly
exploited and still face rampant sexual harassment and violence on
the job. For years, human rights groups have specifically shined light
on the astronomically high rates of sexual abuse that migrant women,
who are predominantly domestic and farm workers, face in the workplace. According to a 2012 Human Rights Watch report, most interviewed
women farmworkers said they had experienced sexual harassment and
violence on the job, but "they had not reported these or other workplace
abuses, fearing reprisals." Anecdotes in the report include a woman in
California whose supervisor at a lettuce company raped her and later
told her she "should remember it's because of him that [she has] this job."
Another farmworker in New York told Human Rights Watch her supervisor repeatedly groped her and other women, and if they resisted, he
threatened to call Immigration or fire them. What does the existence of a
female CEO, a female billionaire, a female president or vice president of
an irrevocably imperialist nation-state, do to materially improve the lives
of these women?

As Angela Davis writes in *Freedom Is a Constant Struggle*, oppression
"does not necessarily depend on the individual actors, but rather is deeply
embedded in the apparatus." Women lawmakers have historically, help-
fully placed greater focus on legislating around reproductive health care,
gender-based violence, and other often overlooked, innately gendered

issues. But in plenty of cases, women politicians, too, are key architects in enforcing reproductive oppression, empowering the carceral capitalist police state, and dismantling the welfare state, to the detriment of the women with the least resources and victims of gender-based violence. Davis concludes, "It doesn't matter that a Black woman heads the police. The technology, the regimes, the targets are still the same."[7]

Women leaders can and often do wield their gender to shill for rape culture and abusers. Hillary Clinton, again, has repeatedly used her power to dismiss the credibility of women who have accused her husband of misconduct and predation. The Trump administration and campaign staff, while overwhelmingly white and male, included just enough women mouthpieces through which Trump could attempt to gaslight American women into buying his administration's condescending narrative of conservative feminism. Feminist women politicians lined up to dismiss women who accused Joe Biden of abuse, and it's these same feminist political leaders who have unquestioningly propped up and voted for the Violence Against Women Act, despite how it bolsters a fundamentally misogynist carceral system.

The disappointingly few women with power in politics are often forced to gain and maintain this power through protecting and enabling men with *more* power. Men who posture as progressive—from Franken to Minnesota Attorney General Keith Ellison to former Michigan Rep. John Conyers—are all too often alleged to be abusers themselves. And it's within this devastating ecosystem that we require victims and survivors of abuse to put everything on the line to come forward, only to later be accused of political agendas. Victims are told that if they don't come forward, it's their fault when abusers face no consequences or further consolidate political power. Yet when victims do come forward, they're left vulnerable, threatened, harmed, or forced to watch as powerful men respond to their claims with gaslighting and character attacks that hurt all victims and survivors. When women and survivors do vote for abusive male candidates who may be the less harmful option among what we're offered in our restrictive, capitalist, misogynist political system, they're accused of enabling abuse. Electoral politics—especially at the federal level—is a thorny, unwinnable, often unfixably degrading labyrinth for survivors. This doesn't mean elections—particularly on the local and state level—can't bring about meaningful change to improve victims' lives. They absolutely can. But as an electorate, we have to collectively recognize that federal and presidential electoral politics are not a cure-all to enacting long-term, transformative change or to meaningfully advance survivor justice. There are no saviors—only movements and solidarity.

8

THE CULTURE WAR

In July 2022 Johnny Depp privately settled with a notably male crew member who alleged the actor had physically assaulted him while they were filming the thriller *City of Lies* in 2017.

Gregg "Rocky" Brooks had first sued Depp in 2018, alleging that Depp became angry while they were filming a scene, punched Brooks twice in the ribs, and screamed, "Who the fuck are you? You have no right to tell me what to do."[1] According to Brooks, Depp then offered him $100,000 to fight back and punch Depp, an offer Brooks declined. Brooks reportedly sought protection from an LAPD officer, and Depp's own bodyguards removed him from the set.

Following the settlement in 2022, curiously enough, Brooks wasn't called a liar for claiming Depp had harmed him. We weren't treated to details about an alleged, salacious extramarital affair between Brooks and James Franco, nor did we hear of any history of mental illness that made him too crazy to be credible. There was no wave of TikTok videos and Twitter threads purporting to debunk his claims about using makeup to cover up the injuries he sustained from Depp's assault, nor any other online harassment campaigns. There were no lengthy social media posts from Depp's A-lister celebrity friends detailing anecdotes of all the times Depp has been wonderful to them or their children, meaning he couldn't possibly be violent with someone else.

If you're curious about the noted lack of smear campaign targeting Brooks for accusing a powerful male celebrity of harming him, it's simple, really: Brooks is a man. He wasn't alleging sexual or domestic violence, so his claims were never going to be held to the same innately sexist scrutiny that's reserved for women who say famous men have harmed them. His lawsuit against Depp isn't seen as an overarching threat to the power and privilege of all men—particularly wealthy, powerful, white men—to do whatever they want to women and still somehow emerge as the victim when women speak out against them.

If you'd like a glimpse of what that might look like, look no further than Depp's victory over ex-wife Amber Heard in his televised, much-publicized defamation lawsuit against her, months before he settled with Brooks. The trial ultimately concerned whether Heard had lied about being abused by Depp, and it was rife with scorched-earth tactics deployed by his legal team, as well as harmful myths about domestic violence that will inevitably help abusers across the country for years to come. Yet early on, even advocates for survivor justice who might otherwise support women and victims in Heard's position seemed uninterested in defending her, allowing Depp's supporters to run away with the public narrative via vicious online harassment campaigns. At least initially, some self-identified feminists wrote off the spectacle as merely "celebrity news"—"Who fucking gives a fuck? Women are losing rights for their bodies, so why are we talking about celebrities' divorce trials? Who gives a shit? Let them figure it out on their own," singer Billie Eilish said of the trial at the time.[2] But this line of thinking ignores the inextricably linked fates of all victims and survivors.

Heard presented more evidence that Depp had physically abused and sexually assaulted her than most victims are able to provide—witness accounts, therapy notes, photos of injuries, text messages, threatening audio—but she was excoriated, called a liar and worse, publicly humiliated, forced to pay a man who she said had nearly killed her north of

$10 million. Victims being ordered to pay their abusers isn't an anomaly. This verdict came roughly one year after former Congress member Katie Hill, who was driven out of Congress after her abusive ex-husband allegedly shared nude photos of Hill with right-wing media outlets that shared these photos with the world, was ordered by a judge to pay more than $200,000 in legal fees to those same right-wing outlets and their lawyers. After Hill sued the publications, a judge ruled that the photos of Hill had been rightfully published because Hill was a public figure, and the photos were a matter of "public interest," and therefore, Hill needed to cover their legal fees.

In the fall of 2022, shortly after the conclusion of Heard and Depp's trial, a similar narrative took hold around the legal conflict between Angelina Jolie and ex-husband Brad Pitt, who Jolie alleges physically assaulted both her and their kids on a private plane in 2016. At the time, I naively hoped that the public reaction would be different given how publicly Jolie and Pitt's shared kids stood by Jolie since the couple separated. Yet if anything, Jolie's strong presence in the kids' lives and Pitt's very obvious absence were weaponized against her.

Just as the public painted Depp as Heard's victim because she fought back or resisted harm he inflicted on her, social media users seemed eager to portray Pitt as yet another male victim—this time, the victim of a spiteful ex who stole his kids by lying and cunningly hiring a top-tier legal team. By popularizing the deceptive term "mutual abuse" that equates victims' resistance with abuse, Depp's lawyers paved a way for subsequent public abuse trials: Powerful men will always be the "victims" when women dare to even try to defend themselves—or in Jolie's case, her children.

If our legal system and general public treat wealthy white women like this, how are victims with significantly less power and fewer resources being treated? And what happens to all victims now that the public has been so sold on victim-blaming myths like "mutual abuse"?

Shortly after the verdict of the Depp-Heard trial, in which a predominantly male jury sided with Depp, online men's rights activists began resurfacing the case of the late Gabby Petito and her abusive boyfriend Brian Laundrie. Laundrie killed Petito in the summer of 2021, shortly after police who confronted the couple days earlier had deemed *Petito* to be *Laundrie's* abuser, because they witnessed her fight back against him; they threatened Petito with arrest and put Laundrie up in a hotel that night. In the subsequent months, he, too, went missing. When his remains were found along with a written confession to killing Petito, his death was ruled a suicide. According to men's rights activists, it was Laundrie who had been treated unfairly. One particular tweet from the summer of 2022, shortly after Depp and Heard's trial concluded, stood out to me: "Gabby Petito did abuse Brian. They likely got in a physical altercation she started and he pushed her back too hard, ultimately killed her. Society condemned him before a trial, so he killed himself because he'd never win that case." When I first read this tweet, as much as I'd wanted to dismiss it as the fringe ravings of one, lone internet lunatic, I knew better: This line of thinking is the natural endgame of the "mutual abuse" lie. There is still lack of broad, cultural understanding about the prevalence of gender-based violence in our patriarchal society that frequently gaslights women and victims into believing they *aren't* victims—nonetheless, whether acknowledged or not, gender-based violence is pervasive, and if every victim who fought back were treated and penalized as the real abuser, the toll of this would be immeasurable.

Simultaneously, many of the men and people who celebrate fathers or brothers or male family members who beat up "their" daughters' or sisters' abusers are the same people who flooded social media platforms calling Amber Heard an abuser for fighting back against Depp. Our perceptions of what is and isn't abuse center around agency: Women and non-cis, straight men are only believable victims if they forfeit theirs. And even then, they're still disbelieved or dismissed, pressed about why they didn't just leave, why they *didn't* fight back—if they stayed in a relationship with their abuser, surely it's because they wanted to? Amid the Depp-Heard trial, the loudest purveyors of the mutual abuse argument chose to ignore altogether that the ability to abuse someone requires holding power over that victim in the first place.

As the rehashing of Petito and Laundrie's story around the same time as Depp and Heard's trial suggests, the trial wasn't just dismissible, irrelevant celebrity gossip; rather, it carried substantial material impact on the safety and lives of women and victims everywhere. Nor was the trial some isolated incident: Courts, police, and the legal system routinely perpetuate mutual abuse myths that ruin victims' lives, either by doing nothing, like the cops who pulled over Petito and Laundrie, and opening the door for their abusers to kill them, or by actively punishing them. I've previously referenced a 2015 study that found 24 percent of surveyed women who called police to report sexual assault and intimate partner violence and seek help were either arrested or threatened with arrest. There is an organization—Survived and Punished—specifically dedicated to advocating for victims of gender-based violence or trafficking who are criminalized and incarcerated for fighting back against abusers. These victims are often women, girls, femmes, trans, and LGBTQ people of color, like Cyntoia Brown, Marissa Alexander, Nan-Hui Jo, and Marcela Rodriguez, to name just a few. In 2012 Marissa Alexander defended herself from her abusive husband by firing a warning shot that caused no physical harm. She was prosecuted and sentenced to a mandatory minimum sentence of twenty years in prison. In 2014 Nan-Hui Jo escaped her abusive, American-citizen partner and took her young child to seek safety. She was consequently arrested for child abduction and portrayed by prosecutors as a manipulative "illegal immigrant" attempting to cheat the US immigration systems, rather than a victim. Also in 2014 Marcela Rodriguez called the police for help during a domestic violence incident. Instead, the police arrested and turned her over to ICE, which then forced her into deportation proceedings. Each of these women of color, Survived and Punished said, was incarcerated for fighting back against abusers who had raped or almost killed them.

To be unequivocally clear, male survivors of domestic and sexual violence exist, and they are all too often dismissed by our patriarchal culture. I can't emphasize this enough: Men are more likely to experience sexual abuse than be falsely accused of it. At the same time, the idea that mutual abuse occurs stems from a dangerously juvenile analysis of power dynamics that frames men's "right" to hit women as the truest form of gender equality. Earlier in this book, I include pieces of my conversations with domestic violence experts Amanda Kippert and Ruth Glenn about abuse. Kippert also told me that while interest in the term "mutual abuse" skyrocketed over the course of the trial, the impulse to find any reason to write off women who say they were harmed, itself, isn't new. Women who don't meet our sexist, racist, classist, ableist, and heteronormative expectations of a "perfect victim" have always been dismissed or attacked. "There's this idea that a victim needs to be this sort of meek, quiet, complacent victim, so when someone fights back, uses a self-defense tactic, or God forbid, has an emotional reaction, we say, 'Well, she can't possibly be telling the truth,'" Kippert said.

Lies about mutual abuse ruin lives and, in Petito's case, can kill. The Depp-Heard trial amplified this lie like never before and set victims' rights and survivor justice movements back generations. It was never merely celebrity gossip, fodder for a slow news day for TMZ—it was the culmination of a years-long political war on victims' rights, a war waged on all fronts: in electoral politics, in dinner-table family arguments about MeToo, and certainly, in the culture we consume.

The backlash that bubbled over and exploded in the Heard-Depp trial had been simmering for years: Roughly one year after reports that self-identified comedian Louis CK had sexually harassed multiple women throughout his career, in the fall of 2018, he resumed performing comedy shows, jokingly complaining about enduring a "hell" year and losing "$35 million in one hour."[3] At the height of his return, he was back to cracking jokes about Asian men ("women with really big clits") and "trans retarded boys" to sold-out crowds; like numerous other famous men accused of egregious, exploitative sexual behaviors, at the drop of a hat he'd switched from vehement apologies to open rebellion against the idea that any acts he'd admitted to were even wrong. The comedian's return to public life that year marked the anniversary of MeToo's emergence into the mainstream. And it came at roughly the same time as the confirmation of Brett Kavanaugh to the Supreme Court. One year before Depp's defamation suit against Heard would go to trial, Bill

Cosby—accused of sexual abuse by dozens of women over the course of decades—was released from prison on a technicality in 2021 after serving just one year. The backlash sent a clear message: The notion that women were allowed to even publicly speak about abuse and gender-based violence was perceived as a threat so disruptive and terrifying that it required equally violent correction.

Amid Depp and Heard's defamation trial, actor Courtney Love offered a very personal account of Depp saving her life and being a supportive, almost parental figure to her daughter and, of course, accused Heard of exploiting "queer feminist intersectional spaces" for "personal gain" in an Instagram Live video. Love's anecdotes were almost immediately weaponized by Depp supporters, building upon a frustrating pattern that's always plagued MeToo in the entertainment industry and beyond: Individual women's testimonies about positive experiences with an abusive man are used to discredit women who say they were harmed by him. Numerous women who went to prep school with Kavanaugh in 2018 signed a letter stating that he didn't assault them, as if their individual experiences with him somehow automatically rendered Dr. Christine Blasey Ford a liar. In 2021 actor Dakota Johnson bemoaned how actors like Armie Hammer and Shia LaBeouf, both accused of sexual battery and domestic violence, had been victimized by "cancel culture," citing her individual positive experiences working with them as iron-clad proof of their innocence.[4]

The unspoken idea here is that if a man hasn't abused every single woman he's encountered in his entire life, it then follows that he's never abused any woman. This "logic" is only applied to gender-based violence and not any other crime or form of harm. All people—men, women, absolutely anyone—with personal relationships to someone who's been accused of abuse might naturally be inclined to universalize their individual experience with them. But this just isn't how human relationships, or reality in general, work. People contain multitudes. That means the same person who may have been extraordinarily kind to you, perhaps even saved your life, can be abusive to someone else. It's entirely human to want to feel like you know who someone truly is—but that shouldn't be the basis for appraising whether someone who says they've been harmed is credible, or whether someone accused of harm is held accountable.

MeToo: TRIALS AND TRIBULATIONS

For all the internet hot takes about how terrified men supposedly are about being falsely accused of abuse post-MeToo, breeding the short-lived 2018 hashtag #HimToo, it's indisputable that MeToo has changed many women's day-to-day lives for the better. Alarmist prioritization of an infrequent male experience of being falsely accused can't erase the positive impact this women-led movement has had on society, and certainly on women's lives.

Yet despite the revelations and deeply important triumphs of MeToo, we're painfully confronted with the institutional power of backlash against the movement. MeToo has been rendered severely dependent on whether powerful men, who are far too often enablers or perpetrators of sexual abuse themselves, have consciences or moral backbones. We're at the mercy of said powerful men choosing to do the right thing—senators choosing to reject a Supreme Court justice nominee accused of abuse, network executives severing ties with abusers. For all men's claims of MeToo ruining their lives, the movement's power has generally been limited to some social repercussions, five minutes of outrage in a fast-paced news cycle. Meanwhile, because of the priorities of our patriarchal government and its reliance on carceral rather than transformative solutions to violence, victims of abuse still aren't getting what they need to heal, and are still left unprotected.

As often as we hear MeToo has "gone too far," or what a "scary time" it is "for young men," to quote our former president, we rarely hear the perspectives of women who feel safer today because of MeToo. When we hear about "lives being ruined," the lives in question are abusive men's—we rarely hear about the lives of women and girls that are ruined by the lifelong impacts of surviving sexual harm, or the opportunities women are denied by men who are too "scared" of MeToo to hire them. As a result of MeToo, some men were forced for the first time in their lives to think of how their words and actions might make women around them feel; this—conscientiousness—was apparently too much to ask for. Why ask men to think about their actions, when we could instead maintain a world in which women, girls, and femmes are forced to live in a perennial state of discomfort and fear?

Amid endemic male hysteria about abusers facing consequences, we rarely hear about the ways sexual violence is actually expanding rather than narrowing in scope—alarming surges in online sexual harassment; cyber rape, or "revenge porn," the nonconsensual distribution of women's nude photos on the internet; deepfake artificial intelligence-generated porn depicting real individuals without their consent; and new, "trendy" forms of rape like stealthing, when a man removes the condom without his partner's knowledge or consent. Stealthing, which first entered the cultural lexicon largely because of Reddit discourse in the 2010s, amounts to rape because the victim consented to intercourse on the condition that it would involve use of a condom. On the state and federal levels, victims of online harassment, cyber rape, and forms of sexual assault like stealthing often have limited legal protections, as geriatric lawmakers struggle to catch up with the times and adapt to the new forms of sexual violence in a digital age.

Speaking of the growing threat of gendered cyber harassment, within weeks of Depp and Heard's trial, an extensive report confirmed what many of us had witnessed or even experienced firsthand: Users who posted anything even vaguely supportive of Heard on social media were subjected to a deluge of targeted online harassment, often from newly created accounts specifically dedicated to vilifying Heard. Per the research firm Bot Sentinel's report released in July 2022, analysis of more than 14,000 tweets that included one of four viral hashtags (#AmberHeardIsAnAbuser, #AmberHeardLsAnAbuser, #AmberHeardIsALiar, and #AmberHeardLsALiar) characterizing Heard as a liar or the "real" abuser revealed that one in five of the accounts appeared to be "dedicated to spamming."[5] The report also analyzed different methods deployed by aggressive pro-Depp accounts, including doxing and what the firm called "copypasta," or repeatedly copying, pasting, and tweeting identical content attacking Heard and her supporters. People who expressed support for Heard, or merely expressed that they believed her allegations, "were attacked relentlessly" with tweets using particularly "vulgar and threatening language," the report said.

According to Bot Sentinel, one anti-Heard user "used a photo of a woman's deceased child to create a fake account and troll the woman," solely because of her tweets in support of Heard. These trolls "didn't limit their abuse to women" who supported the actress—they "also targeted their family members." One user, Ella Dawson, told CBS at the time that nearly two months after the verdict of the trial, she was "still getting people tweeting at me, calling me weird, heinous stuff" over tweets she shared that were supportive of Heard and other domestic violence victims. "It's been weeks and weeks," and she remained "bombarded by people every day for weeks on end saying that Amber Heard is a liar and women lie, and I am an abuse apologist who must be lying."[6]

Shauna Thomas, co-founder and executive director of the national feminist organization UltraViolet, told *USA Today* that she "was served an unbelievable amount of content from so-called survivors and feminists taking Johnny Depp's side." She explained, "The actual latent sexism in society that exists was being tapped into and weaponized, and it was being permitted and amplified by social media platforms." Further, as Bot Sentinel would eventually report in its research, Thomas added, "There was nothing authentic about it. I think once people realized that, they did start weighing in in [Heard's] defense. But at that point, it was too late."[7]

UltraViolet's research in 2021 found a third of women under the age of thirty-five and 70 percent of LGBTQ adults report being harassed online; 61 percent of women compared with 48 percent of men characterize online harassment as a "major problem."[8] In its report, Bot Sentinel said it found hundreds of Twitter accounts "violated multiple rules and policies of the platform, including but not limited to violent threats, abuse/harassment, hateful conduct, private information, and platform manipulation and spam," in the context of the Depp-Heard trial. Yet Twitter "didn't do enough to mitigate the platform manipulation and did very little to stop the abuse and targeted harassment," essentially "[leaving] the women to fend for themselves with little to no support from the platform."

It wasn't just Bot Sentinel's report—other reporting from Vice News that year showed the right-wing news outlet the Daily Wire had funneled thousands of dollars toward promoting misleading anti-Amber Heard propaganda on social media. Another report showed former aides to alleged rapist President Trump had been critical to spearheading Depp's online redemption campaign. These were the architects of the misogynist spectacle of Heard and Depp's trial: seasoned, right-wing political agitators. And they took such great interest in the trial because they knew it was about more than popular culture, more than two rich actors. It was about hard-launching the practical strategies to silence victims broadly, using Heard as a stand-in for all women, a catch-all net for generations of deep-seated, violent misogyny.

Women and survivors with the least privilege stood to lose the most from the spectacle of the trial, its verdict, and the precedent it set, particularly pertaining to defamation suits. As one campus survivor justice organization, Know Your IX, highlighted at the time, the verdict aimed an especially targeted threat at campus sexual assault survivors, who are frequently subject to defamation lawsuits and peer-led smear campaigns. A 2021 survey by the organization found 23 percent of student survivors said their assailant or assailant's attorney threatened to sue them for defamation, 19 percent said they were warned by their school of the possibility of defamation suits, and 10 percent have faced "retaliatory complaints" filed by their assailants.[9] That same year, I also reported for Jezebel on a rising tide of increasingly successful "anti-male bias" lawsuits in response to disciplinary action around campus sexual assaults—one database claims more than 700 Title IX-related lawsuits alleging anti-male bias have been filed since 2013, though it's not clear how many have been thrown out or privately settled.[10]

Sage Carson, a co-author of Know Your IX's extensive 2021 report on the consequences student survivors face for reporting, told me that the entire purpose of defamation suits and the mere threat of them is to silence victims. And it's not just famous perpetrators or "those with political power" who have this tool in their arsenal: "With the rise of MeToo, famous men accused of sexual harm—Jeffrey Epstein, Andrew Cuomo, Bill Cosby, Harvey Weinstein—have all popularized a strategy to evade accountability by launching smear campaigns to undermine the victims' credibility, then coming after those victims in court," Carson said. "This campaign of retaliation we see folks using like Depp did is intended to silence victims by making the cost of reporting too high to bear."[11]

According to Carson, the survivors interviewed by Know Your IX primarily faced threats of defamation suits rather than actual defamation suits, but that alone can chill speech. And when defamation suits move forward, even when survivors "win," they still ultimately lose due to "the economic weight, how the legal fight strips them of resources." Know Your IX's research shows that most student survivors weren't subjected to defamation lawsuits or threats because they named their abuser publicly online, but simply because they told their friends and campus communities they had been assaulted. They were being punished for seeking community after experiencing trauma.

One survivor Carson interviewed, who was assaulted in her freshman year of college and whose assailant was found responsible by the school, said that her assailant proceeded to launch a "four-year smear campaign" against her, including a defamation lawsuit that followed her the rest of her college career. Through the lawsuit, he was able to "access her medical records, school records, even her sexual history," and his retaliation eventually forced her to transfer schools, delay her graduation, and spend over $100,000 trying to protect herself from his attacks. It's worth noting 34 percent of campus sexual assault survivors are forced to drop out of school.

The smear campaign Depp's team deployed against Heard mirrored tactics that campus sexual assault survivors' abusers deploy against them. One survivor interviewed by Know Your IX said her assailant and all his fraternity brothers "posted anonymous, horrible stories about her, slut-shamed her, made threats as they walked past her on the street." Other student survivors were subjected to similar stalking and very public harassment campaigns targeting them as well as their friends and family, sometimes forcing them to fear for their physical safety. Unsealed court documents after the Heard-Depp trial concluded revealed Depp's legal team's original plan to use Heard's nude photos against her in court. (Also notable: The unsealed documents showed Depp's assistant apologizing to Heard for Depp beating her the day before, back in 2014.)

Ninety percent of campus sexual assaults are already unreported. After the nightmarish Depp-Heard trial, and with the looming threat of costly defamation lawsuits and aggressive public smear campaigns, the rate of unreported assaults could surge even further. Defamation suits aren't "just about silencing celebrities—it's about silencing all survivors," Carson told me.

Alexandra Brodsky, author of *Sexual Justice*, first noticed the growing success of "anti-male bias" litigation in circuit courts in 2017. A few such cases Brodsky and her co-authors highlight in a 2021 paper on the subject are *Doe v. Purdue University, Doe v. Oberlin College*, and *Doe v. University of the Sciences*.[12] The male plaintiffs of these cases are students who were accused of and penalized for sexual misconduct at their schools, and they allege that Title IX policies violated their rights specifically because of their gender.

Circuit courts ruled in favor of all aforementioned plaintiffs. As Brodsky's paper notes, "this backward reasoning suggests that civil rights enforcement is a form of discrimination against dominant groups." Following the logic of this rising trend in Title IX litigation, workplace supports for pregnant people are discrimination against non-pregnant people, and supports for people with disabilities are discrimination against people without disabilities. Her research found that at the heart of these cases was the plaintiffs' broad equation of accused parties with male identity, despite how students accused of sexual misconduct aren't always men. Contrary to popular men's rights talking points, men, again, are statistically more likely to be victims of sexual harm than falsely accused of it.

Anti-male bias claims once seemed like fringe rants coming from niche men's rights subreddits—until suddenly they were launched into the national spotlight amid the Depp and Heard defamation trial. But in recent years, particularly amid massive public backlash to MeToo, the idea that even considering claims of sexual misconduct amounts to radical misandrist oppression has become more widely accepted than ever. This idea has also been implicitly and explicitly parroted out by mainstream and legacy media for years: "Does anyone still take both sexual assault and due process seriously?" one 2018 *Atlantic* article posited, amid the Kavanaugh hearings in 2018. The year before, author Ijeoma Oluo said *USA Today* asked her to write a counter op-ed to their editorial board on the need for "due process" for men accused of sexual assault, about her supposed opposition to due process. According to Oluo, the newspaper then rescinded the invitation when she made it clear she did, in fact, support due process. The insinuation was that feminism and survivor justice are inherently at odds with due process. To be clear, due process is violated by the government denying someone their rights or a fair trial, *not* members of the general public taking sexual misconduct claims seriously.

"As we're seeing courts applying more generous standards—really uniquely generous standards—to lawsuits brought by students and staff accused of sexual harassment, that stands in contrast with really onerous legal standards that have been applied for students who are survivors," Brodsky said. "The result could be that schools may look at the case law and say, to minimize our liability, our best bet is to decide that no sexual harassment occurred so we can avoid a lawsuit from the accused student that could likely succeed."

Rarely did we hear about stories like this in the context of Heard and Depp's defamation trial, the ripple effects it carried for everyday people—particularly young people and students with the least power—who would be swallowed whole by the misogynist, victim-blaming spectacle the trial fed. But the uniquely high-profile nature of that trial and its ramifications for everyday victims weren't lost on victims' rights advocate Amanda Kippert. "For a lot of fans, it's inconvenient for us to believe that a celebrity we like is guilty—we've seen this many, many times before," she said, "and it's incredibly harmful." The positioning of Depp as a sort of martyr, not just among online men's rights extremists but in the mainstream too, stemmed from a broader issue: the idolization of celebrities. Consider NBA players like Kobe Bryant and Derrick Rose, pioneering male comedians like Cosby and Louis CK, popular artists like Chris Brown, beloved actors like James Franco.

In the years since these men were credibly accused of violence, their lives and careers went on, some benefiting from controversy. Because all these men are icons to primarily male fans who idolize them, women's ostensibly trivial complaints about them are irrelevant—a culture that endorses celebrification and idolatry is inherently at odds with survivor justice and will always contribute to the widespread enabling of gender-based violence.

This is even true of highly visible celebrities who vocally advocate for survivor justice. The hyperfixation on highly public cases of gender-based violence and "victories"—like the years-in-the-making demise of Harvey Weinstein—has convinced many that survivor justice is broadly popular, that we've won this fight now that a few famously bad men are locked up, and we can slip into the very complicity that men's rights activists have thrived on. This couldn't be further from the truth.

MeToo AND THE SILICON VALLEY

The celebrification of MeToo in 2017—or the mass of highly visible celebrities who spoke up about their experiences with sexual misconduct and advocated for victims and survivors—inevitably contributed to its commodification. Companies and brands were compelled to publicly take a stand on the issue to continue to line their pockets. From Reese Witherspoon to Kerry Washington, top women in the entertainment industry were pivotal to the creation of the Time's Up Legal Defense Fund. But the organization ultimately fell apart by the summer of 2021, when its executive director actively defended former New York Gov. Andrew Cuomo amid the numerous sexual misconduct allegations against him.

Lyft, in particular, excelled at feminist corporate spin. In 2019 the company launched a partnership with top sexual violence advocacy organization RAINN to "create a culture of safety for drivers and riders." Around the same time, Lyft also very publicly donated $1 million to Planned Parenthood. But like nearly all brands that tried to capitalize on MeToo, the company's words didn't match its actions.

When Alison Turkos got into her Lyft in 2017, she told me that at the time, she had complete trust in this corporation—it had publicly opposed former President Trump's Muslim ban and donated to the ACLU, among other strides toward social justice.

The events of that evening changed her life. Turkos would be held at gunpoint and kidnapped by her Lyft driver, then taken to a park and gang-raped.

In 2019 Turkos filed a lawsuit against Lyft, joining thirteen other women who separately filed claims saying they were raped or sexually assaulted by their Lyft drivers. All of them were ignored or steamrolled by the company for years, all while it continued to outwardly posture as progressive. Then, in 2022, Lyft agreed to a $25 million settlement to resolve claims from its shareholders that the company failed to be transparent about "safety problems"—phrasing that relegated over a dozen reported sexual assaults to an inconvenient footnote. Lyft shareholders claimed that by concealing these issues and misleadingly posing as a socially conscious alternative to Uber, the company's actions posed an "existential risk" to shareholders' profits when Lyft went public in 2019. Around the same time that the lawsuits emerged, the company's value almost immediately tanked and never recovered.

Lyft shareholders called the 2022 settlement an "excellent" result. In contrast, according to Turkos, neither she nor any of the other survivors harmed by Lyft received a dime from this settlement, despite how many people who saw the news may have read the headline and concluded that Lyft was paying survivors.[13]

It wasn't.

Instead, Lyft was paying its ultra-rich shareholders $25 million. The only correspondence Turkos said she'd ever received from Lyft was a statement it shared to The Verge in 2019, essentially writing off sexual assault as inevitable: "The unfortunate fact remains that one in six women will face some form of sexual violence in their lives—behavior that's unacceptable for our society and on our platform." But because Turkos's driver had "passed the New York City TLC's background check and was permitted to drive," the company seemed to shrug off all responsibility.

"Shareholders quite literally profited off of my kidnapping, off of my multiple rapes, off of the violent crime that was committed against me," Turkos said. She noted that the company was "making money until stock prices fell" amid the backlash against Lyft for the sexual assault lawsuit, and only then did shareholders begin to take issue with the company's actions—not for its treatment of women like her, but their loss of money. "With this $25 million settlement, rich people are again getting richer because of what happened to me in 2017."

Lyft, Turkos said, doesn't value her or any other survivors—it values "people who will give them money and make them money." Since her experience, Turkos has has become dedicated to organizing for survivor justice and trying to hold Lyft accountable. As much as she loves this work, it's exhausting and retraumatizing, and she still hasn't been paid a cent. "I don't get paid to be a public-facing survivor who rips herself open to tell her story. It's a full-time job, and it feels like I'm being constantly gaslit, slapped in the face by a company that says, 'Safety is our number one priority.'"

Lyft's deference to its exorbitantly wealthy shareholders—but not the survivors permanently scarred by Lyft rides—reflects a broader issue of corporations creating situations that endanger women and victims, and then harming, silencing, and dismissing them. Lyft is one of many Silicon Valley tech giants that have weaponized NDAs to establish cultures of fear and silence and consequently cover up rampant sexual misconduct.

As usual, companies want to appear progressive, to support survivors, without doing the work. Corporate statements and policies motivated by a desire to match celebrity activism, to profit off major cultural moments, often conceal darker truths. "You have to name what happened to be able to address it," Turkos said. But years after her kidnapping and rape, Lyft's shareholders have continued to fall back on platitudes and language that erase and therefore compound the trauma of survivors like her. They'll never have to face "the lives lost, the people who had to move because their driver knows where they live," Turkos told me. "They don't see that we cannot show up as our full selves in our relationships and our friendships with our families. We can't sleep through the night."

SURVIVOR JUSTICE IN THE MAINSTREAM

Turkos's story and the persistence of corporate hypocrisy extends from a greater issue: Beyond the glamorous magazine covers of celebrity activists, beyond the surface-level empowerment rhetoric deployed by influencers and millionaire actors, survivor justice movements haven't actually progressed that far in the mainstream, contrary to narratives that it's progressed "*too* far." It's been well over a decade now since a Nebraska judge in 2008 prohibited a rape victim from even using the word "rape" during her testimony—she was one of several women told during their 2000s trials to use the more palatable term "sexual assault" instead, ostensibly to help their case. Not much has changed nearly two decades later.

On the 2021 HBO miniseries *Catch and Kill*, an exploration of the rigorous journalism that led to Weinstein's undoing, *New Yorker* deputy editor Deirdre Foley-Mendelssohn recalled at one point, "Weinstein's team was pushing very, very hard for us to not use the term rape, to use assault—and it seemed that was the direction things were going." Tammy Kim, a *New Yorker* fact checker, added, "There were a couple colleagues who were skeptical or thought readers would be skeptical if we characterized certain acts as rape."

"Would using the term be sensationalist?" journalist Ronan Farrow then asked Kim and *New Yorker* head of research Fergus McIntosh, who were responsible for fact-checking the Weinstein report. McIntosh responded, "Being cautious about something isn't an excuse for not telling the truth about it. Being cautious means being really sure about what happened."

As *Catch and Kill* and the US Department of Justice explain, sexual assault is legally defined as "an attempt or apparent attempt to inflict bodily injury upon another by using unlawful force, accompanied by the apparent ability to injure that person if not prevented." Rape is legally defined as an "act of unlawful sexual intercourse accompanied through force or threat of force by one party and implying lack of consent and resistance by the other party."

The extensive conversations that guided the *New Yorker*'s editorial choice to specify that several women alleged Weinstein had *raped* them are a focal point of that particular *Catch and Kill* episode. But even beyond the docuseries, the policing of victims and survivors' language and characterizations of their lived experiences persists all around us.

In the introduction of Chanel Miller's memoir *Know My Name*, in which Miller recounts her story of surviving sexual assault perpetrated by Stanford rapist Brock Turner, she writes: "The FBI defines rape as any kind of penetration. But in California, rape is narrowly defined as the act of sexual intercourse. For a long time I refrained from calling [Turner] a rapist, afraid of being corrected. Legal definitions are important. So is mine. He filled a cavity in my body with his hands. I believe he is not absolved of the title simply because he ran out of time."[14]

Miller's self-described fear "of being corrected" is highly resonant for victims of violence—it's certainly resonant to me—and even more so for those with high-profile cases, who often have to hear their own stories retold and picked apart by other people, over and over again. Sexual violence necessarily makes for challenging reporting. Fact-checking is essential, but it can be difficult to adhere to legal standards that are inherently cold, distant, even dehumanizing. How can anyone claim to know more about survivors' trauma than they themselves do? As McIntosh notes in *Catch and Kill*, there's an important distinction between "being cautious" and just "not telling the truth."

When we hyperfixate on correcting the language survivors use that feels most honest and true to their lived experience with trauma, what we may be striving for is accuracy and a patriarchal conception of objectivity—but really, we're just reinforcing the ways that patriarchy protects abusers by casting doubt on victims and their credibility.

Whenever survivors speak up, they're frequently forced to hear some condescending argument about how false accusations happen—and they do—but without the crucial context that all credible research shows this is highly rare, and there is nothing to gain and everything to lose from coming forward about experiencing sexual assault. When we focus on a very narrow set of experiences over a far more common one—that one in five women is a victim of completed or attempted rape—this is a direct manifestation of violent, sexist power dynamics.

The maintenance of these power dynamics relies on the implicit and explicit characterization of women and victims as untrustworthy. They are either purposeful liars or, at best, irrational, overly emotional, and likely to exaggerate—for example, by erroneously calling their experience a rape. HBO's *Catch and Kill* is deeply honest about this conflict, and about the media's frustrating skepticism, as well as the vital importance of letting survivors speak and characterize our own truths. The show shined light on the highly arbitrary ways in which we assign credibility to victims of abuse, and the ways our culture, media objectivity standards, and legal definitions can police and invalidate survivors. Legal definitions should protect victims rather than poke any holes possible to distract from the harmful acts committed by the perpetrator.

Dated understandings of media objectivity continue to carry sexist, illogical impacts on women and survivors. Felicia Sonmez, a former reporter at the *Washington Post*, in 2021 filed a lawsuit against her employer for its policy that had barred her from reporting on news involving sexual assault because Sonmez had previously disclosed that she was a survivor herself. Her complaint alleged a fellow *Post* reporter had sent an unsolicited lewd photo to another journalist and was still allowed to continue reporting without restriction after being accused of sexual misconduct. In contrast, Sonmez claimed that after she came forward about her assault, her editors accused her of trying to make herself the "star" of her sexual assault story and asked why she hadn't reported it to the police.

The newspaper said its policy prevented bias in reporting, but as Sonmez's lawsuit notes, it's been applied inconsistently. The *Post*'s policy didn't ban reporters who had experienced medical emergencies from covering health care issues. Instead, this rule was specifically weaponized against gendered experiences. There's a fundamental one-sidedness to how we define objectivity and pin the term "bias" to any identity or experience that deviates from whiteness and maleness, without considering how white-ness and maleness are identities that come with their own biases. Because these identities are treated as the default by traditional reporting conven-tion, they're privileged with being treated as neutral and impartial.

Sonmez is by no means the only female reporter who's experienced sexual violence, even if she's one of few who's spoken up publicly. "If you removed sexual assault survivors from newsrooms, how many women would actually remain?" victim rights lawyer Carrie Goldberg told me for an article in Salon in 2021. "That's what's so naïve about *WaPo*'s actions—they treat Ms. Sonmez as though surviving a sexual assault is rare."[15]

Just as surviving sexual violence—not to mention nearly routine sexual harassment—isn't uncommon for female journalists, plenty of male reporters are and have been publicly outed as perpetrators of sexual misconduct themselves. In 2020 the *New Yorker*'s Jeffrey Toobin was caught masturbating on a Zoom call—only to return to a contributor role on CNN the following year. Before that, MSNBC's Chris Matthews was accused of sexual harassment by several women, notably after using his platform to defend sexual abusers. And before them, Matt Lauer of NBC was one of the first powerful men in media ousted for misconduct at the height of MeToo in 2017, accused of sexually assaulting several women in his office, after years of sexist media commentary.

Sonmez's suit was eventually thrown out when a judge sided with her employer. Stories that meaningfully challenge rape culture or analyze the political conditions of survivors are consequently left untold when they're excluded from newsrooms. And when survivors' stories and expe-riences with marginalization go untold, cycles of erasure and cultural complacency persist.

A VICTIM-BLAMING MEDIA ECOSYSTEM

It's not just exclusionary policies, tone-policing, and discriminatory prac-tices in journalism that victims and survivors are forced to contend with—it's a culture and mass media landscape in general that transform the violence we've experienced into spectacle for consumption, that manipulate us into questioning the severity and legitimacy of our own experiences.

Cable news media responses to allegations against abusive men, for example, reliably offer abusers a platform to harass, attack, and demonize their victims, or welcome wealthy, powerful white men and political operatives to speculate and pontificate on the credibility of victims, reducing them and their trauma to the objects of political analysis. On TV and in film, depictions of gendered violence and abuse continue to rely on shock factor that desensitizes us to the everyday pain of real-life victims. Consider the gratuitous gender-based violence, at least in the first season of the Netflix series *You*—the drama-thriller was marketed as shocking and subversive, despite how we live in a world where women are statistically more likely to be killed by an intimate partner or ex-partner than anyone else. Sexual violence and patriarchal renderings of it exist all around us, particularly within the media that male, non-victim audiences have the privilege of being able to consume as escapism.

Consider the repetitive, normalized rape scenes and disturbing, needless depictions of violence against women and girls in HBO's *Game of Thrones*. Through scene after scene of rape and gender-based violence, the series' male writers attempted to depict a "bygone" historical era—as if we live in a modern world where gender-based violence no longer happens. Using rape and violence as central points in storytelling for female characters isn't just retraumatizing for audience members who are survivors; it's also reductive of the fullness of women's lives. In a wholly fictionalized fantasy world, why are we allowed dragons and magic but not liberated women? Rape, in these male writers' eyes, is treated as the only plot device that can accord female characters humanity, dimension, and growth. On top of this laziness, the explanation that rape was prevalent in historical societies, in the past tense, is plainly insulting: The insinuation is that we, as modern women, have it so good, we couldn't possibly wrap our heads around historical reality. Yet in a real-life world where sexual assault remains endemic, sexual violence isn't just a lazy storytelling trope—it's something many of us have infinitely more experience with than the male TV writers telling us to stop complaining.

Just as frustrating, depictions of sexual and domestic violence as exclusively grotesque acts of rape, beatings, assaults, and killings like those depicted in *Game of Thrones* have the effect of gaslighting women, victims, and society at large about what real-life abuse entails. Gender-based violence can look wildly different from the overt physical violence of what we see onscreen; it can be—and often is—any exploitation of power to pressure or coerce someone to engage in sexual activities, or any act of taking advantage of someone while they aren't in a state of being able to consent freely and enthusiastically. When popular imagination frames sexual and domestic abuse exclusively as the extremes we see on our television and movie screens, we tell victims that if their experience wasn't like that, then they have nothing to complain about.

In 2021 Olympic gymnast and survivor justice activist Aly Raisman partnered with MeToo founder Tarana Burke in the documentary *Darkness to Light*, which follows Raisman as she travels across the country to meet with survivors and discuss healing. Raisman herself is one of dozens of young, female gymnasts who were sexually assaulted by former US Olympic doctor Larry Nassar, who was enabled to prey on young women and girls for years by the USA Gymnastics organization and Michigan State University, as they brushed complaints about him under the rug. Early on in *Darkness to Light*, Raisman emphasizes that hearing "graphic details" of other survivors' assaults can be highly triggering to her, staying with her for weeks and bringing her intense anxiety and discomfort. Raisman and the survivors she connects with, as well as the experts interviewed by the documentary, discuss how specific, highly personal triggers can take survivors right back to the moment of their assault even years later.

The first time I experienced sexual assault, someone I had invited into my home and initiated some sexual contact with repeatedly ignored my objections to continuing the encounter. Even as the experience left me traumatized, I still couldn't fully discern whether what had happened was a sexual assault because I had let the person into my home. I was also one of many victims who have prior, often intimate relationships with their attacker, and I couldn't wrap my head around seeing this person as an abuser—not when rapists and assailants on TV shows and in movies I'd seen were portrayed as violent strangers rather than classmates and peers.

A few years later, I experienced sexual assault again at a party in my freshman year of college, when someone I didn't know in a dark room groped me while I vomited over a trash can, heavily intoxicated. I understood that experience as an assault but didn't even consider taking action, as it hadn't felt "severe" enough to justify dragging myself through what would certainly be an exhausting and retraumatizing bureaucratic process.

Domestic abuse isn't always the assaults and stalking inflicted on Jennifer Lopez's housewife-pushed-to-the-brink in *Enough* in 2002, nor King Henry VIII's execution of not one but two wives in *The Tudors* (and, well, in sixteenth-century England), or the fictionalized marital rape of Georgina Cavendish in the eighteenth-century period piece *The Duchess*. Nor is all abuse the supposedly darkly humorous mistreatment of *The Office*'s Michael Scott by his partner and former boss, Jan, who famously coerced him to undergo repeated vasectomies; or—circling back to *You*— Joe Goldberg's murder and attempted murders of previous girlfriends, among several other women. Domestic abuse can also entail emotional manipulation and coercion, not unlike Danny Castellano's attempts to force partner Mindy Lahiri to quit her job and tamper with her birth control on *The Mindy Project*.

In contrast, the adult cartoon comedy *Tuca & Bertie* exemplifies how TV and movies can include storylines that address sexual violence in thoughtful and respectful ways. In season one of the show, Bertie, a perennially anxious song thrush, opens up to her best friend Tuca, a free-spirited, exuberant toucan, about her experience being sexually assaulted as a child by her lifeguard. The trauma of the assault stopped Bertie from swimming for years until that episode. The show didn't depict a scene of the assault, or even name or identify the character who harmed Bertie. As some eagle-eyed audience members pointed out, it also didn't include a single male character. *Tuca & Bertie*, a show about two thirty-something animated bird women, presented a way forward for sexual assault storytelling where we don't need triggering, violent assault scenes constructed for the male gaze and can instead center survivors.

Tuca & Bertie creator Lisa Hanawalt spoke to *TV Guide* on the decision to not include a scene of the assault or bring to life Bertie's attacker "because [she] didn't want anyone to judge whether or not [Bertie] overreacted to it." She explained, "We just wanted to say, 'You know what? Something happened, and it traumatized her. And it really doesn't matter what those specifics are.'"[16] All too often, if survivors' accounts of their trauma *are* believed, their stories are heavily scrutinized or compared to other supposedly more violent scenarios, with survivors implicitly or explicitly told they're overreacting, as Hanawalt suggested.

If someone comes forward about their experience with assault in a show or movie, or certainly real life, the only information we really need is that they were harmed and deserve our support—we don't need and shouldn't ask for more details than that. Allowing survivors to anonymize their abuser is crucial to supporting and helping survivors feel comfortable and safe to speak on what happened to them, without pressure to disclose more details than they wish, and potentially retraumatize or endanger themselves in the process.

The 2020 movie *Promising Young Woman*, which follows a young woman's quest to avenge her friend who was raped at a party in medical school, centers around a rape that's never shown, and maddeningly portrays the unforgivable violence of everyday male complicity as an extension of rape culture. Throughout the film, Carey Mulligan as Cassandra feigns intoxication at bars to expose men as sexual predators and confronts and punishes those who harmed or denied justice to her late friend. Absence of a scene of the rape itself seems to strengthen the film's storytelling power, as it focuses instead on the intensity of the aftermath of sexual violence for both victims and their loved ones. HBO's *I May Destroy You*, also from 2020, follows an author named Arabella as she navigates life, friendship, and her career after a sexual assault at a bar that she struggles to remember. Like *Promising Young Woman* and *Tuca & Bertie*, the show explores how the emotional violence of sexual assault outlasts the physical act itself.

Many survivors of sexual violence have spent countless hours dissecting and questioning our own experiences, our memory, the proportionality of our reactions or emotional responses. We consume news media that pieces apart our credibility, as well as television and film that normalize our trauma for ratings and shock factor—all while convincing us that if our experiences aren't exactly like the grisly rapes and killings of women depicted onscreen, then we aren't truly victims.

ANTI-"CANCEL CULTURE" BACKLASH PROTECTS ABUSERS

Culture and politics take their cues from each other.

In 2020 nineteen-year-old Aaron Coleman won his primary race to represent the 37th district of the Kansas state House. Coleman, a Democratic-socialist, had shared nude photos of a twelve-year-old girl when he was fourteen, and had harassed and pressured her to commit suicide. In 2019, at eighteen, he allegedly strangled and assaulted his then-girlfriend. The *New York Times* reported that, years later, Coleman sent a message to a relative of one of his victims that read: "I've moved on. They call the past the past for a reason because that's where you are supposed to leave things. At this point you shouldn't move on for me, you should move on for yourself."

Shortly after the allegations surfaced, Coleman continued to show little remorse, briefly withdrawing from the race with an embittered statement blaming feminism for supposedly doing more to harm progressive causes than the right. But within days of withdrawing, Coleman rejoined the race, announcing his reentrance with a bizarre statement equating his experience being pressured to step down for his record of abuse to "undoing democracy." In the entirety of Coleman's statement, he attempts to treat his "platform" as somehow separate from his violent actions, as if an agenda of equity and justice for all can be achieved under the stewardship of an unrepentant sexual abuser:

> They said that they did not vote for me expecting that I was a perfect person. They told me that all of us have sinned, and we all make mistakes. My withdrawal would immediately return to power the same corporatist, out-of-touch seven-term incumbent that voters just rejected. They did not

only vote for me but they voted for my platform and for change for our community. We cannot undo democracy because I am a flawed individual who has made mistakes.

Coleman's return was widely supported by mostly male social media users (including men who identify as progressive and leftist, and even prominent male journalists) who insisted that his life had been unfairly ruined, simply because he was no longer a popular candidate after we had learned more about who he was. That same outrage on behalf of his teenage victims was essentially nonexistent. Media narratives that assign victimhood to powerful men who are held accountable for their treatment of women and girls inevitably bleed into politics, and these narratives write the playbook for male politicians like Coleman.

Contrary to liberal feminist misrepresentations of the Democratic Party as the savior of women, sexual misconduct and misogynist behaviors aren't partisan. In my experience and those of close friends and family, toxic behaviors—from the condescending phenomenon "mansplaining" to sexual assault—are limited to no political party or ideology. People's public personas and public politics can dramatically diverge from how they treat people in their private lives. Men with feminist politics— notably, like the ex-boyfriend of one of my loved ones who voted for and supported Democratic-socialist candidate Bernie Sanders while subjecting her to emotional and physical abuse—are capable of the same violence and toxicity as any other men. People and communities representing all political ideologies often fail to protect victims.

Not bestowing public office upon a nineteen-year-old who not so long ago committed egregious acts of violence and showed no remorse isn't the same thing as sending him to prison or "ruining his life." Elected office is a privilege, not a right, and certainly not a right for people who have committed acts of sexual harm. The defenses of Coleman were predictable, recycled through the varying scandals of numerous celebrities and famous men who preceded him—"MeToo has gone too far" or "it was a long time ago, he was so young." Coleman's victims were teenage girls, now subjected to a lifetime of trauma—where was this same sympathy for them?

Supposedly progressive, male journalists lamented the impact of the allegations of violence on Coleman's "promising career," while Glenn Greenwald, co-founder of The Intercept, mourned that Coleman had been "sabotaged" over "middle school misconduct," without acknowledging what that "misconduct" entailed. Another male reporter expressed dismayed shock at Coleman being shamed into dropping from the race, asking on Twitter, "We're just done with him forever?" Another argued it was "horrific and intolerant" to have past behavior "held against you in perpetuity."

That summer, defenses of Coleman from internet men on the left were especially upsetting because they were rooted in the same twisted and misogynist logic we so often encounter from men in leftist and frankly all political spaces: that women's safety and dignity—from abortion rights to safety from harassment and violence—are secondary to or expendable for broader, more "important" political goals. We see this when liberal and progressive politicians suggest they can relegate reproductive rights to bargaining chips and embrace anti-abortion candidates in their own party, like "Democrat" Henry Cuellar, reelected to a tenth term in Congress, within months of *Roe* being overturned. We see this when allegations of sexual harassment and abuse directed at male politicians are dismissed or swept under the rug for some nebulous, ever-evasive "greater good."

In the weeks leading up to his 2020 bid for the presidency, Bernie Sanders faced questions and confrontation from former staff about a culture of casual sexual harassment—even sexual assault—and misogyny on his 2016 campaign team. Specifically, twenty-four individuals—men and women—had signed a letter calling for a meeting with the senator about the "toxic environment" that developed over the course of his 2016 primary campaign. The *New York Times* reported that, according to several women who had come forward, "women were groped and mocked for reporting misconduct," paid thousands of dollars less than male colleagues with similar jobs, or punished when they refused to share hotel rooms with managers. In 2022 Sanders wrote an op-ed arguing Democrats shouldn't run solely on abortion—something that wasn't happening—and should focus instead on economic issues, as if they're separable from each other, as if the ability to decide whether or when to start a family isn't the ultimate economic issue.

The Sanders staffers who came forward were clear they did not want to characterize Sanders and his supporters as unilaterally, unfixably sexist, and criticized the "Bernie Bro" stereotype; they also acknowledged sexual harassment is endemic to political campaigns everywhere. And they're absolutely right.

In a January 2019 interview about the allegations, Sanders denied knowing about the harassment and broader workplace culture issues and suggested this was a distraction from his ostensibly more important work—"I was a little busy running around the country trying to make the case." Ultimately, he apologized "to any woman who felt that she was not treated appropriately," more or less shifting the burden of the problem onto those who "felt" they had been mistreated, rather than simply stating point-blank that multiple women had been harmed, and he needed to take action to do better.

This crisis—of both endemic campaign-trail sexual misconduct and politicians' failure to accept responsibility—is not unique to the Sanders campaign, nor is it unique to one political affiliation. The nonpartisan nature of enabling workplace sexual abuse and misogyny further extends to how politicians of all parties rail against so-called "cancel culture," the mythic idea that abusers and powerful men who harm others are being unfairly punished when they face any sort of critical response or consequence.

Conservative culture warriors and political candidates have embedded outrage and misleading narratives about "cancel culture" at the heart of their political platforms. In 2021 the Conservative Political Action Committee (CPAC) quite literally named its annual conference "America Uncanceled," because, following their thinking, the world's foremost wealth-hoarding, colonizing superpower has been "canceled" by critical academics, activists, and snarky social media users. Even Pope Francis got in on the discourse: In January 2022—fresh off telling married couples everywhere that if they have pets instead of children, they're responsible for the downfall of humanity[17]—he declared that cancel culture is "a form of ideological colonization, one that leaves no room for freedom of expression." The Catholic Church, mind you, happens to be history's greatest and most ruthless colonizer. From around the 1400s onward, people across Africa, Asia, the Americas, and everywhere were killed, enslaved, tortured, and "converted" to Catholicism by varying European colonial superpowers. And the legacy of colonization persists to this day with white savior complex-driven missionary projects in non-white countries, on top of persistent church sexual abuse. But, sure—accountability for abusers and neo-Nazis is the real colonization.

Conservatives and religious figures are by no means the only ones who have been critical of our perceived descent into "cancel culture." President Obama criticized the phenomenon while speaking at an event in early 2020: "I do get a sense sometimes now among certain young people, and this is accelerated by social media, there is this sense sometimes of: 'The way of me making change is to be as judgmental as possible about other people, and that's enough.'"[18]

He added, "Like, if I tweet or hashtag about how you didn't do something right or used the wrong verb, then I can sit back and feel pretty good about myself, cause, 'Man, you see how woke I was, I called you out.' This idea of purity and you're never compromised and you're always politically 'woke' and all that stuff. . . . The world is messy; there are ambiguities. People who do really good stuff have flaws. People who you are fighting may love their kids, and share certain things with you."

To Obama's point, words and tweets and sweeping judgments of people can be futile and ineffective in the absence of performing additional work offline. But considering that victims and women of color often have less access to traditional, white male–led media and cultural spaces or leadership positions in general, social media is often the only place they can be heard, where they can tell their stories and seek any form of justice and support. Deriding social media–based activism dismisses the fact that, for many marginalized people, it's one of the only options available to them to demand change.

Let's not forget that it's often women, victims, and marginalized people who are "canceled," rather than the people who abuse them. Again, it was Democratic Rep. Katie Hill, one year into her first term, who was forced to resign from her office over nude photos—not Florida Republican Rep. Matt Gaetz, alleged in 2021 to have committed statutory rape and under investigation for sex trafficking, or Ohio Republican Rep. Jim Jordan, alleged to have helped cover up sexual abuse in Ohio State University's wrestling program.

When conservatives and many liberals offer blistering critiques of our "cancel culture," "political correctness," and war on "free speech," they are centering the experiences of powerful, male abusers who face critique. They aren't thinking of women, people of color, and other marginalized people who, like Hill, only get one chance to wield power, and are all too often literally, *actually* canceled—not just criticized in progressive social media spaces—unlike their white, male, abusive counterparts. And they certainly aren't thinking of what life will be like for the victims and survivors of the powerful men who *aren't* "canceled" and subsequently continue to harm and abuse with impunity.

We encounter similar, inherently violent power dynamics in the right's beloved "marketplace of ideas," which not only advantages but empowers abusers. In this so-called marketplace, all ideas, from revolutionary eco-socialist, feminist liberation to white supremacy, can supposedly compete on an equal level for support among the masses. But it's wealthy, white men who control the platforms on which we share these ideas and engage these conversations. They determine who is and isn't heard, they have the power to bury victims of sexual violence who come forward, and that's often exactly what they do.

Obama is right in some regards—the world is "messy," there are "ambiguities." When it comes to determining how many "chances" anyone deserves, or navigating the nuance and complexity of human imperfection, of how to effectively and compassionately facilitate growth for victim, perpetrator, and society, no case is entirely like another. Determining how harm can be repaired, and how accountability can be rendered without further empowering a system that is fundamentally built to punish and harm victims, requires difficult conversations and open-mindedness. When punishment of an assailant is regarded as a higher priority than supporting the safety and needs of the victim, we've failed as a community to deliver justice. Uniform responses to violence often fail or further harm victims, or treat their unique, individual needs to heal and move forward as tangential. Critics of "cancel culture" are right that we should question and interrogate punitive responses to sexual harm—but this doesn't mean sexual harm shouldn't be met with accountability.

Often, I think of the term "political correctness" and frequent connotations that basic respect for marginalized people has somehow been taken too far, or is simply asking for too much. The term "political correctness," like "cancel culture," exists solely to validate the people who believe that "inconvenient" and inclusive words, or mainstream strides toward social justice, are somehow equally as oppressive as systemic, violent racism and misogyny.

While backlash against so-called political correctness has been construed as frustration with what can no longer be said or done in today's soft, coddled liberal dystopia, I've come to understand it more as frustration and bitterness about what now, today, *can* be said—by women and marginalized people. Groups that have traditionally been expected to accept oppression and bigotry as inherent to their existence, without a word of complaint or any meaningful option for recourse, have become increasingly empowered to respond to oppressive acts, to speak up about bigoted comments and harmful actions, and to seek respect, even justice. More trans people feel empowered to demand respect for their gender identities; more people of color feel empowered to ask for their names to be pronounced correctly; more women and survivors feel empowered to speak up about sexual misconduct.

It seems all the time we hear about the importance of preserving free speech in the context of people with privilege no longer being able to share awful, dehumanizing ideas, to tell cruel and bigoted jokes, to harass and abuse, without facing any social and professional consequences. Rarely do we hear praise of a broad cultural shift moving us slowly— sometimes *painfully* slowly—but surely toward inclusivity, thoughtfulness, respect, and safety.

MEN'S RIGHTS ASIANS
AND INTRA-RACIAL MISOGYNY

In our policy landscape more intent on protecting abusers than meeting the basic needs of victims of abuse, women and survivors of color are forced to navigate cultural spaces equally bent on our erasure and dehumanization in our own racial communities. Speaking up about these experiences with intra-racial bullying and oppression, most often perpetrated by men in our communities, can exacerbate the harassment or often enough land us the "race traitor" label. This is true within all communities of color, and I've certainly experienced it and watched other Asian women, particularly more famous Asian women, be subjected to harassment for speaking out about misogyny among Asian men. Social media has worsened this issue, allowing misogynist men with shared racial identities to convene and coordinate racist, sexist harassment campaigns against "their" women with punishing efficiency.

When Sunisa Lee, a Hmong American, Olympic-gold-medalist gymnast, went public with her relationship in December 2021, she faced a brutal and immediate harassment campaign, and for Asian women who witnessed the hatred, it wasn't hard to guess why: Lee was in an interracial relationship with Jaylin Smith, a Black man and fellow student athlete. When a fan posted a TikTok video in support of Lee, writing, "I know that Sunisa will be judged by certain eyes in the Hmong Community because her man is Black. LOVE is LOVE, no matter what race or gender you are," Lee responded with the comment: "This makes me so happy. I've received so much hate. . . . They support me when it's beneficial for them never when it comes to my happiness. Thank you!"

As Lee's reply implied, much of the "hate" she received came from her own racial community. Many Asian women are accused, often by Asian men, of "hating" ourselves, or, again, being "race traitors," if we're partnered with non-Asian men. In recent years, some of the leading perpetrators of this racist, sexist targeted harassment are the increasingly vocal "MRAsians," or "men's rights Asians," who have primarily convened in Asian-identity Reddit threads. They purport to fight back against the very real issue of anti-Asian racism, but more often than not, their "activism" exclusively entails bullying Asian women for allegedly choosing white men or non-Asian men over them. Case in point: The toxic and frankly disturbing r/AsianMasculinity Reddit thread quickly became a breeding ground for horrific comments about Lee over her reply to the afore-mentioned TikTok video, with many of the comments parroting familiar MRAsian talking points about Asian women's supposed failure to support Asian men.

Eileen Huang, an Asian American digital organizer who focuses on AAPI issues, has also been the subject of significant online harassment campaigns from MRAsians. Huang's writing and social media posts exploring anti-Asian racism, anti-imperialism, and anti-Blackness within Asian communities first began going viral in 2020 amid ongoing racial justice protests. Huang, who is nonbinary, told me for an article in Jezebel in 2022 that they learned about MRAsians when these men started to "harass, dox, send rape and sexual violence threats" to Huang and led other online campaigns to intimidate and "psychologically torture" them.

Huang's criticisms of Asian communities for anti-Blackness and other problematic online behaviors came at the same time as a rise in anti-Asian violence, making Huang particularly vulnerable to MRAsians' retaliation. Speaking of "cancel culture," MRAsians plotted on Reddit about how to "cancel" Huang, contacting Yale (their school at the time), mass-reporting Huang on Twitter to ultimately get their account suspended, and trying to get Huang fired from their internship. One Reddit user claimed Huang has "blood on her hands," misgendering them. In MRAsians' eyes, Huang, not institutionalized white supremacy, was the real enemy.

"The first thing I saw was them screenshotting pictures of me with white people, or friends or ex-partners, and they would be like, 'Oh, look at her, how can you complain about white supremacy when you sleep with white men or want to sleep with them?'" Huang said. The screen-shots wound up on fake Instagram pages impersonating Huang and on Asian-identity Reddit threads where Huang's harassers assembled to mock and coordinate attacks on them. MRAsians make this argument against seemingly every Asian woman or femme they come across, regardless of whether there's a white boyfriend in their photos, Huang said, because "in reality it doesn't even matter who an Asian woman dates—if you provoke MRAsians, that's how they'll attack you."

Many MRAsians see themselves as fighting white supremacy and even advancing the rights and status of Asian Americans by targeting and harassing Asian women—particularly those perceived to have non-Asian partners—because they see these two identities as a conjoined, singular evil. Asian women with non-Asian partners, even just Asian women who criticize Asian men for misogyny, *are* white people to MRAsians.

Asian American feminist activist and writer Jenn Fang shared with me similar insights about her experiences with MRAsians' harassment. The pervading political ideology espoused by these men is that Asian men and Asian women "need to practice political authenticity through their personal lives, and their sex lives in particular," because MRAsians see "Asian men as emasculated in American society." This, Fang said, creates a responsibility, in Asian men's rights activists' eyes, for Asian women "to promote Asian men as worthy sex partners, which is Asian women's most useful form of activism." Any Asian woman who isn't adequately wielding their sexuality on behalf of Asian men is thus "inauthentic," a "sellout."

I, too, have been among the ranks of Asian women and femmes assigned an imaginary white boyfriend by MRAsians. In the summer of 2021, shortly after I wrote an article questioning why Shang-Chi was the protagonist of the Marvel Studios movie *Shang-Chi and the Legend of the Ten Rings*, when his sister was objectively cooler, the article was shared in an MRAsian TikTok video that went viral, and my online accounts were flooded with very specific, targeted, and graphic messages insisting I was a "white man's whore," and that I had a white boyfriend I somehow didn't know existed.

Notably, even before Lee's relationship became Instagram official at the end of 2021, the champion gymnast opened up about personally facing anti-Asian racism when she and a group of Asian women friends had been called racial slurs and were pepper-sprayed when they went out one night. Her experiences underscored how Asian women simultane-ously experience anti-Asian racism from outside their communities and misogyny from within their communities.

In 2021 and 2022 in particular, MRAsians seized an opportunity to become louder online as a sharp rise in anti-Asian violence in the US finally gained national attention. Mainstream media didn't exactly make it hard for them: Coverage of anti-Asian racism rarely if ever considered the unique dimensions of oppression Asian women face under white supremacy and patriarchy, nor how the majority of reported anti-Asian hate incidents victimized women.[19] Instead, coverage focused on sur-face-level complaints from more privileged Asians that could be made digestible to white people on social media. Incidents of violence were framed as "violent attacks against individuals without any discussion about structural oppression, settler colonialism, military imperialism, patriarchy, ableism—any of these things that help us to understand social injustice as intersectional," Fang told me. And as Huang noted to me, coverage of the #StopAsianHate movement problematically focused on Hollywood representation, or selectively fixated on "hate crimes" by Black and other people of color, perpetuating racist tropes about Black-Asian conflict and fueling harmful calls for more carceral responses.

Even after a fatal shooting in an Atlanta massage parlor perpetrated by a white man who called Asian women a sexual "temptation" in March 2021, legacy media coverage of anti-Asian racism often failed to contex-tualize the day-to-day, racialized misogyny Asian women face, and the routine violence that Asian sex workers or Asian people perceived to be sex workers experience. This resulted in a systemic failure to investigate the violent fetishization of Asian feminine identity—which can be traced back to hundreds of years of Western imperialism and the sexual enslave-ment of colonized Asian women by the US military—at a critical cultural moment, and how this has contributed to the victim-blaming and erasure of Asian sexual assault survivors.

When media coverage of anti-Asian racism neglects to interrogate the heightened oppressions Asian women and femmes face, this allows

MRAsians to harass us with little pushback. To them, Asian women are more powerful than Asian men in American society, specifically because of white men's famed fetishization. This fetishization is a compliment in their view; it's flattery, privilege, status. MRAsians erroneously "conflate being sexually desirable to someone with agency and power," Huang said, and consequently, the entire scope of what they perceive as anti-Asian oppression is that Asian women don't automatically sleep with them because they're Asian. Their grand calculus of determining oppression vs. privilege within their communities at no point considers the possibility that MRAsians are rejected by women because of their insufferable, abusive behaviors, rather than racial identity.

There are real and important ways that cisgender, straight Asian men and Asian men broadly are oppressed and wronged by white supremacy, which invalidates and punishes non-white expressions of masculinity and feminizes Asian men. The backlash against Lee and her relationship with a Black man was deeply rooted in anti-Blackness that's endemic among MRAsians, as well as many Asian communities in general. This anti-Blackness, in particular, Huang told me, comes at least in part from MRAsians' insecurities about their desirability under white supremacy. "They'll stereotype Black men as hypermasculine and aggressive, and more sexually desirable, and that's something they want," Huang said, citing extensive commentary in MRAsian Reddit threads and social media. "They'll tell themselves that the people who are perpetrating the most hatred toward Asians are Black people. They'll overall just ignore white supremacy as the actual root of any of this." White supremacy harms Asian men. But being racist toward other people of color, or verbally assaulting Asian feminists and Asian women with non-Asian partners, merely fractures the solidarity that's essential to dismantling dual white-supremacist and patriarchal oppressions. Backlash and militancy from MRAsians present just one, chilling example of how women of color experience targeted misogyny internally and externally from our communities, and digital culture exacerbates these threats. Often enough, we're left with nowhere and no one to turn to but each other.

CAN RAPE JOKES BE FUNNY?

The year 2022 marked one decade since white, male "comedian" Daniel Tosh directed a gang rape joke in his stand-up set at a female audience member after she told him rape jokes aren't funny.

"Wouldn't it be funny if that girl got raped by, like, five guys right now?" he "joked." What ensued was a one-dimensional, characteristically 2012 debate about rape jokes and the usual male hysteria about the "thought police"—2012's version of the "woke mob"—coming for men's sacred birthright to mock and degrade whoever they please without criticism for the sake of "comedy." As recently as the summer of 2021, *Saturday Night Live*'s Michael Che posted "jokes" mocking Olympic gymnast Simone Biles, a survivor of Larry Nassar, to his Instagram story and faced no consequences for this. Che's "jokes" reflected the worst and most reductive interpretation of comedy possible—the punchline of choice was a young, Black sexual assault victim.

To state the obvious, this is what traditional, sexist rape jokes are all about; their purpose is to embarrass and exert social power over rape victims. Embarrassment is a natural feeling and instinctive response to when someone degrades you or takes away your power. And it's precisely the intention of perpetrators of sexual harm to make their victims feel embarrassed to silence them. It's this embarrassment, this culture of stigma and shame, that's long protected abusers from any sort of accountability.

Despite "jokes" like Che's, since the reckoning of 2012, the discourse around rape jokes has become substantially more productive, as more comedians who are survivors have entered the fold with their own jokes. Enter: Kelly Bachman and Dylan Adler's two-person musical comedy show from 2021, *Rape Victims Are Horny Too*. I interviewed Bachman and Adler for Jezebel that year.

"We wanted to show survivors are not just, like, wilted flowers, who are sad, suffering, victims all the time," Bachman, a comedian and rape survivor, told me. "For Dylan and me, we're laughing. We're silly people, joyful people. And we're sort of defiantly joyful in the way we deal with our own pain."[20]

Before Bachman met and began working with Adler, a fellow survivor-comedian and musician, Bachman was one of several women comics who confronted Harvey Weinstein as he sat in the audience at a stand-up show in New York City in 2019. "I didn't know that we have to bring our own mace and rape whistles to Actor's Hour," she said of Weinstein while performing her set. Bachman, like other women who called out Weinstein's presence, was booed and told to "shut up" by some at the venue.

"Yes, we experienced trauma, we're still mourning, and that can make it confusing that we still have desires, want to be admired, but also not wanting to be pursued," Adler said of the duo's 2021 show. But for all these conflicting feelings and anxieties, survivors can still be and often are sexual beings, contrary to popular culture narratives that frame survivors as innately asexual.

"When I was getting raped four years ago—that's one leap year ago—I just kept thinking to myself the whole time, I can't wait to use this to get ahead in comedy! They're gonna see my name in lights, it's gonna be 'Victim,'" Bachman joked in a live show the duo performed in 2020. Rape culture and the objectively stupid idea that victims benefit from experiencing and talking about sexual violence are the object of the duo's comedy—*not* victims.

Adler told me he knew the show wasn't going to be for everyone. They'd reflected on the show's name for some time before ultimately landing on *Rape Victims Are Horny Too*, aware of the innately triggering nature of the word "rape." But they said it was important for them to be authentic to their experiences, and the experiences of many survivors who are told they weren't actually raped. "When Kelly and I were talking about the show, we had so many shared experiences and know how it feels when people say their rape was much worse, or when people try to gaslight and belittle your experience," he said. "We learned so many other survivors have felt that way too, and we had to put it in there, and just let people know what the show is about."

"Rape" can be a hard word to hear, as Bachman and Adler explore in their honest, no-holds-barred comedy. But as more media and institutions dilute people's experiences with rape and assault with more palatable, nebulous terms like "sexual misconduct" or even "harass-ment," the comics hope their show validates rape survivors by directly naming their experience.

"People a lot of times will kind of ask me if I'm a comedian because of trauma, and things like that, and no, actually. I'm funny because I'm funny," Bachman told me. A lot of survivors are funny, she added—but it's not because they're survivors. It's because that's who they are, before and after surviving rape. "Survivors aren't a monolith—a lot of survivors are queer, trans, lesbian, straight men, nonbinary people, gay men, people of all races," Adler said.

As their show ran throughout 2021 and returned in the summer of 2022, Adler and Bachman reflected on how the comedy space had become embroiled in a frustrating culture war over comedians like Dave Chappelle supposedly being censored or canceled for their bullying of marginalized people—particularly trans people—dressed, of course, as the noble art of comedy rather than bullying. But neither censorship nor cancelation was actually happening, here. "If people don't want to be offended, they shouldn't go to comedy clubs? Maybe," comedian and *Shrill* author Lindy West wrote for Jezebel in 2012. "But if you don't want people to react to your jokes, you shouldn't get on stage and tell your jokes to people."

In a comedy special called *Rape Jokes*, performed in 2018, comedian and survivor Cameron Esposito recounts the story of her own sexual assault, her life after it, and throws in jokes about how sexual assault is portrayed onscreen. "She's assaulted and then she becomes very good at swords," Esposito said. "That was not my experience. I stayed the same amount good at swords: expert." She also slammed male comics who have cried "censorship" when faced with backlash over their offensive "jokes" or behaviors. "That's the wrong word," Esposito said. "Feedback. You have gotten feedback."

Despite how comedy remains bogged down by the same infantile "censorship" and "free speech" debates that erupted in 2012 following Tosh's rape "joke," Bachman and Adler said they still see progress in how sexual violence has been treated in comedy and culture over the last decade. There is a deepening understanding that rape jokes that criticize unequal power dynamics, that prompt us to laugh at the ridiculousness of rape culture and demand change, can be funny. Rape jokes have historically been used to mock and consequently shame and silence victims through humiliation and domination—today, many comedians are survivors who are flipping the script.

Arguably the most reliable cultural bellwether that exists is comedy, collective understandings of what is and isn't culturally acceptable for society to laugh at. That the last decade has seen a shift in jokes being made at the expense of victims to jokes made at the expense of rape culture itself doesn't singlehandedly spell victory in the greater movement for survivor justice. But it is certainly cause for hope—perhaps even laughter.

9

SURVIVOR JUSTICE

In the previous chapter, I recounted an anecdote shared with me by Sage Carson, an organizer at Know Your IX who co-authored its 2021 report about the plight of student survivors. Carson herself is a survivor who reported her sexual assault to her school and was warned that she could face a defamation lawsuit and extensive retaliation if she pressed on. One survivor Carson interviewed had been assaulted in her freshman year of college, and although her assailant was found responsible by the school, he continued to terrorize her, filing a defamation lawsuit, accessing her medical records, and eventually forcing her to transfer schools, delay her graduation, and spend over $100,000 trying to protect herself from his attacks.

What does accountability mean for an assailant like this?

There is a misconception that supporting abolition and decarceration means being opposed to accountability. No victims' paths to healing will ever look entirely the same—but many would agree that repeated claims of innocence from their perpetrators, accusations that they are liars, prolonged and retraumatizing trials and adjudication, inflict greater harm on them. What many survivors are seeking is some form of apology and remedy, some acknowledgment from their perpetrator of the harm they've committed. But the threat of incarceration and a lifetime of punishment obviously has the impact of discouraging this outcome, if not rendering it altogether impossible.

Punishment for perpetrators can certainly, understandably bring satisfaction for both victims and their supporters. But as abolitionist scholar-activist Mariame Kaba has argued, personal anger and vendettas shouldn't be the driving force behind policymaking. "It's not wrong to feel what you feel—relief, or even happiness—when the system snaps up the powerful, but the only way to achieve real justice is to build it ourselves, outside of the system," Kaba has said. "Abolitionism is not a politics mediated by emotional responses."[1] State-rendered punishment for abusers also doesn't improve the material conditions of victims' lives; it doesn't provide them with mental health services or other health care, or address the economic ramifications of surviving abuse by compensating them in any way.

As the abolitionist writer Micah Herskind has written, "Our response to harm does not need to be either a cage or doing nothing at all, though these are generally the only options on offer from the state." Further, "punishment, consequences, and accountability are distinct categories." And while abolitionists oppose policies rooted in punishment—"the infliction of cruelty and suffering on people"—they "firmly believe in consequences (requirements for and demands made of those who have caused harm), which are determined in direct relationship to the harm in question," Herskind wrote. These processes involve all who were impacted by the harm in question to collectively determine steps toward accountability and call on the perpetrator to "[take] responsibility for harm caused and [work] toward repair and changed behavior."[2]

Anti-carceral scholars and advocates have put forth frameworks known as transformative justice and restorative justice to address and repair harm without further reproducing harm or relying on processes that retraumatize victims. Restorative justice brings together the victim, perpetrator, and the community without imposing the involvement of state actors or law enforcement. It centers the victim and their needs to heal and determines how the perpetrator can make amends as well as what needs to be done to ensure the community at large feels safe. Transformative justice is broader—it requires us to proactively work to change the social conditions and systemic inequities that cause harm to happen in the first place. "Transformative justice asks how we can respond to harm without creating more harm and transform the conditions that led to harm. A transformative justice framework rejects the victim-perpetrator binary in recognition that we all experience and cause harm," Herskind wrote. Restorative justice and transformative justice go hand in hand. They're rooted in an understanding that the carceral state is fundamentally unequipped to address issues of interpersonal violence and harm; instead it reproduces the conditions that lead to violence—the funding of prisons and policing at the expense of community resources—and disproportionately, deliberately targets people of color and marginalized people. As I've explored at length in this book, state violence and interpersonal violence are inseparable from each other—as a result, the state can never be a reliable arbiter to address interpersonal harm and violence.

In 2021 I spoke with L. Tomay Douglas, a restorative justice practitioner working for the Center for Restorative Justice at the University of San Diego, about her work to promote restorative justice practices on campus. Douglas believes a common misconception about restorative justice is that it's a "soft science" and gives perpetrators of harm an "easy out." Instead, she says, on some level, it can present an even greater challenge than carceral "solutions"—it forces perpetrators to reflect deeply, to sincerely acknowledge and reckon with the reality that they've harmed someone and must take meaningful steps to fix this. "That thinking—of restorative justice as 'soft'—is the result of a punitive mindset," Douglas said. "What [restorative justice] does is give agency to the survivor. It's the community coming together to heal itself, not including institutions and police that reproduce harm." Restorative justice is essential to create an environment where survivors of sexual harm can feel safe coming forward without fear of retraumatization, Douglas explained.

Marilyn Armour, director of the Institute for Restorative Justice and Restorative Dialogue at the University of Texas at Austin, School of Social Work, has also written on popular misconceptions about transformative and restorative justice. "Restorative justice views crime not as a depersonalized breaking of the law but as a wrong against another person," Armour wrote for Charter for Compassion, an international organization that advocates for and educates about restorative justice. "Accordingly, restorative justice seeks to elevate the role of crime victims and community members; hold offenders directly accountable to the people they have harmed; and restore, to the extent possible, the emotional and material losses of victims by providing a range of opportunities for dialogue, negotiation, and problem solving."[3]

Armour notes that in 1994 restorative justice "took a giant step toward becoming mainstream when the American Bar Association endorsed victim-offender mediation, a program usually associated with first-time offenders and minor crimes," and later when the United Nations, the Council of Europe, and the European Union all "committed to promote restorative practices."

Mainstream support for abolition has been steadily rising since the eruption of 2020's national and global racial justice protests, and it was at this time that many people were first exposed to terms like restorative and transformative justice. Yet clearly, as Armour explains, these frameworks have existed and received support from institutions as influential as the United Nations for decades. Leading American universities, including Stanford, Brown, Skidmore College, the Universities of Colorado, Michigan, Kentucky, and Vermont, have already experimented with methods shifting away from traditional, adversarial Title IX processes that can leave victims retraumatized and unsupported; some of these universities have claimed to embrace restorative justice models to address harm.

The American College Personnel Association has written of Title IX procedures: "Whether one is a fan of the Obama-era Title IX guidance or a critic, the debate about campus sexual assault has been narrowly framed in terms of an adversarial process that leaves only winners and losers, often ending with the 'winners' as just as miserable as the 'losers.'

Adjusting policy and procedure to tip slightly in favor of the complainant or the accused does not remove an intractable dynamic of secondary victimization, collective distrust, frustration, dissatisfaction, and professional burnout."[4] The American Bar Association 2017 Task Force on College Due Process Rights and Victim Protections explicitly called for a shift to restorative justice practices in response to endemic campus sexual assault.

Still, claiming support for restorative justice practices is one thing—actually providing this support is another. What does "restorative justice" in words mean when nearly all universities that have attempted to co-opt this term still fund and employ campus police officers, or contract with local police departments, inevitably causing survivors and particularly those of color to feel unsafe? Following the election of Joe Biden, survivor justice advocates including those at Know Your IX called for the new administration to go beyond merely reversing the Trump administration's harmful Title IX policies, which included allowing schools to avoid investigating off-campus assaults, and even allowing alleged assailants to cross-examine victims. As an anti-carceral organization, Know Your IX also called for the new administration to challenge policies that require universities to report sexual assaults to police, as well as remove police from campuses, and repeal mandatory-minimum and minimum-sanction policies that require punitive measures be taken against the assailant, consequently discouraging survivors from coming forward.

In 2021 another Know Your IX organizer, Emma Levine, told me the Biden administration could shape its Title IX policy around restorative justice principles by investing more funding toward community-based mediators to support campus sexual assault survivors. Mediators offer support through both formal adjudication processes and informal resolutions, pending what the survivor chooses. According to Levine, this investment could offer survivors a broader range of options to seek justice and healing in a way that feels comfortable and safe for them. "That really is a survivor-specific, situation-specific decision to make, whether they want to pursue a formal or informal adjudication process," Levine said, noting that the formal adjudication process for survivors facilitated by schools can sometimes render them vulnerable to retraumatization. Levine added that schools that claim to apply restorative and transformative justice principles shouldn't also have the aforementioned mandatory police referrals, police presence on campus, or mandatory minimum policies.

Douglas similarly emphasized that beyond casually throwing around terms like "restorative justice," schools need to put their money where their mouth is: Title IX officers at universities should partner with diverse student organizations to empower "the community to heal the community and sustain these partnerships with trainings, workshops, campaigns, and hiring processes on restorative justice." Survivor-centric language, alone, won't suffice.

College campuses are a prime example of spaces where communities can practice different restorative justice practices and work to address harm and abuse via community-based, anti-carceral approaches. Alexandra Brodsky explores the wide range of anti-carceral solutions to addressing interpersonal conflict and sexual misconduct in *Sexual Justice*. She argues that the perpetual framing of sexual violence as a criminal rather than civil issue has harmed victims of sexual violence for years, forever holding them to unattainable evidentiary standards, retraumatizing and subjecting them to the brutality of the criminal legal system. Recall, for example, the Ohio judge who in 2010 called for four teenage rape victims to be required to undergo polygraph tests, even though their attackers had already been found guilty; or the Illinois judge who in 2022 overturned an eighteen-year-old rapist's prison sentence and blamed the sixteen-year-old victim's parents for allowing her to attend a party with alcohol. These cases are prime examples of the harm and retaliation that victims often face in criminal courts that are designed to treat them as liars.

When sexual violence is exclusively understood as a criminal issue, this bolsters mainstream narratives that position victims who come forward as "accusers" trying to ruin innocent men's lives, rather than human beings who have been harmed and are merely seeking remedy. To that end, Brodsky advocates for broader understanding of sexual violence as a matter for civil litigation, which gives survivors the opportunity to seek damages that can materially improve their lives and holds them to the more reasonable "clear and convincing" civil evidentiary standard rather than the criminal "beyond a reasonable doubt" standard. Brodsky's research also spotlights how organizations and communities ranging from schools, churches, and workplaces to, say, video game fan communities and other interest groups and spaces, can adjudicate sexual misconduct allegations and more immediately protect victims than the slow-moving, punishing criminal system. Victims sometimes simply need distance from their abusers or assailants; employers and churches can easily enough call for the removal of abusive employees or members, at least for a certain amount of time, or facilitate necessary trainings and education to prevent future incidents.

One video game fan community that Brodsky highlights ruled that a member who had sexually harassed another member couldn't attend the annual convention for a designated period. "[Survivor justice] movements have always been doing a lot of work to talk about what justice means beyond punishment," Brodsky told me in 2022 for my reporting in Jezebel. "I've seen organizers increasingly focused on everything that schools can do to help survivors learn and thrive that have nothing, or very little, to do with punishment." This can entail simply "asking schools to offer survivors counseling, change their schedules so they don't have to see their harasser in the hallway, or provide tutoring to help a survivor catch up in a class that they missed in the wake of their assault," she said. "Title IX is an education civil rights statute—discipline is only one of many parts to realizing that vision."

Abolitionist, anti-carceral values, and the acknowledgment that everyone can grow, change, and redeem themselves, may mean that in some cases, the perpetrator can be given the opportunity to learn and do better. In other cases, to protect victims and other vulnerable members of a community, the perpetrator must give up their power, lose a leadership position they may hold, or leave the community altogether.

All victims and survivors have different needs and preferences for the processes, supports, and outcomes that will help them heal. Contrary to the arbitrary nature of the carceral system, which often yields racist impacts and criminalizes or retraumatizes sexual violence victims, our own communities are the safest and most reliable spaces to seek justice and support. Healing and solutions for sexual harm—or any interpersonal harm—aren't one-size-fits-all. We deserve to be cared for and supported by communities that have our safety and best interests at heart—not a criminal system that exists to dehumanize, surveil, and dole out punishment.

SURVIVOR JUSTICE WITHOUT STATE PUNISHMENT

Survivor justice has always relied on mutual aid, or community members pooling their resources and services to care for one another in the face of ongoing state failures and neglect. Abuse victims are often forced to rely on their communities and support systems to escape their abusers, which is a central reason that abusers focus so heavily on isolating victims from friends, family, and the outside world. Because the government fails to provide reliable access to shelter, money, health care, and other essential resources for low-income victims, mutual aid and community care have always been essential to victims' safety.

The state will not save us. It certainly won't save the same victims of gender-based violence that it subjugates and entraps in abusive situations via neoliberal policies and the threat of criminalization. Historically, few institutions have understood and exemplified this reality better than the Black Panther Party, which launched and continues to maintain community-based survival programs across the country that provide children with hot lunches, organize child care, maintain community gardens for fresh produce, and offer other vital, everyday resources. Their acts of community care reflect the reality that violent state neglect has never been race-neutral, purposefully targeting Black communities and other marginalized people who have little option but to respond by internally organizing.

Specific to mutual aid systems that support survivors, volunteers run national hotlines specifically to connect victims to local advocates and create individualized plans for them to get to safety. Volunteers ask victims what their individual needs are, help assess the threat level of one's abuser, sometimes come up with alibis and credible reasons to leave the house that account for the safety of victims' children, and determine where the victim can seek immediate shelter—sometimes from trusted volunteers—among other supports.

Filling gaps in the advocacy of national victim rights' organizations like RAINN, mutual aid networks like the Ahimsa Collective, formerly called MARJ, are funded and operated solely by community members. Ahmisa was founded in 2020 during the pandemic by Bay Area–based organizers "for anyone in need, with a focus on those impacted by violence and trauma, crime survivors, formerly incarcerated people, and those with incarcerated loved ones." There is, of course, significant overlap between gender-based violence survivors and incarcerated people. Ahmisa also offers community check-in circles and a locally run hotline for people experiencing sexual or domestic violence in real time.

In the face of repeated failures by the state to house and adequately support the most marginalized among us, and certainly, victims of domestic abuse, mutual aid and collective care have been a staple of the movement for survivor justice. As elected officials routinely fall short, and people of color and abuse victims remain excluded from voting and democracy, mutual aid makes up for the day-to-day critical gaps in direct services for victims.

Mutual aid is as simple as a neighbor delivering a hot meal when someone is too sick to get out of bed. It's buying groceries for someone who is struggling financially, staying up late talking with a friend in crisis, helping someone move, giving a neighbor a ride to the doctor. It can entail intervening in abusive situations to protect someone who is experiencing gender-based violence without involving law enforcement, or it can be helping someone whose abuser is trying to prevent them from voting make sure their ballot counted. The state is not fulfilling our massive, big-picture needs; it certainly isn't taking into consideration the everyday struggles of victims and survivors. That's what makes mutual aid so indispensable and powerful: its adaptability, its specificity, its lack of arbitrary, dehumanizing state-based evaluations of whether "need" for help is sufficient.

Abortion funds—locally run groups that fundraise to cover the wide range of costs for people seeking abortion care—exemplify the power of mutual aid. Before *Roe v. Wade* created a now-defunct federal right to abortion nearly fifty years ago, abortion funds like the underground Jane Collective helped community members with unwanted pregnancies safely get the abortion care they needed. After *Roe* was decided, the barriers to care remained massive, even with the legal right in place: 90 percent of US counties lacked abortion providers, while a handful of states had just one. Federal law prohibited public funding of most abortion care. Abortion funds have always existed to move mountains for people to be able to afford abortion procedures and medications, or the costs of travel, lodging, child care, and lost income from missing work to have the abortion. Across the country, the National Network of Abortion Funds' ninety-two member funds supported close to 200,000 callers seeking abortion care and dispersed $9,437,004 to callers between July 2019 and June 2020 alone.

One particular abortion fund, North Dakota's Women in Need (WIN) Fund, covers the costs of abortion care for survivors of sexual violence, emphasizing that the eradication of reproductive rights carries disproportionate harm for victims and survivors of abuse. Destini Spaeth, a volunteer at WIN Fund who used to work at an independent abortion clinic, told me in 2022 that well-funded, national anti-rape organizations have often fallen short at supporting access to reproductive care despite their tremendous resources, including state funding.

Spaeth explained she doesn't think "there's a lack of advocacy" around reproductive justice from these groups, so much as a "lack of education and knowledge" about the connections between issues of abortion access and gender-based violence. "I feel like if they understood what does happen when people are denied abortions—the repercussions from that in terms of domestic violence, people having to stay in unsafe homes— they would be a bit louder about reproductive rights." As I've previously noted, being denied a wanted abortion places someone at greater risk of long-term domestic violence; pregnant people are all too often killed by abusive partners who don't want them to be pregnant. When victims do birth a rapist or abuser's child, they may find themselves embroiled in years-long, retraumatizing custody battles, like Analyn Megison, or forced to co-parent with their rapist, like Darcy Benoit. Not to mention, forced pregnancy itself is an act of state gender-based violence that's all the more traumatic for those who have already survived sexual assault.

Instead of organizations like RAINN or the National Sexual Violence Resource Center, it's mutual aid groups like local abortion funds that survivors and victims find themselves turning to for urgently needed reproductive care. Mutual aid in support of abortion access is particularly important given the utter failures of electoral politics and federal lawmakers to take this issue seriously. Prior to the eventual overturning of *Roe*, for years Democratic politicians in Congress and the White House fundraised off the perpetual threat to abortion rights—to be able to fundraise off that threat, they needed it to exist, purposefully enabling it through each election cycle. As journalist Danielle Tcholakian pointed out in an essay in the spring of 2022, Democrats held almost total power on the federal level in the early years of the Obama era to federally codify *Roe*; they declined, and President Obama stated outright that abortion rights were "not a priority" for his administration in 2009. Tcholakian wrote:

> Democrats had the opportunity to codify Roe *years ago, and they've had the ability to scrap the filibuster in order to do it since then, and they've refused to, because it was more politically expedient to win votes by fear.* Vote for Democrats so Roe doesn't get overturned *was their preferred way, always the Democratic way. Why achieve new things, why take risks, why try, when you could just scare people away from a potential brighter future with the fear of a darker one? We won't do anything, but the other side will and it'll be bad, so please click this donation button and turn out to vote.*[5]

Indeed, within moments of *Roe* being overturned, we were told to simply vote to save ourselves. House Speaker Nancy Pelosi sent out a fundraising email within minutes of the decision. Democratic House Majority Whip

James Clyburn called the decision "anticlimactic," when, as majority whip, he *could* have been applying pressure to get his caucus to take meaningful, climactic action. Texas Rep. Henry Cuellar—a proud anti-abortion "Democrat" who continued to enjoy support from Pelosi and other top Democrats even when *Roe* fell—responded by reiterating he's "pro-life." President Biden doubled down on opposing calls to expand and balance the Supreme Court, and he refused to support eliminating the Senate filibuster, which was stopping Democrats from passing abortion rights legislation despite their majority.

For decades, anti-abortion lawmakers at every level of government have led a scorched-earth campaign to make abortion as inaccessible and stigmatized as possible across the country. Congress effectively banned abortion for poor people with the Hyde Amendment, and state legislatures have enacted over 1,300 bans and restrictions since 1973, when *Roe* was originally decided. For the most part, the Democratic Party responded to this strategy with impotent exploratory committees, strongly worded statements, and refusals to say the word "abortion." Shortly after *Roe* was overturned, the Democratic-controlled Senate Judiciary Committee announced it would "hold a hearing next month to explore the grim reality of a post-*Roe* America." In other words, pregnant people had been stripped of all rights and reduced to state-controlled incubators. But a polite discussion of that would simply have to wait for the Senate to return from summer recess.

At the risk of sounding controversial, voting is good. In fact, organizing and voting—in addition to voter suppression, gerrymandering, and an overall highly undemocratic political system—are how the anti-abortion movement pulled off *Roe*'s fall in the first place. But given Democratic leaders' immediate responses to the fall of *Roe*, it was clear from the start that they had no tangible plan to save our reproductive rights. Our rights cannot just be a fundraising ploy for powerful elites. We should continue to vote, but also question how the same "allies" in federal office who did virtually nothing to prevent this outcome consistently tell us that voting for them is the only solution—particularly in a country where voter suppression and white-supremacist minority rule are so deeply institutionalized. The least politicians can do, if they're so determined to do nothing but issue platitudes, is say the word "abortion" out loud rather than rely on euphemisms that further perpetuate stigma by implying abortion is too undignified a word to speak.

In the last several decades, there simply hasn't been a credible opposition party to anti-abortion Republicans on the federal level—but I emphasize federal level, because voting and organizing on the local and state level can be transformative. As previously noted, even with *Roe* in place for nearly fifty years, instead of looking to the government and elections for saviors, people seeking abortion care have long created solutions within their own communities: abortion funds, which meet the unique needs of the localities they serve. And these funds have sometimes worked with municipal governments to create public city abortion funds, like we've seen in Austin, Portland, and New York.

In the immediate aftermath of *Roe* being overturned, as well as the weeks and months leading up to it, states with Democratic-majority legislatures got to work, demonstrating the power and exponentially greater responsibility of local and state-level lawmakers to protect reproductive rights. California passed legislation to expand who's eligible to offer abortion care and cover more costs of abortion for California and out-of-state residents under the state's MediCal program. Connecticut passed legislation to protect people who travel out of state for abortion from criminalization. Vermont—along with California and Michigan—created a ballot measure to enshrine the right to abortion in the state constitution. Massachusetts introduced legislation to provide access to medication abortion in state universities' health centers. Portland, Oregon, which had recently established a public abortion fund in the city, also became one of three cities in the US at the time to offer paid leave to those who have abortions.

And state attorneys general hold tremendous power to prevent the prosecution of pregnancy loss or abortion by issuing directives to local law enforcement. Pregnancy and abortion criminalization are often a highly localized issue determined by individual police departments, which have free rein to misapply fetal homicide laws to criminalize pregnant people. State legislators, particularly in states with Democratic majorities in the legislature, are also taking action to protect pregnant people from crim-inalization in post-*Roe* America. In California's legislature, for example, Assemblymember Buffy Wicks introduced a bill in 2022 to explicitly decriminalize pregnancy loss and self-managed abortion, which aren't crimes in the first place.

For better and worse, local-level policymaking is powerful—while cities are voting to publicly fund abortion, other cities are electing coun-cil members who have voted to make their cities "sanctuary cities for the unborn," where abortion is outlawed. By the end of 2021, the *Guardian* reported, nearly thirty cities had voted to outlaw abortion. After the fall of *Roe*, several abortion clinics in states where abortion was banned planned to move their clinics to operate in border towns near impacted states; in November 2022 city council members in two conservative border towns in New Mexico close to Texas voted to become sanctuary cities, ahead of one abortion clinic's planned move there.

Federal-level politics are entirely worthy of scorn and cynicism—but vote if for no other reason than to complete the local- and state-level por-tions of your ballot.

None of this is to say federal rights aren't important. It's impossible to overstate just *how* important legislation to guarantee a federal right to abortion and federal decriminalization of pregnancy outcomes are. But for years now, on the federal level, we've instead witnessed massive, sys-temic failure to protect reproductive rights, and failure to protect abuse victims and survivors, rendering them vulnerable to forced pregnancy. As a result, survivor justice and reproductive justice require us to orga-nize our communities and fight for our own reproductive rights—by any means necessary.

In the absence of *Roe v. Wade*, the responsibility to protect abortion rights has expanded beyond the state and local level, inevitably bleed-ing into the private sector. You'll recall that shortly after the Supreme Court overturned *Roe*, companies across the country including Disney, Netflix, Paramount, Meta, Nike, AT&T, and even Dick's Sporting Goods announced widely praised moves to cover employees' costs of abortion and out-of-state travel to access the procedure. Other companies, including Yelp, Citibank, Starbucks, and Amazon, made similar moves even before the decision, while Lyft and Uber said they would cover legal fees for drivers in Texas and other states if they're hit with costly lawsuits for driving someone to get an abortion because of SB 8.

But no one should have to ask their boss for an abortion. It's incredibly bleak that access to care could ever depend on your employer, at all, or whether you have the privilege of employer-provided health insurance. Those who are most impacted by abortion bans are also the most likely to be unemployed, underemployed, or lower paid, likely lacking paid time off or insurance to cover abortion-related costs. Privatized "solutions" like this will just worsen the inequities in who can and can't afford abortion.

These abortion coverage policies would be rendered irrelevant altogether if some of these companies hadn't donated hundreds of thousands of dollars to anti-abortion politicians who paved the way for the fall of *Roe*. Public records show Yelp, Citigroup, Uber, and Lyft alone have donated hundreds of thousands to Republican politicians ranging from former President Donald Trump—who appointed three of the nine Supreme Court justices in one term—to the National Republican Senatorial Committee and the National Republican Congressional Committee in recent election cycles. Prior to Disney's spring 2022 announcement that it would no longer donate to any politicians, it donated $452,650 to anti-abortion politicians in 2020 alone; that same year, Nike donated $267,633 and AT&T donated a whopping $4,992,266 to anti-abortion politicians, according to the women's rights watchdog UltraViolet.[6]

As previously noted, Meta's social platforms, Facebook and Instagram, were exposed for helping anti-abortion crisis pregnancy centers collect the personal data of people seeking abortion care, which could be used against them in criminal proceedings, just weeks before *Roe* was overturned. In May 2022 a Meta executive specifically instructed employees to not talk about abortion on Workplace, its internal company chat and task management system. Months later, after *Roe* fell, the company handed over a Nebraska teen's text communications and other data to law enforcement, who arrested and criminalized the teen for a self-managed abortion.

None of this is to say employers and corporations shouldn't be covering abortion care and associated costs for their employees—but if they really want to help address the national abortion crisis and its disproportionate impacts on low-income people of color, they could start by donating to abortion funds. In doing so, they could ensure they're helping more people access care than just members of the professional managerial class under their employ. At the very least, corporations could expand whose abortion-related costs they cover to include not just employees with health insurance but also lower-wage employees and their family members and dependents.

In the absence of *Roe*, corporations hold more power over our reproductive rights and ability to get reproductive care than ever. Companies like Meta and Google have the resources and power to determine whether an abuse victim whose abuser is stalking, suing, or trying to incriminate them for getting an abortion can access damning evidence to punish their victim. It's not just lawmakers—our advocacy and public pressure campaigns increasingly must be applied to the private sector, too.

We've already seen that these campaigns can be successful.

Weeks before *Roe* was overturned, Democratic members of Congress including Reps. Alexandria Ocasio-Cortez and Ayanna Pressley and Sens. Bernie Sanders and Elizabeth Warren wrote a letter addressed to Google, urging the company to cease collecting and storing location data of abortion patients, as this can contribute to the threat of pregnancy criminalization: "We are concerned that, in a world in which abortion could be made illegal, Google's current practice of collecting and retaining extensive records of cell phone location data will allow it to become a tool for far-right extremists looking to crack down on people seeking reproductive health care."

The letter also noted that while the company collects customer data for "various business purposes" such as targeted ads, this data is also routinely used by law enforcement officials, who "obtain court orders forcing Google to turn over its customers' location information." The

Democrats cited data published by Google that found one-quarter of the law enforcement orders the company receives each year are for location data through geofence warrants (11,554 such warrants in 2020 alone). "If abortion is made illegal by the far-right Supreme Court and Republican lawmakers, it is inevitable that right-wing prosecutors will obtain legal warrants to hunt down, prosecute and jail women for obtaining critical reproductive health care," the letter states. "The only way to protect your customers' location data from such outrageous government surveillance is to not keep it in the first place."

They were right: As I've previously reported, online search history and location data have long been used to target and surveil pregnant people and those seeking abortion care. When the reversal of *Roe* opened the door for states to reduce pregnant people's bodies to literal crime scenes, it also increased the likelihood of these cases. Reporting from around when *Roe* was overturned revealed that you could purchase the extensive location data of individuals who had just visited abortion clinics for as little as $160 from a private data company—just imagine what abusive partners and law enforcement, two sides of the same coin, can do with this easily accessible information.

For years, Google allowed itself to be complicit in the possible criminalization of abortion and pregnancy loss. It wasn't until rigorous reporting, public outcry, and consequently pushes from lawmakers that the company finally announced changes in July 2022: Going forward, the company said, it would automatically delete location data of users who visit medical facilities like abortion clinics, fertility centers, domestic violence shelters, counseling centers, and other sensitive locations. It wasn't a perfect promise. Google didn't go into detail about how it would respond to future requests for information from law enforcement, offering the vague promise that it would "continue to oppose demands that are overly broad or otherwise legally objectionable." Further, the company continues to bolster anti-abortion surveillance through its search engine and Maps app, which widely promote anti-abortion "crisis pregnancy centers"—nearly half of search results for "abortion" on Google Maps in abortion-hostile states direct people to fake clinics, whose websites collect and store their personal data. Nonetheless, Google's pledge was a start, born of aggressive activism and movement journalism. The company's enduring shortcomings are a reminder that neither the state nor corporations will save us: We will.

Where abortion funds offer direct support to people seeking abortion care, If/When/How's Repro Legal Defense Fund (RLDF) and Pregnancy Justice offer direct support to people in need of legal representation when faced with criminal charges for their pregnancy outcomes. RLDF covers the costs of bail and legal representation for people who are being investigated or have been arrested and prosecuted for self-managed abortion. The organization also connects people to expert legal representation and trains attorneys to handle pregnancy criminalization cases, and offers expert witnesses to people who are being prosecuted. Further, it tracks and holds law enforcement agencies accountable for targeting pregnant people. Without *Roe*, RLDF director Rafa Kidvai told me, "we're going to see a lot more cases" of pregnancy criminalization as well as a "culture of fear that's out of control for pregnant people," rendering the work of her organization especially vital—and especially in need of monetary support.

Pregnancy Justice's legal advocacy for pregnant people facing criminal charges or investigation for their pregnancy outcomes includes direct representation of clients; connecting pregnant people to pro bono experts; offering advice and model briefs to lawyers; and conducting research and drafting court papers. The group also works extensively with medical and public health experts to educate the public and lawmakers about the rising threat of pregnancy criminalization.

In April 2022, shortly after Lizelle Herrera was briefly jailed in Texas, charged with homicide for allegedly self-managing an abortion, I wrote a detailed guide on how pregnant and pregnant-capable people can protect ourselves from being investigated and criminalized for our abortions and pregnancy outcomes.[7] In writing the guide, I emphasized in the strongest terms that no one is ever to blame for losing their pregnancy—an experience that can be traumatic enough in its own right, without criminalization. Additionally, no one should be victim-blamed for facing criminal charges for this experience. But there are crucial steps we can take to minimize our risk of criminalization and arrest at this increasingly dangerous time for pregnant people in the US—and it's vitally important for us to not just educate ourselves but also share knowledge and resources within our communities.

The list of reasons pregnant people have faced arrest is endless: surviving violence that results in miscarriage, experiencing stillbirth and "improperly" disposing of fetal remains, or even having a home birth with complications. The medical system has always colluded with law enforcement to police pregnant people—nonconsensual drug testing of pregnant patients is rampant and has consistently discouraged people with substance use struggles from seeking essential prenatal care. As I've previously mentioned, reporting from doctors, social workers, and acquaintances is the primary means through which pregnancy loss and abortion come to the attention of law enforcement. Community members need to be educated about the pivotal role they play in preventing carceral outcomes for pregnant people.

The following is a brief recap of my guide:

- **Minimize your digital footprint when searching for information about abortion:** Use public computers at the library, or virtual private networks (VPNs) on your personal devices. Use encrypted messaging apps like Signal or Google Voice to contact medical experts with questions about self-managed abortion and miscarriage. Any other communications can be obtained and cited as criminal evidence.

- **Know how to use abortion pills:** Medication abortion pills are highly safe and effective to end a pregnancy, but it's crucial to follow all instructions when using them to minimize risk of complications that could possibly require an emergency room visit and consequent exposure to doctors and law enforcement. Additionally, take the pills orally instead of inserting them in the vagina, as they can leave residue in the vagina that can appear during a pelvic exam or other medical exams. Groups like Women on Web, Planned Parenthood, Reproaction, Shout Your Abortion, and Plan C Pills offer detailed step-by-step guides to obtain and safely take the pills.

- **Avoid risk of contact with anti-abortion doctors:** In the event of complications or confusion related to a self-managed abortion or miscarriage, turn to pro-abortion medical experts at groups like the M+A Hotline or Plan C Pills for medical advice.

- **Don't incriminate yourself:** Know that if police officers ask for your phone or other evidence that could be used against you, you have the right to refuse.

Donate to legal defense funds for pregnant people. Apply pressure to state-level lawmakers and state attorneys general to decriminalize abortion and pregnancy loss. Know your rights and the best practices to protect yourself from pregnancy-related state surveillance and punishment. Ensure that others know their rights, too.

The state doesn't exist to serve victims and survivors or pregnant people, who are all too often the same people. Law enforcement, criminal courts, and prisons won't save us. Brands and corporations won't save us. Liberal politicians won't save us. We have only ourselves and our communities to rely on for safety, accountability, resources, knowledge, and support. And that's plenty.

10

ANOTHER WORLD

Throughout the early 2020s, the 1990s suddenly made a triumphant comeback. In addition to bell-bottoms, graphic tees, and every other iconic fashion staple, there was the 2021 limited series *Impeachment: American Crime Story*, which took us back to the 1998 impeachment of President Bill Clinton. This portrayal of the landmark moment in American history was fundamentally modern in its multilayered character explorations of the women who helped screw over former White House intern Monica Lewinsky. One of those women is Susan Carpenter-McMillan, president of the conservative Women's Coalition; advisor to Paula Jones, whose testimony alleging Clinton had harassed her would spark his impeachment; and—you guessed it—a leading anti-abortion activist. She tells Paula in the second episode of *Impeachment*, "People get confused when I tell them I'm a conservative feminist. But you don't have to be a lesbian or an abortionist to believe a woman deserves equal respect to a man."

The line is haunting in its present-day relevance: Where, historically, the anti-abortion movement railed against feminism, it's more recently rebranded via shifts in language and leadership to embrace feminism, desperate to court young people and exploit their well-documented affinity for social justice. Phyllis Schlafly, the face of the conservative women's movement to defeat the Equal Rights Amendment by arguing it would allow women to leave their houses and get abortions, spent the last decades until her 2016 death accusing feminism of making women "unhappy." Fast-forward to today, as leading anti-abortion activists, like the on-screen Carpenter-McMillan, are increasingly women who have learned to brand themselves as the "real" feminists.

Shortly after the Supreme Court heard oral arguments for *Dobbs v. Jackson Women's Health*—the case that would end *Roe*—in 2021, the *New York Times* published an op-ed by an anti-abortion author and priest titled "Why the Feminist Movement Needs Pro-Life People." The Lily published a controversial profile of the notably female attorney general of Mississippi, who litigated *Jackson* to overturn *Roe*, and suggested her gender necessarily made this fight a feminist undertaking. A separate *Washington Post* article headline from the fall of 2021 reads "The New Face of the Antiabortion Movement Is a Young Mom of Six Who Listens to Lizzo"—this headline laughably obscured how the "young mom of six" in question was trying to take the R&B artist's reproductive rights away. And in the summer of 2021, a "feminist" author and Catholic scholar published a whole book that attempts to make the case for "pro-life feminism." All these sentiments echo a 2018 radio segment in which the president of the anti-abortion group Human Coalition assured listeners that someday we'd all look back and recognize the "original feminists were pro-life."

"Pro-life feminism" has increasingly become a fixture in electoral politics, too. In 2016 Republican presidential candidate Carly Fiorina branded herself as pro-women while fanatically claiming she had witnessed video proof of Planned Parenthood "harvesting" aborted fetuses' brains." (Sure, Jan.) Throughout her father's presidency, Ivanka Trump appointed herself the White House women's rights czar and simultaneously, aggressively stumped for female anti-abortion politicians throughout the Trump presidency. In the wake of Texas's SB 8 abortion ban in 2021, former Republican vice presidential nominee Sarah Palin called herself the "real feminist," compared to fake feminists like Rep. Alexandria Ocasio-Cortez, who "milk the whole female thing" with their support for reproductive rights and sexual assault survivors.

In reality, "pro-life feminism" is a misnomer—the two ideologies are mutually exclusive. The phrase makes as much sense as a nightmarish *1984* tagline to the effect of 2+2=5. Contrary to the increasingly commercialized, depoliticized sentiments of conservative and many liberal strains of feminism that regard women wearing power suits and running exploitative corporations as "feminist," feminism is a set of actual values to advance gender and social justice rather than anything an individual woman says or does. And believe it or not, forcing women and pregnant people to give birth against their will, criminalizing people for their pregnancy outcomes including abortion, and consequently placing pregnant people at greater risk of domestic violence and maternal death, all fall squarely in the anti-feminist category.

"Anything that might compromise our abilities to make our own choices that are best for us is simply contrary to feminism," Kwajelyn Jackson, executive director of the Feminist Women's Health Center in Atlanta, told me in 2022. Her reproductive health clinic, which provided abortion services prior to Georgia's statewide, post-*Roe* abortion ban, is part of a nationwide network that was founded in the 1970s when feminist organizers "became interested in developing health centers and spaces where women could have the autonomy and authority to direct their own health care and fix the ways paternalism and patriarchy have existed in traditional health systems," she said.

"At my clinic, we've always said we want people to have a multitude of choices, and we don't want people to be limited in the options they have available to them," Jackson continued. "We're supporting people in their pregnancies, whether they're wanted and planned or unintended, to have all the resources they need to deliver safely, to have a healthy community to raise children. But abortion cannot be off the table if we're going to have real feminist spaces." In other words, even if anti-abortion activists did support a robust social safety net (they very much do not), the availability of abortion remains essential to the dignity and safety of pregnant people, regardless of any other resources they're offered. In reality, they advocate abortion bans to force poor people to give birth and remain trapped in poverty.

In 2018 at the height of MeToo, Republican and Democratic women senators unanimously backed an effort to crack down on Congressional sexual harassment. At the time, it seemed like a unifying, special moment. On the surface, liberal and conservative so-called feminists alike purported to care about sexual harassment. But when feminism is a branding moniker rather than an ideology for gender justice, its stated values are seldom ever enforced. Instead, political opportunists of all genders, and across the ideological spectrum, selectively target and hold accountable some alleged abusers but not others, pending their politics. Women leaders across both parties have unabashedly stood by men in their respective parties who are credibly accused of abuse—as have numerous, vocal "feminist" celebrities who placed themselves front and center in the celebrity MeToo movement, only to stand by the likes of Johnny Depp, Woody Allen, Elon Musk (accused of a 2016 sexual assault in 2022), and President Joe Biden, all accused of sexual misconduct.

This, of course, brings us back to Carpenter-McMillan. Perhaps she was right to take action against Bill Clinton, but she was transparently motivated by her aspirations to end legal abortion, not help sexual harassment victims. Her unflinching opportunism in *Impeachment* is emblematic of conservative "feminism" as a whole. Beneath layers of shallow empowerment rhetoric, conservative "feminism" is really just conservatism—specifically, conservatism that implores women to happily give up their rights rather than have them forcefully seized.

We can only begin to eradicate our rape culture and address the interpersonal and institutionalized systems of state violence that enact harm on women, victims, and especially women and victims of color, by placing our greatest focus on those with the least resources and social capital—not charismatic women politicians, nor wealthy celebrity feminists. Mind you, in 2019 Alyssa Milano's proposed solution to the wave of state-level abortion bans sweeping the country was a women-led sex strike—as if sex is solely for the enjoyment of cis men and not women, which is a line of thinking that inevitably contributes to the passage of abortion bans by implying women only have sex to procreate. Milano and women like her shouldn't be the face of liberatory feminist movements. The liberation of those with the least privilege and resources means liberation for all; nothing less can be accepted in any movement or space that purports to advance feminist values.

Nancy Fraser, a co-author of the 2019 anti-capitalist, feminist manifesto *Feminism for the 99%*, once spoke to *Jacobin* about the importance of understanding MeToo as a labor struggle that centers the poor and the most marginalized:

> *The public image of this movement [#MeToo] is focused on Hollywood, highly paid actresses, entertainers, the media, and so on. But the broad mass of much less privileged women is even more vulnerable to sexual assault and harassment at work. . . . The #MeToo movement, if you think about it more broadly, is a labor struggle. It's a struggle for a safe workplace where you are not subject to abuse. That the media focuses only on the top tier is unfortunate, for it makes it look like it's not a class struggle.*[1]

Survivor justice isn't survivor justice, at all, if it's won only for a narrow sect of the wealthiest, most powerful women. We can't orient this movement around exacting vengeance on a small handful of individual, terrible men who hurt wealthy, famous women—we need guarantees of safety, resources, and liberation for all.

In 2021 I had the opportunity to speak to author, activist, scholar, and domestic violence survivor Rafia Zakaria about her book *Against White Feminism* and increasingly hollow, depoliticized strains of modern feminism, for an article in Salon. Throughout the book, Zakaria analyzes the historical ties between white women–led suffrage and imperialism, the dangers of global philanthropy that doesn't seek input from its supposed beneficiaries in formerly colonized countries, and the opportunism of white women who have installed themselves as the saviors of women in Southwest Asian and North African countries by advocating military action. She calls on Western readers to interrogate everyday norms, like why we normalize and define certain cultural crimes as "honor killings" while treating frequent, white-perpetrated intimate partner violence as an aberration in the Western world.

"The whole project of the book was essentially to put the fangs back in feminism. By that I mean very pointedly reinvigorating feminism as a political movement, and not just as any choice that any woman makes," Zakaria told me. "I don't believe in choice feminism, I don't believe all choices women make are somehow right and feminist because a woman made them."

Zakaria's words—on the importance of putting "fangs back in feminism"—resonated deeply with me, particularly as I was working on this book at the time. True political empowerment for the most marginalized victims of abuse becomes possible when we understand and respect them as a collective and inherently political demographic. The interpersonal violence they face can no longer be dismissed as intimate, as private, as personal and therefore apolitical, but rather, inextricably, irrevocably connected to institutionalized state oppression.

To respect victims' and survivors' collective humanity requires us to respect their nuanced needs to experience justice and healing, not write them off as a singular, hapless unit in need of one-size-fits-all, carceral solutions. And more than that, survivor justice requires us to build another world altogether where victims and survivors can experience meaningful political power—a world where they are safe and free from criminalization, from the violence of poverty, economic disenfranchisement, and sexual and reproductive coercion; a world where they're free to vote, free to organize, and free to not just participate in but actively shape democracy.

Abolitionist scholar-activist Ruth Wilson Gilmore often says that abolition is a place, a *physical* place—that is, it's a set of material conditions, not platitudes and niceties from ultra-rich politicians. "'Freedom is a place' means we combine resources, ingenuity, and commitment to produce the conditions in which life is precious for all," Gilmore told me in a conversation about her 2022 book *Abolition Geography*. "So, no matter the struggle, freedom is happening somewhere. Through different forces and relations to power, the people are constantly figuring out how to shift, how to build, how to consolidate the capacity for people to flourish, to mobilize our communities, and stay in motion until satisfied."[2]

Freedom is, indeed, happening somewhere. Even as millions remain caged and entrapped within the prison system, many of them victims of jarring state and interpersonal gender-based violence, activists are continually rising up and organizing their communities to free them. Survived and Punished, an abolitionist collective mentioned earlier, "focuses on criminalized survivors to raise awareness about the integrated relationship between systems of punishment and the pervasiveness of gender violence," its website states. The collective, which has chapters in New York, California, and Chicago, "aims to initiate mass defense projects that will free all survivors, which would require the abolition of prisons and other systems of punishment." It asserts that "prisons, detention centers, all forms of law enforcement, and punitive prosecution are rooted in systems of violence, including racial, anti-trans/queer, sexual, and domestic violence."

Survived and Punished began as a campaign to free Marissa Alexander, a Black woman who was criminalized and jailed after she let out a warning shot when her abusive husband threatened to kill her in 2010, as well as several other women and survivors of color who faced criminalization as a direct result of the abuse they experienced. As this book has detailed at length, this is by no means an uncommon experience. Interpersonal gender-based violence and state-sanctioned gender-based violence—what the abolitionist group Sisters Inside calls "state sexual assault"—are all too often conjoined forces of oppression.

There's always more work to be done, but groups like Survived and Punished and other community organizers have experienced exciting success in recent years: Cyntoia Brown, imprisoned for over a decade for killing her abuser in self-defense as a teen, had her sentence commuted by Tennessee's Republican governor in 2019. Teresa Paulinkonis had her sentence commuted by California Gov. Gavin Newsom in 2020 after spending thirty-one years in prison for killing her abusive stepfather in 1989, also in self-defense. In April 2022 the state of Texas halted Melissa Lucio's impending execution, after advocates stressed for years that police had coerced her to falsely confess to her daughter's killing, when Lucio was an abuse victim herself.

Nonetheless, as abolitionist Mariame Kaba has pointed out, win-lose binaries are counterproductive in liberatory organizing: "Often when we engage in campaigns, we lose. But any organizer worth their salt knows that it's much more complex than a simple win-loss calculus," she wrote in an essay in *We Do This 'Til We Free Us*.[3] Instead, Kaba calls on us to consider whether we mobilized new people, built solidarity, and raised political consciousness, whether we resisted the status quo and learned new lessons for future fights.

Survived and Punished is clear-eyed about the reality that only complete overhaul of the criminal legal system and carceral police state could ever free the most vulnerable survivors and victims. This is precisely why organizers and advocates strive toward abolition, freeing as many incarcerated survivors as possible in the meantime, and reject the idea of freeing only particularly sympathetic incarcerated people within a fundamentally white-supremacist society. The group identifies this as the "politics of exceptionalism" on its website:

> The "politics of exceptionalism" occurs when people advocate for the freedom of an individual only because they are considered exceptional to other imprisoned people—for example, the perfect survivor, the perfect immigrant, etc. S&P does not get down like that. When we support individual defense campaigns, or when we call for the freedom of "survivors" in particular, we promote a "politics of relationality," or strategies that help people engage the broader crisis of criminalization, and help create a public context for others to talk about their own experiences of surviving violence and being punished for that survival.[4]

Building a new world for victims and survivors of abuse to experience safety and thrive requires an end to the "politics of exceptionalism," an end to fighting only for the liberation of the most traditionally respectable victims. Further, it requires us to rethink who we center in feminist movements broadly, to reject capitalist "feminisms" that individualize success, failure, and, consequently, victimhood.

In her 2020 essay "The End of the Girlboss Is Here," author Leigh Stein critiques how corporate, "girlboss" feminism has presented "gender disparities . . . as a war to be fought on a personal level," and how the rise and glorification of women-led, supposedly feminist companies and corporations is a direct consequence of the erosion of public trust in the state to fulfill its duties to the most vulnerable. "The rise and fall of the girlboss is about how comfortable we've become mixing capitalism with social justice. We looked to corporations to implement social changes because we lost faith in our public institutions to do so," Stein wrote. She continued:

> *Until this country is willing to reckon with its extraordinary wealth inequality, and our government requires corporations to pay their fair share in taxes, we will continue to see reincarnations of the girlboss because she's a manifestation of the American myth that says if you're not succeeding, it must be because you're not trying hard enough.*[5]

In the US there is greater profit incentive to criminalize, incarcerate, and exploit victims of abuse than to protect, house, and provide them with material supports to live with dignity. Capitalism is fundamentally incompatible with survivor justice and a politically conscious feminist movement that doesn't center around notions of "choice" and celebrity. In a society like this, where health care, shelter, and dignified wages aren't human rights, the state all but forces the most marginalized—women and femmes of color, undocumented people, queer and trans people, sex workers, and all who struggle to make ends meet—who are struggling with abuse to remain in violent or exploitative relationships, whether with partners or employers, and remain reliant on them or lose access to the basic resources they need to live.

The crisis of our rape culture, and the punitive violence enacted on victims by our electoral system and capitalist police state simultaneously, will never be solved exclusively by those of us who are trying to survive these conditions. Rape culture and violence against women pervade—within our homes, our communities, the mass media we consume. Only solidarity, mass movements, and collective action, especially from those with more privilege, can bring about the necessary change in our culture and politics. This transformation of our society must begin with all of us imagining and building toward another world from the bottom up.

Interpersonal violence is inextricably bound to the routine violence executed by a state that empowers individuals and corporations to amass unthinkable amounts of wealth through exploitation and theft, and hoard this wealth, while the most vulnerable among us, and certainly victims of sexual and domestic abuse, are purposefully neglected. Survivor justice necessitates massive wealth redistribution and publicly funded health care, housing, livable universal basic income, dignified wages, education, and child care. It necessitates sweeping policy changes to guarantee abortion and reproductive health care access for all; decriminalization of pregnancy and abortion; comprehensive, LGBTQ-inclusive, and consent-based sexual health education; decriminalization of sex work; decriminalization of self-defense by victims of abuse; and the total dismantling of the carceral, capitalist police state that criminalizes rather than protects the most vulnerable.

The inability of many victims of abuse to vote, participate in democracy, and practice political autonomy means that too many of them are unable to play a role in changing their political realities and changing the electoral and policy landscapes that have entrapped them in cycles of dehumanization and abuse. That's why mutual aid and community care play an indispensable and immediate role in meeting victims' needs and helping support them financially, as we simultaneously organize toward systemic change that politically empowers and offers them safety and security.

The personal is the political. This foundational rallying cry of the feminist movement first emerged in the 1960s, and it remains prescient and valuable to this day, in a society where our bodies, health, lives— even our innermost thoughts and desires for ourselves—are shaped and controlled by politics and the state, all while abuse and interpersonal violence remain treated as separable from public policy and democracy. Our home lives and relationships are inextricably shaped by public policy, and simultaneously, our domestic situations impact our ability to fully participate in society and change our lives and political representation.

To state that the personal is the political also necessarily acknowledges that a wide variety of lived experiences shape and forge our political standings. This is contrary to monolithic thinking about what abuse entails, and, perhaps more importantly, monolithic thinking about who victims are. About who people who have abortions are. About who people who struggle under capitalist, carceral patriarchy are. Reductive, victim-blaming thinking inevitably leads to dehumanizing narratives, which then lead to dehumanizing policies.

The overturning of *Roe* in the summer of 2022 marked about one year since I had interviewed a handful of people of faith who have had abortions about how their conceptions of religion guided them to seek abortion care for a Salon article. CoWanda Rusk was weeks away from graduating from her Texas high school, preparing for college, and in the midst of an abusive relationship when she learned she was pregnant, and she immediately got "on the floor and started praying" the moment after her pregnancy test was positive. "I know God was with me in all of those moments, and I know I had the love and support and the guidance of something bigger than myself," she told me. When Rusk heard Pope Francis's message in 2016 that people who had abortions should be forgiven, she told me she "cringed."

"Forgiveness happens on a personal level," she said. "I absolutely do not agree with needing forgiveness from God nor other people for making a decision to take care of yourself. That is the most ridiculous thing, the most shaming thing. You did nothing wrong by accessing health care." If anything, Rusk told me, "Religious leaders should be asking for your forgiveness for not using their powers to make sure people have access to basic needs and health care."

In contrast with Rusk's experience, Tohan, another Christian woman I spoke with, told me her decision to have an abortion "was very personal— nothing to do with religion." People who have abortions don't exist within simplistic binaries about religion and opposition to religion; even those who are people of faith and have sought abortion care conceive of their experiences in different ways. This is just one, singular example of how groups who are often forced to take center stage in conversations about their oppression are infinitely more human than these conversations allow them to be.

Our identities aren't neat talking points and props for politicians who are ultimately more interested in being reelected than helping us. Identity is messy, and even messier when it's a composite of seemingly vastly conflicting experiences and positions. My own identity provides an imperfect glimpse of this: As an Asian American woman and daughter of immigrants navigating a time of rising violence targeting Asian communities and particularly Asian women and femmes, I'm horrified by continual efforts from lawmakers to weaponize this trauma to advance the carceral state, via insidious hate-crime legislation that further invests both public resources and public faith in policing. As a matter of personal preference, I avoid publicly or even privately speaking about my experience with abortion care but adore campaigns like Shout Your Abortion to destigmatize this vital, necessary health service by proudly sharing the full range of abortion stories, including those that are celebratory and empowering. And as a survivor of sexual violence, all these years later, I am still constantly reckoning with what the word "survivor" even means—as if trauma begins and ends with a simple act of violence and doesn't bleed into every aspect of how you interact with the world for the rest of your life.

When I think about survival, when I think about all the other jagged, misfitted pieces of my identities, about agency, progress, power, I think about a passage from Chanel Miller's *Know My Name* reflecting on what healing has looked like for her:

> *I am not sure exactly what healing is or looks like, what form it comes in, what it should feel like. I do know that when I was four I could not lift a gallon of milk, could not believe how heavy it was, that white sloshing boulder. I'd pull up a wooden chair to stand over the counter, pouring the milk with two shaking arms, wetting the cereal, spilling. Looking back I don't remember the day I lifted it with ease. All I know is that now I do it without thinking, can do it one-handed, on the phone, in a rush. I believe*

the same rules apply, that one day I'll be able to tell this story without it shaking my foundation. Each time will not require an entire production, a spilling, a sweating forehead, a mess to clean up, sopping paper towels. It will just be a part of my life, every day lighter to lift. . . .

I don't believe it was my fate to be raped. But I do believe that here we are is all we have. For a long time, it was too painful to be here. . . . From grief, confidence has grown, remembering what I've endured. From anger, stemmed purpose. To tuck them away would mean to neglect the most valuable tools this experience has given me.[6]

Survival and struggle are complicated, non-monolithic, nonlinear. But I do know this: Victims and survivors deserve better than the inadequate policies, one-dimensional narratives, and apathetic culture we've been dealt.

Just as the system we currently live in anchors itself in our oppression and subjugation, those of us marginalized by white supremacy and patriarchy—women, survivors, people of color, and queer and trans people—must anchor ourselves in each other and draw our strength from our relationships and communities. And it's through this strength that we can build toward a new world in which we're safe from violence in all its wide-ranging forms, and in charge of our own political destinies.

ACKNOWLEDGMENTS

I want to extend my deepest gratitude to the team at North Atlantic Books for converting yet another unhinged, misandrist rant of mine into a real book. In particular, thank you to Shayna Keyles, my editor, for your patience, kindness, and support in getting this project across the finish line, and helping make this manuscript what it is (which, I hope, is good!). Thank you to my literary agent, Mina Hamedi, for believing in this book—and me—and finding it a home. And I cannot thank enough the women and survivors who shared their stories with me for this project as well as my prior reporting; I hope I've honored your bravery and trust. To my friends and family, the co-workers and mentors I'm always learning from, and the scholars and activists whose invaluable work is cited throughout this text, I'm indebted to all of you, too. In particular, I want to thank Susan Rinkunas, Caitlin Cruz, and Laura Bassett, whose groundbreaking reporting on reproductive rights has inspired me for much of my career, and who I've been fortunate enough to work with at Jezebel. I'm also eternally inspired by the courage and radical optimism of my dear friends Danni Wang, Sonali Seth, Anya Kushwaha, Nayanika Kapoor, and Clarice Szeto, all working on the frontlines of the collective fights for social justice in their own incredible, indispensable ways. I've always believed that no one achieves anything alone and what makes work worth doing is doing it together—nothing's further solidified this belief than writing this book and being in community with such inspiring people.

The overturning of *Roe v. Wade* in the summer of 2022 heightened the personal stakes for me throughout the process of assembling this book. Popular, even mainstream, anti-abortion perspectives often center around loss—loss of life, loss of potential, loss of a future scientist who might have cured cancer. Instead, I want to talk about what is gained when people have the right to an abortion, the right to plan their futures and lives. This book, and on my best and worst days, everything in my life that matters to me, wouldn't have been possible without abortion. It might not be a cure for cancer, but I hope this text is something that will help survivors of gender-based violence by highlighting their resiliency, and exposing the cruelties of our rape culture, which we all have an obligation to help dismantle. Our lives are more than hypotheticals. I hope that everyone who reads this knows that you deserve agency, health care, and happiness, whatever that may look like for you.

NOTES

Introduction

1 Bruce Gross, "False Rape Allegations: An Assault on Justice," *Forensic Examiner* 18, no. 1 (Spring 2009).

2 Maeve Wallace, Veronica Gillispie-Bell, Kiara Cruz, Kelly Davis, and Dovile Vilda, "Homicide during Pregnancy and the Postpartum Period in the United States, 2018–2019," *Obstetrics & Gynecology* 139, no. 2 (November 2021), www.ncbi.nlm.nih.gov/pmc/articles/PMC9134264/.

3 Maria Sacchetti and Nick Miroff, "Senate Report Details Medical Mistreatment of Female Immigration Detainees," *Washington Post*, November 15, 2022, www.washingtonpost.com/national-security/2022/11/15/ice-amin-women-medical-mistreatment/.

4 "Sexual Assault Statistics in the US," National Sexual Violence Resource Center, 2018, www.nsvrc.org/node/4737.

5 Eleanor Kilbanoff. "Three Texas women are sued for wrongful death after allegedly helping friend obtain abortion medication," *Texas Tribune*. March 10, 2023.

6 "Arrests and Other Deprivations of Liberty of Pregnant Women, 1973–2020," Pregnancy Justice, September 18, 2021, www.nationaladvocatesforpregnantwomen.org/wp-content/uploads/2021/09/FINAL_1600cases-Factsheet.docx.pdf.

7 Samuel L. Dickman et al., "Uncovered Medical Bills after Sexual Assault," *New England Journal of Medicine* 387 (September 15, 2022), www.nejm.org/doi/full/10.1056/NEJMc2207644.

8 T. K. Logan and Roberta Valente, "Who Will Help Me? Domestic Violence Survivors Speak Out about Law Enforcement Responses," National Domestic Violence Hotline, 2015, www.thehotline.org/wp-content/uploads/media/2020/09/NDVH-2015-Law-Enforcement-Survey-Report-2.pdf.

Chapter 1: The Invisible Threat

1 Rebecca Solnit, "How Many Husbands Control the Votes of Their Wives? We'll Never Know," *Guardian*, November 19, 2018, www.theguardian.com /commentisfree/2018/nov/19/voter-intimidation-republicans-democrats -midterm-elections.

2 Diana Greene Foster, *The Turnaway Study: Ten Years, a Thousand Women, and the Consequences of Having—or Being Denied—an Abortion* (New York: Scribner, 2021).

3 Laura Huss, Farah Diaz-Tello, and Goleen Samari, "Self-Care, Criminalized: August 2022 Preliminary Findings," If/When/How, August 10, 2022, www .ifwhenhow.org/resources/self-care-criminalized-preliminary-findings/.

4 "National Exit Polls: How Different Groups Voted," *New York Times*, November 3, 2020, www.nytimes.com/interactive/2020/11/03/us/elections /exit-polls-president.html.

5 Leslie Kern, *Feminist City* (London: Verso, 2020), 98.

6 Kern, *Feminist City*, 147.

7 "National Intimate Partner and Sexual Violence Survey, 2010," Centers for Disease Control and Prevention, www.cdc.gov/violenceprevention/pdf /nisvs_report2010-a.pdf; Shane Goldmacher, "America Hits New Landmark: 200 Million Registered Voters," Politico, October 19, 2016, www.politico.com /story/2016/10/how-many-registered-voters-are-in-america-2016-229993.

8 Kylie Cheung, "Domestic Violence Is a Form of Voter Suppression," *Dame*, May 26, 2020, www.damemagazine.com/2020/05/26/domestic-violence-is-a -form-of-voter-suppression/.

9 Amy Dellinger Page, "True Colors: Police Officers and Rape Myth Acceptance," *Feminist Criminology* 5, no. 4 (2010); *On the Front Lines: Police Stress and Family Well-Being: Hearing before the Select Committee on Children, Youth, and Families*, House of Representatives, 102nd Cong., 1991.

10 Sequoia Carrillo, "Even Divorce Might Not Free You from Your Ex's Student Loan Debt," NPR, February 8, 2022, www.npr.org/2022/02/08/1063655620 /student-loans-married.

11 Kylie Cheung, "When Your Partner Tries to Control Your Reproductive Choices," Rewire News Group, April 6, 2021, https://rewirenewsgroup .com/2021/04/06/when-your-partner-tries-to-control-your-reproductive -choices/.

12 "Professor Meier Identifies How Family Courts Treat Abuse and Accusations of Alienation," George Washington University Law School, October 6,

2017, www.law.gwu.edu/professor-meier-identifies-how-family-courts-treat
-abuse-and-accusations-alienation.

13 Albert Samaha, "An 18-Year-Old Said She Was Raped While in Police Custody.
The Officers Say She Consented," Buzzfeed News, February 7, 2018, www
.buzzfeednews.com/article/albertsamaha/this-teenager-accused-two-on
-duty-cops-of-rape-she-had-no.

14 Elizabeth Swavola, Kristi Riley, and Ram Subramanian, *Overlooked: Women
and Jails in an Era of Reform*, Vera Institute, August 2016, www.vera.org
/publications/overlooked-women-and-jails-report.

15 *Sexual Victimization in Prisons and Jails Reported by Inmates, 2011–2012*,
Department of Justice, Office of Justice Programs, Bureau of Justice Statistics, 2013, https://bjs.ojp.gov/library/publications/sexual-victimization
-prisons-and-jails-reported-inmates-2011-12-update.

16 Wanda Bertram and Wendy Sawyer, "Prisons and Jails Will Separate Millions of Mothers from Their Children in 2021," Prison Policy Initiative,
May 5, 2021, www.prisonpolicy.org/blog/2021/05/05/mothers-day-2021/.

17 Kern, *Feminist City*, 65.

18 Brad Boserup, Mark McKenney, and Adel Elkbuli, "Alarming Trends in US
Domestic Violence during the COVID-19 Pandemic," *American Journal of
Emergency Medicine* 38, no. 12 (2020), https://doi.org/10.1016%2Fj
.ajem.2020.04.077.

19 Donna St. George. "Teen girls 'engulfed' in violence and trauma, CDC finds,"
Washington Post, Feb. 13, 2023.

20 "Economic Distress and Intimate Partner Violence," Department of Justice,
National Institute of Justice, January 4, 2009, https://nij.ojp.gov/topics/articles
/economic-distress-and-intimate-partner-violence.

21 Chad D. Cotti et al., "The Relationship between In-Person Voting, Consoli-
dated Polling Locations, and Absentee Voting on COVID-19: Evidence from
the Wisconsin Primary," National Bureau of Economic Research, 2020,
www.nber.org/papers/w27187.

22 Dickman, "Uncovered Medical Bills."

23 "Women of Color More Likely to Be Uninsured or Covered by Medicaid,"
Kaiser Family Foundation, 2022, www.kff.org/women-of-color-more-likely
-to-be-uninsured-or-covered-by-medicaid-womenshealth/; Centers for Disease
Control and Prevention, "Intimate Partner and Sexual Violence Survey."

24 "The Extent and Costs of Crime Victimization: A New Look," Department
of Justice, National Institute of Justice, 1996, www.ojp.gov/pdffiles1/nij
/155282rp.pdf.

25 Amy E. Bonomi et al., "Health Care Utilization and Costs Associated with Physical and Nonphysical-Only Intimate Partner Violence," *Health Services Research* 44, no. 3 (2009), https://doi.org/10.1111/j.1475-6773.2009.00955.x.

26 Munira Z. Gunja, Evan D. Gumas, and Reginald D. Williams II, "The U.S. Maternal Mortality Crisis Continues to Worsen: An International Comparison," Commonwealth Fund, December 1, 2022, www.commonwealthfund.org /blog/2022/us-maternal-mortality-crisis-continues-worsen-international -comparison.

27 Donna L. Hoyert, "Maternal Mortality Rates in the United States, 2020," National Center for Health Statistics, Centers for Disease Control and Prevention, February 2022, www.cdc.gov/nchs/data/hestat/maternal-mortality /2020/maternal-mortality-rates-2020.htm.

28 Alexandra Brodsky, "Why So Many Survivors Choose Not to Report Sexual Assault to the Police," Literary Hub, August 24, 2021, https://lithub.com/why -so-many-survivors-choose-not-to-report-sexual-assault-to-the-police/.

29 Kylie Cheung, "'Fetal Personhood' Questions to Ketanji Brown Jackson Should Terrify Us," Jezebel, March, 24, 2022, https://jezebel.com/fetal-personhood -questions-to-ketanji-brown-jackson-sho-1848698963.

30 Anjali Fleury, "Fleeing to Mexico for Safety: The Perilous Journey for Migrant Women," United Nations University, May 4, 2016, https://unu.edu /publications/articles/fleeing-to-mexico-for-safety-the-perilous-journey-for -migrant-women.html.

31 Alexandria Doty, "ICE Detainees Denied Access to Abortion," Immigration and Human Rights Law Review, March 25, 2022, https://lawblogs.uc.edu /ihrlr/2022/03/25/ice-detainees-denied-access-to-abortion/.

32 "Border Patrol Official: Young Girls Illegally Entering US Given Birth Control, Plan B," CBS News, June 19, 2018, www.cbsnews.com/losangeles/news/border -patrol-immigration-plan-b-birth-control/.

33 Alice Speri, "Detained, Then Violated," The Intercept, April 11, 2018, https:// theintercept.com/2018/04/11/immigration-detention-sexual-abuse-ice-dhs/.

34 Matthew Haag, "Thousands of Immigrant Children Said They Were Sexually Abused in U.S. Detention Centers, Report Says," *New York Times*, February 27, 2019, www.nytimes.com/2019/02/27/us/immigrant-children -sexual-abuse.html.

35 "Sex Workers Project," Urban Justice Center, https://swp.urbanjustice.org /category/resources/.

36 Chelsia Rose Marcius, "Hundreds of Women Set to Sue New York over Allegations of Prison Sex Abuse," *New York Times*, November 16, 2022, www.nytimes.com/2022/11/16/nyregion/new-york-prison-sex-abuse.html.

37 Carolyn Sufrin, Rachel K. Jones, Lauren Beal, William D. Mosher, and
    Suzanne Bell, "Abortion Access for Incarcerated People," *Obstetrics &
    Gynecology* 138, no. 3 (2021), https://doi.org/10.1097/aog.0000000000004497.

38 Jimmy Jenkins. "Arizona inducing the labor of pregnant prisoners against
    their will," Arizona Republic. Jan. 2, 2023.

39 Judith Levine and Erica R. Meiners, *The Feminist and the Sex Offender*
    (London: Verso, 2020), 5.

40 Solnit, "How Many Husbands."

Chapter 2: Carceral Feminism and the Violence Against Women Act

1   Jim Mustian, "Woman's Rape Cries Go Unheard in Unmonitored Drug
    Sting," Associated Press, September 13, 2022, https://apnews.com/article
    /crime-alexandria-5fdc645d413aaec5b4078b2f23579149.

2   Lesley McMillan, "Police Officers' Perceptions of False Allegations of Rape,"
    Journal of Gender Studies 27, no. 1 (2018), https://doi.org/10.1080/09589236.2016
    .1194260.

3   Blake Sammann and Jason Lewton, "Judge's Reversal in Criminal Sexual
    Assault Case Draws Ire," WGEM, January 11, 2022, www.wgem.com/2022/01/12
    /judges-reversal-criminal-sexual-assault-case-draws-ire/.

4   Hannah Knowles, "A Domestic Violence Shelter Put up Black Lives Matter
    Signs, and Law Enforcement Revolted," *Washington Post*, October 17, 2020,
    www.washingtonpost.com/nation/2020/10/17/embrace-black-lives-matter/.

5   Maya Schenwar and Victoria Law, *Prison by Any Other Name* (New York:
    New Press, 2020), 11.

6   Jackie Wang, "Against Innocence: Race, Gender, and the Politics of Safety,"
    LIES 1 (2012), www.liesjournal.net/volume1-10-againstinnocence.html.

7   Levine and Meiners, *Feminist and the Sex Offender*.

8   Courtney Tanner, "Moab Officer Was 'Biased' against Gabby Petito
    Because of His Past, Her Parents Claim in New Lawsuit," *Salt Lake Tribune*,
    November 3, 2022, www.sltrib.com/news/2022/11/03/moab-officer-was
    -biased-against/.

9   Lawrence William Henry, "A Silent Dilemma: The Challenges Black Collegiate
    Women Face Disclosing Sexual Victimization" (PhD diss., Nova Southeast-
    ern University, 2020), https://nsuworks.nova.edu/shss_dcar_etd/159.

10 Rafia Zakaria, *Against White Feminism* (New York: W. W. Norton, 2021), 1.

11 "The Sexual Abuse to Prison Pipeline," Rights4Girls, 2012, https://rights
    4girls.org/wp-content/uploads/2018/09/SAPP-UPDATED-SEPT-2020
    _Final-3-1.pdf.

12 Leila Morsy and Richard Rothstein, *Mass Incarceration and Children's Outcomes*, Economic Policy Institute, December 15, 2016, www.epi.org/publication/mass-incarceration-and-childrens-outcomes/.

13 Levine and Meiners, 41.

14 "The Facts on Violence Against American Indian/Alaskan Native Women," Futures without Violence, 2012, www.futureswithoutviolence.org/the-facts-on-violence-against-american-indian-alaskan-native-women.

15 "Maze of Injustice," Amnesty International, August 8, 2011, www.amnestyusa.org/reports/maze-of-injustice/.

Chapter 3: Intimate Damage

1 "Sexual Assault," RAINN, www.rainn.org/articles/sexual-assault.

2 "State-by-State Statistics on Domestic Violence," National Coalition against Domestic Violence, https://ncadv.org/state-by-state.

3 Madison Pauly, "It's 2019, and States Are Still Making Exceptions for Spousal Rape," *Mother Jones*, November 21, 2019, www.motherjones.com/crime-justice/2019/11/deval-patrick-spousal-rape-laws/.

4 John Knefel, "After Roe, Conservatives Set Their Sights on Ending No-Fault Divorce Laws," Media Matters for America, August 2, 2022, www.mediamatters.org/tim-pool/after-roe-conservatives-set-their-sights-ending-no-fault-divorce-laws.

5 "Report of the Permanent 2022 Platform & Resolutions Committee," Republican Party of Texas, https://texasgop.org/wp-content/uploads/2022/06/6-Permanent-Platform-Committee-FINAL-REPORT-6-16-2022.pdf.

6 "Prison Population by State," World Population Review, 2022, https://worldpopulationreview.com/state-rankings/prison-population-by-state.

7 Kyla Bishop, "A Reflection on the History of Sexual Assault Laws in the United States," *Arkansas Journal of Social Change and Public Service*, April 15, 2018, https://ualr.edu/socialchange/2018/04/15/reflection-history-sexual-assault-laws-united-states/.

8 "The Criminal Justice System: Statistics," RAINN, www.rainn.org/statistics/criminal-justice-system.

Chapter 4: Reproducing State Violence

1 "Voting Laws Roundup: December 2021," Brennan Center for Justice, December 21, 2021, www.brennancenter.org/our-work/research-reports/voting-laws-roundup-december-2021.

2 "Debunking the Voter Fraud Myth," Brennan Center for Justice, January 31, 2017, www.brennancenter.org/our-work/research-reports/debunking-voter -fraud-myth.

3 Kylie Cheung, "Women Secretaries of State Are the 'Last Line of Defense' against Far Right Lies," Jezebel, May 20, 2022, https://jezebel.com/women -secretaries-of-state-are-the-last-line-of-defens-1848898338.

4 "Block the Vote: How Politicians Are Trying to Block Voters from the Ballot Box," American Civil Liberties Union, August 18, 2021, www.aclu.org/news /civil-liberties/block-the-vote-voter-suppression-in-2020.

5 Ari Berman, "How Gerrymandering and Voter Suppression Paved the Way for Abortion Bans," *Mother Jones*, May 17, 2019, www.motherjones.com/politics /2019/05/gerrymandering-voter-suppression-abortion-heartbeat-bills/.

6 Todd J. Gillman, "Texas Democrats Won 47 Percent of the Vote Statewide, but Picked Up Only 13 of the State's 36 Congressional Seats," *Dallas Morning News*, November 24, 2018, www.dallasnews.com/news/politics/2018/11/24 /texas-democrats-won-47-of-votes-in-congressional-races-should-they-have -more-than-13-of-36-seats/.

7 "Fact Sheet: About the Hyde Amendment," All* Above All, https://allaboveall .org/resource/hyde-amendment-fact-sheet/.

8 Beverly M. Black and Cecilia Mengo, "Violence Victimization on a College Campus: Impact on GPA and School Dropout," *Journal of College Student Retention* 18, no. 2 (May 11, 2015), https://doi.org/10.1177/1521025115584750.

9 Paul Specht, "Fact Check: How Many Student Loan Borrowers Failed to Finish College?," WRAL, February 15, 2021, www.wral.com/fact-check-how -many-student-loan-borrowers-failed-to-finish-college/19524091/.

10 "Deeper in Debt: 2021 Update," American Association of University Women, 2021, www.aauw.org/app/uploads/2021/05/Deeper_In_Debt_2021.pdf; Jessica Harris, "Women of Color Undergraduate Students' Experiences with Campus Sexual Assault: An Intersectional Analysis," *Review of Higher Education* 44, no. 1 (Fall 2020), https://doi.org/10.1353/rhe.2020.0033.

11 Seung Min Kim, "Neomi Rao, Trump's Nominee for D.C. Appeals Court, Apologizes for Past Writing on Date Rape," *Washington Post*, February 11, 2019, www.washingtonpost.com/politics/neomi-rao-trumps-nominee-for -dc-appeals-court-apologizes-for-past-writing-on-date-rape/2019/02/11 /2733c384-2e58-11e9-ac6c-14eea99d5e24_story.html.

12 Kylie Cheung, "Lyft Pays Shareholders $25 Million for Driver Sexual Assaults—but Nothing for Survivors," Jezebel, June 16, 2022, https:// jezebel.com/lyft-pays-shareholders-25-million-for-driver-sexual-as -1849074186.

13 Kylie Cheung, "Stop Telling People in Red States to Move When They're Faced with Devastating Bans," Jezebel, May 3, 2022, https://jezebel.com /red-state-abortion-seekers-trans-people-advocates-best-1848841000.

Chapter 5: Rape Culture in the Carceral Capitalist Police State

1 "Mapping Police Violence," May 31, 2022, www.mappingpoliceviolence.org.
2 "What Is the Backlog?" End the Backlog, www.endthebacklog.org/what-is -the-backlog/.
3 Angela Davis, *Women, Race and Class* (New York: Random House, 1981), 190–91.
4 Eliott C. McLaughlin, Sara Sidner, and Michael Martinez, "Oklahoma City Cop Convicted of Rape Sentenced to 263 Years in Prison," CNN, January 21, 2016, www.cnn.com/2016/01/21/us/oklahoma-city-officer-daniel-holtzclaw -rape-sentencing/index.html.
5 Ariane Lange, "Cops Had a Warrant to Arrest a Stalker. Nine Days Later, He Was Free, and She Was Dead," Buzzfeed News, October 30, 2018, www .buzzfeednews.com/article/arianelange/rosemarie-reilly-kelley-mcluskey -stalking-murder-lawsuit.
6 Anastasia Dawson, "New Port Richey Officer Fired amid Allegations of Fondling Girl in Custody," *Tampa Bay Times*, September 9, 2022, www .tampabay.com/news/crime/2022/09/09/new-port-richey-officer-fired-amid -allegations-of-fondling-girl-in-custody/.
7 Meg O'Connor, "City to Approve $125,000 Settlement for Woman Who Says Phoenix Cop Stalked Her," *Phoenix New Times*, 2019, www.phoenixnewtimes .com/news/phoenix-set-to-approve-125000-settlement-over-alleged-stalker -cop-11366768; Aaron Farrar and Kiley Thomas, "Ringgold Police: Officer Fired for Inappropriate Contact with Women in Person, Online," WTVC, August 6, 2019, https://newschannel9.com/news/local/ringgold-police -officer-fired-for-inappropriate-contact-with-women-online; Phil Davis, "Baltimore Police Trainee Arrested and Charged with Harassing Women Who Wouldn't Invite Him to Party, Court Records Show," *Baltimore Sun*, February 7, 2021, www.baltimoresun.com/news/crime/bs-md-ci-cr-baltimore-bpd -trainee-arrest-20210207-vzjtaa2gh5a7pe7gwgjykehi3i-story.html; "Wichita Police Officer Arrested, Accused of Stalking Woman," Associated Press, October 3, 2020, https://apnews.com/article/arrests-wichita-0a44ac67045 4c33cf5658f66f590d708.
8 Chelsia Rose Marcius, "Hundreds of Women Set to Sue New York over Allegations of Prison Sex Abuse," *New York Times*, November 16, 2022, www.nytimes.com/2022/11/16/nyregion/new-york-prison-sex-abuse.html.

9 Derek Hawkins, "Judge to Inmates: Get Sterilized and I'll Shave off Jail Time," *Washington Post*, July 21, 2017, www.washingtonpost.com/news /morning-mix/wp/2017/07/21/judge-to-inmates-get-sterilized-and-ill -shave-off-jail-time/.

10 Sacchetti and Miroff, "Senate Report Details Medical Mistreatment."

11 Jerome Hunt and Aisha C. Moodie-Mills, "The Unfair Criminalization of Gay and Transgender Youth," Center for American Progress, June 29, 2012, www.americanprogress.org/article/the-unfair-criminalization-of-gay-and -transgender-youth/.

12 "Police Response to Survivors, 2020 Survey," Women's Justice NOW, August 2021, https://nownyc.org/womens-justice-now/issues/law-enforcement -response-to-survivors-survey-2020/.

13 Jackie Wang, *Carceral Capitalism* (South Pasadena, CA: Semiotext(e)), 2018.

14 Dave McKenna (@djmckenna00), Twitter, June 7, 2020, https://twitter.com /djmckenna00/status/1269579021148446721.

15 Abbas Muntaqim, "Good Cops Do Not Exist," Medium, March 5, 2017, https:// medium.com/@BlakeDontCrack/good-cops-do-not-exist-43be29096b86.

16 Christopher Uggen, Ryan Larson, Sarah Shannon, and Robert Stewart, *Locked Out 2020: Estimates of People Denied Voting Rights Due to a Felony Conviction*, The Sentencing Project, October 30, 2020, www.sentencingproject .org/reports/locked-out-2022-estimates-of-people-denied-voting-rights/.

17 Jessica Mindlin, Leslye E. Orloff, Sameera Pochiraju, Amanda Baran, and Ericka Echavarria, *Dynamics of Sexual Assault and the Implications for Immigrant Women*, National Immigrant Women's Advocacy Policy, American University, 2013, https://niwaplibrary.wcl.american.edu/wp-content /uploads/2015/Ch1-DyanimcsSexualAssaultImplications-07.10.13.pdf.

18 Esther Wang, "Judge Is Nice to a Teen Accused of Rape Because He Came from a 'Good Family,'" Jezebel, July 3, 2019, https://jezebel.com/judge-is -nice-to-a-teen-accused-of-rape-because-he-came-1836073053.

Chapter 6: Seizing the Means of Reproduction

1 "Report: Abortion Costs U.S. Economy $6.9 Trillion," Republican Party, Committee on Ways and Means, House of Representatives, June 16, 2022, https:// gop-waysandmeans.house.gov/report-abortion-costs-u-s-economy-6-9-trillion/.

2 "Forced Sterilization of Disabled People in the United States," National Women's Law Center and Autistic Women and Nonbinary Network, January 2022, https://nwlc.org/resource/forced-sterilization-of-disabled-people -in-the-united-states/.

3 "Uninsured Rates for the Nonelderly by Race/Ethnicity," Kaiser Family Foundation, 2019, www.kff.org/uninsured/state-indicator/nonelderly -uninsured-rate-by-raceethnicity/.

4 Katie McDonough, "Study on Reproductive Rights and Domestic Violence: Being Denied an Abortion 'Tethered Women to Violent Men,'" Salon, September 29, 2014, www.salon.com/2014/09/29/study_on_reproductive _rights_and_domestic_violence_being_denied_an_abortion_tethered _women_to_violent_men/.

5 Dellinger Page, "Police Officers and Rape Myth Acceptance."

6 Elizabeth Miller et al., "Pregnancy Coercion, Intimate Partner Violence, and Unintended Pregnancy," January 2010, www.ncbi.nlm.nih.gov/pmc /articles/PMC2896047/.

7 Tessa Stuart, "She Wanted an Abortion. Now the Embryo Is Suing Her Doctors," *Rolling Stone*, September 23, 2022, www.rollingstone.com/politics /politics-features/abortion-arizona-personhood-roe-wade-1234598516/.

8 Mia Salenetri, "Do These Five States Prevent Pregnant Couples from Getting Divorced?," WUSA9/CBS, June 1, 2022, www.wusa9.com/article/news/verify /states-prevent-pregnant-people-from-getting-divorced-arkansas-florida -arizona-missouri-texas-fact-check-roe-v-wade/65-58964075-6127-40e4-a2ac -4aaf75c25217; Justia US Law, A.Z. vs. B.Z., March 31, 2000, www.law.justia .com/cases/massachusetts/supreme-court/volumes/431/431mass150.html; Maura Dolan, "Divorced Couple's Frozen Embryos Must Be 'Thawed and Discarded,' Judge Rules," *Los Angeles Times,* November 18, 2015, www.latimes .com/local/lanow/la-me-ln-frozen-embryos-20151118-story.html; Roy Strom, "SCOTUS Ends Long Illinois Embryo Battle," *Chicago Daily Law Bulletin,* March 2, 2016, www.chicagolawbulletin.com/archives/2016/03/02/embryo -03-02-16; Sheryl Rentz, "Frozen Pre-Embryos Awarded to Wife in Penn-sylvania Court Case," *The Law Offices of Sheryl R. Rentz,* April 27, 2012, www.srrentzlaw.com/blog/family-law/frozen-pre-embryos-awarded -wife-pennsylvania-court-case; Dakin Andone, "An Arizona Woman Can't Use Her Frozen Embryos after Divorce, State Supreme Court Rules," CNN, January 27, 2020, www.cnn.com/2020/01/26/health/arizona-embryo-court -ruling-trnd/index.

9 "The Hyde Amendment Creates an Unacceptable Barrier to Women Getting Abortions," National Women's Law Center, 2015, https://nwlc.org /resource/hyde-amendment-creates-unacceptable-barrier-women-getting -abortions/.

10 Anna Betts, "A Young Victim of Incest Was Denied an Abortion in Florida and Forced to Travel for Care, Planned Parenthood Said," Buzzfeed News,

October 13, 2022, www.buzzfeednews.com/article/annabetts/abortion
-florida-ban-incest.

11 Bryan Schott, "Video: GOP Lawmaker Says She Trusts Utah Women to
Control Their 'Intake of Semen' as Abortion Trigger Law Goes into Effect,"
Salt Lake Tribune, June 27, 2022, www.sltrib.com/news/politics/2022/06/24
/utah-republicans-take/.

12 Caitlin Cruz, "Michigan GOP Hopeful: 'If Rape Is Inevitable . . . Lie Back
and Enjoy It,'" Jezebel, March 8, 2022, https://jezebel.com/michigan-gop
-hopeful-if-rape-is-inevitable-lie-back-1848622655.

13 Jonathan Edwards, "Ohio Lawmaker Calls Pregnancies from Rape an 'Opportunity' for Victims," *Washington Post*, April 29, 2022, www.washingtonpost
.com/nation/2022/04/29/ohio-rape-bill-opportunity/.

14 Bryan Anderson, "Bo's Time? NC Republican Political Newcomer Draws
Fire in Bid for Toss-Up Congressional Seat," WRAL, October 21, 2022, www
.wral.com/bo-s-time-nc-republican-political-newcomer-draws-fire-in-bid
-for-toss-up-congressional-seat/20530941/.

15 Susan Rinkunas, "Yes, Women Will Die after Roe—from Pregnancy," Jezebel,
July 14, 2022, https://jezebel.com/abortion-bans-pregnancy-deaths-1849175032.

16 Bud Foster, "14-Year-Old Girl Denied Medication Because of New Abortion
Law Speaks Out," KOLD, October 3, 2022, www.kold.com/2022/10/04/14-year
-old-girl-denied-medication-because-new-abortion-law-speaks-out/.

17 Lorena O'Neil, "Louisiana Doctors: We're Choosing between Saving a Life
or Going to Jail," Jezebel, July 6, 2022, https://jezebel.com/louisiana-doctors
-we-re-choosing-between-saving-a-life-1849150116.

18 "Woman Dies in Poland after Having to Carry Dead Foetus for Seven
Days," Notes from Poland, January 6, 2022, https://notesfrompoland.com
/2022/01/26/woman-dies-in-poland-after-being-made-to-carry-dead-foetus
-for-seven-days/.

19 Kylie Cheung, "Sexual Assault Survivors Are Being Billed Thousands for
Emergency Care," Jezebel, September 14, 2022, https://jezebel.com/sexual
-assault-survivors-are-being-billed-thousands-for-1849534311.

20 Bradford William Davis, "Insiders Say RAINN, the Nation's Foremost Organization for Victims of Sexual Assault, Is in Crisis over Allegations of Racism
and Sexism," Insider, February 25, 2022, www.businessinsider.com/rainn-crisis
-racism-sexism-employees-say-hollywood-corporate-america-2022-2.

21 Jessica Tebow, "After My Miscarriage, I Wanted to Grieve. California Law
Made Me Give My Embryo to the Police First," *San Francisco Chronicle*,
September 9, 2022, www.sfchronicle.com/opinion/openforum/article/Open
-Forum-abortion-protection-17425633.php.

22 Kylie Cheung, "Most People Criminalized for Inducing Abortion Are Turned in by Doctors, Not Internet Activity," Jezebel, August 9, 2022, www.jezebel.com/most-people-criminalized-for-inducing-abortion-are-turn-1849383477.

23 Christie Renick, "The Nation's First Family Separation Policy," The Imprint, October 9, 2018, https://imprintnews.org/child-welfare-2/nations-first-family-separation-policy-indian-child-welfare-act/32431.

24 Kylie Cheung, "The Policing of Native American Pregnancies Has to Stop," Jezebel, November 25, 2021, https://jezebel.com/the-policing-of-native-american-pregnancies-has-to-stop-1848113033.

25 Charlotte Scott Austin, "Texas Abortion Ban Does Not Impact IVF," Spectrum News 1, July 13, 2022, https://spectrumlocalnews.com/tx/south-texas-el-paso/politics/2022/07/13/texas-abortion-ban-does-not-impact-ivf; "What to Watch in Tonight's Walker-Warnock Debate," *Atlanta Journal-Constitution*, October 14, 2022, www.ajc.com/politics/politics-blog/the-jolt-what-to-watch-in-tonights-walker-warnock-debate/U4ZHMAVEEFHGXHWNZ6UWON32GA/.

26 Kavitha Surana, "'We Need to Defend This Law': Inside an Anti-Abortion Meeting with Tennessee's GOP Lawmakers," ProPublica, November 12, 2022, www.propublica.org/article/inside-anti-abortion-meeting-with-tennessee-republican-lawmakers.

27 *Results from the 2013 National Survey on Drug Use and Health: Summary of National Findings*, Department of Health and Human Services, Substance Abuse and Mental Health Services Administration, 2014, www.samhsa.gov/data/sites/default/files/NSDUHresultsPDFWHTML2013/Web/NSDUHresults2013.pdf.

28 Jessica D. Hanson et al., "Epidemiology of Substance-Exposed Pregnancies at One Great Lakes Hospital That Serves a Large Number of American Indians," *American Indian and Alaska Native Mental Health Research Journal* 23, no. 4 (2016), www.ncbi.nlm.nih.gov/pmc/articles/PMC5011980/.

29 Rachel Simon, Jennifer Giroux, and Julie Chor, "Effects of Substance Use Disorder Criminalization on American Indian Pregnant Individuals," *AMA Journal of Ethics* 22, no. 10 (October 2020), https://journalofethics.ama-assn.org/article/effects-substance-use-disorder-criminalization-american-indian-pregnant-individuals/2020-10.

30 Lindsay Beyerstein, "Part 1: Investigating Big Horn County," in *The Breach*, podcast, September 25, 2018, Rewire News Group, https://rewirenewsgroup.com/2018/09/25/the-breach-season-4-montana-e1/.

31 Cheung, "Stop Telling People in Red States."

32 Sharona Coutts, "Anti-Choice Groups Use Smartphone Surveillance to Target 'Abortion-Minded Women' during Clinic Visits," Rewire News Group, May 25, 2016, https://rewirenewsgroup.com/2016/05/25/anti-choice-groups -deploy-smartphone-surveillance-target-abortion-minded-women-clinic-visits/.

33 "Crisis Pregnancy Centers Research and Report," Women's Law Project, October 2021, www.womenslawproject.org/abortion-reproductive-health /crisis-pregnancy-centers-research-report/.

34 "Anti-Abortion Fake Clinic Report," Centre for Countering Digital Hate, June 2022, https://counterhate.com/wp-content/uploads/2022/06/CCDH -Anti-Abortion-Fake-Clinic-Report.pdf.

35 Susan Rinkunas, "Twitter Flagged a Tweet about Abortion Pills as 'Promoting Self-Harm,'" Jezebel, November 8, 2022, https://jezebel.com/twitter -flagged-a-tweet-about-abortion-pills-as-promoti-1849759714.

36 "2020 Violence and Disruption Statistics," National Abortion Federation, December 2021, https://prochoice.org/wp-content/uploads/2020_NAF_VD _Stats.pdf.

37 "Ted Cruz's History with Anti-Abortion Extremists," Texas Freedom Network, December 2015, https://tfn.org/ted-cruzs-history-with-anti-abortion -extremists/.

38 Anna Merlan, "Exclusive: FBI Warned Law Enforcement Agencies of Threat Posed by Non-Existent 'Pro-Choice Extremists,'" Jezebel, January 31, 2019, https://jezebel.com/exclusive-fbi-warned-law-enforcement-agencies-of-threat -1832134408.

39 Melissa Guida-Richards, "My Birth Mother Didn't Get the Option of Abortion. That's Why I Stand against the Texas Ban," *Independent*, September 3, 2021, www.independent.co.uk/voices/adoption-texas-abortion-ban-international -b1914093.html.

40 "Annual Report 2019–2020," National Network of Abortion Funds, 2021, https://abortionfunds.org/annual-report-fy-2019-20/.

Chapter 7: Against Saviors

1 Angela Davis, *Freedom Is a Constant Struggle: Ferguson, Palestine, and the Foundations of a Movement* (Chicago: Haymarket Books, 2016), 7.

2 Davis, *Freedom Is a Constant Struggle*, 116.

3 Guy Taylor and John Solomon, "Sexual Harassment Complaints at State Department Soar under Clinton, Kerry," *Washington Times*, June 18, 2015, www.washingtontimes.com/news/2015/jun/18/sexual-harassment-complaints -state-department-soar/.

4　Ruby Cramer and Rosie Gray, "Democrats Will Have to Answer Questions about Tara Reade. The Biden Campaign Is Advising Them to Say Her Story 'Did Not Happen,'" Buzzfeed News, April 28, 2020, www.buzzfeednews.com /article/rubycramer/joe-biden-tara-reade-talking-points-campaign-defense.

5　Susan Rinkunas, "Texas AG: Supreme Court Should Let States Ban Same-Sex Intimacy," Jezebel, June 28, 2022, https://jezebel.com/texas-ag-supreme-court -should-let-states-ban-same-sex-1849118394.

6　Cinzia Arruzza, Tithi Bhattacharya, and Nancy Fraser, *Feminism for the 99%* (London: Verso, 2019), 2.

7　Davis, *Freedom Is a Constant Struggle*, 18.

Chapter 8: The Culture War

1　Adam Klasfeld, "Johnny Depp Intends to Settle Suit Accusing Him of Assaulting *City of Lies* Crew Member: Document," Law and Crime Network, July 11, 2022, https://lawandcrime.com/live-trials/johnny-depp/johnny-depp-settle -assault-lawsuit-gregg-rocky-brooks-city-of-lies-crew-member/.

2　Zack Sharf, "Billie Eilish Slams Internet for Caring about Depp-Heard Trial over Abortion Rights: 'Who Gives a F—?,'" *Variety*, June 24, 2022, https:// variety.com/2022/music/news/billie-eilish-johnny-depp-amber-heard -trial-1235302744/.

3　Zack Sharf, "Louis C.K. Says He Lost $35 Million and Went to 'Hell and Back' due to Sexual Misconduct Fallout," IndieWire, October 16, 2018, www.indiewire.com/2018/10/louis-c-k-lost-35-million-went-to-hell-sexual -misconduct-fallout-1202012475/.

4　Tatiana Siegel, "Why Dakota Johnson Is Hollywood's Heiress Apparent," *Hollywood Reporter*, November 3, 2021, www.hollywoodreporter.com/movies /movie-features/dakota-johnson-the-lost-daughter-fifty-shades-of-grey-chris -martin-1235040691/.

5　*Targeted Trolling and Trend Manipulation: How Organized Attacks on Amber Heard and Other Women Thrive on Twitter*, Bot Sentinel, July 2022, https:// botsentinel.com/reports/documents/amber-heard/report-07-18-2022.pdf.

6　Graham Kates, "Report Finds Online Campaign of 'Widespread Targeted Harassment' against Supporters of Amber Heard," CBS News, July 18, 2022, www.cbsnews.com/news/amber-heard-supporters-online-targeted -harassment-campaign-report/.

7　Alia E. Dastagir, "Why We Didn't See Amber Heard Coming and What It Might Mean for Other Women Who Allege Abuse," *USA Today*, June 2, 2022,

www.usatoday.com/story/life/health-wellness/2022/06/02/after-amber
-heard-we-asking-wrong-questions-metoo/7487231001/.

8 *Social Media Fails Women: Transforming Social Media Policies for a Feminist Future*, UltraViolet, November 2021, https://weareultraviolet.org/wp-content /uploads/2021/11/Social-media-fails-women.pdf.

9 *The Cost of Reporting: Perpetrator Retaliation, Institutional Betrayal, and Student Survivor Pushout*, Know Your IX, 2021, https://www.knowyourix.org/wp -content/uploads/2021/03/Know-Your-IX-2021-Report-Final-Copy.pdf.

10 "Title IX Lawsuits Database," Title IX for All, https://titleixforall.com/title-ix -legal-database/.

11 Kylie Cheung, "Campus Sexual Assault Survivors Have Always Feared Defamation Lawsuits," Jezebel, June 2, 2022, https://jezebel.com/campus-sexual -assault-survivors-have-always-feared-defa-1849010239.

12 Dana Bolger, Alexandra Brodsky, and Sejal Singh, "A Tale of Two Title IXs: Title IX Reverse Discrimination Law and Its Trans-Substantive Implications for Civil Rights," *UC Davis Law Review* 55, no. 2 (December 2021), https://lawreview.law.ucdavis.edu/issues/55/2/articles/files/55-2_Bolger _Brodsky_Singh.pdf.

13 Cheung, "Lyft Pays Shareholders $25 Million."

14 Chanel Miller, *Know My Name* (New York: Viking, 2019), viii.

15 Kylie Cheung, "'Being Emotionally Closer to Stories Isn't Weakness': Inside Wapo Reporter's Bombshell Lawsuit," Salon, August 10, 2021, www.salon.com /2021/08/10/felicia-somnez-washington-post-lawsuit-discrimination/.

16 Krutika Mallikarjuna, "Tuca & Bertie Creator Breaks Down That Complicated Sexual Assault Storyline," *TV Guide*, May 6, 2019, www.tvguide.com/news /tuca-and-bertie-lisa-hanawalt-interview/.

17 Elisabetta Povoledo, "Pope Scolds Couples Who Choose Pets over Kids," *New York Times*, January 6, 2022, www.nytimes.com/2022/01/06/world/europe/pope -pets-kids.html.

18 Emily S. Rueb and Derrick Bryson Taylor, "Obama on Call-Out Culture: 'That's Not Activism,'" *New York Times*, October 31, 2019, www.nytimes.com /2019/10/31/us/politics/obama-woke-cancel-culture.html.

19 Erin Donaghue, "Nearly Two-Thirds of Anti-Asian Hate Incidents Reported by Women, New Data Shows," CBS News, May 7, 2021, www.cbsnews.com/news /asian-american-hate-incidents-women-disproportionately-impacted/.

20 Kylie Cheung, "This Survivor Comedy Duo Wants You to Know 'Rape Victims Are Horny Too,'" Jezebel, December 2, 2021, https://jezebel.com/this -survivor-comedy-duo-wants-you-to-know-rape-victim-1848150185.

Chapter 9: Survivor Justice

1 Mariame Kaba, *We Do This 'Til We Free Us* (Chicago: Haymarket Books, 2021).

2 Micah Herskind, "Some Lessons from Mariame Kaba's 'We Do This 'Til We Free Us,'" Medium, March 1, 2021, https://micahherskind.medium.com /some-lessons-from-mariame-kabas-we-do-this-til-we-free-us-4ae4fc9986bb.

3 Marilyn Armour, "Restorative Justice: Some Facts and History," Charter for Compassion, https://charterforcompassion.org/restorative-justice/restorative -justice-some-facts-and-history.

4 "Restorative Justice as a Path Forward for Title IX Cases," American College Personnel Association, September 11, 2018, https://myacpa.org/restorative -justice-as-a-path-forward-for-title-ix-cases/.

5 Danielle Tcholakian, "Oh, *Now* Democrats Want to Codify Roe v. Wade!," Jezebel, May 9, 2022, https://jezebel.com/oh-now-democrats-want-to-codify -roe-v-wade-1848901956.

6 ReproReceipts website, UltraViolet, 2022, https://reproreceipts.com/.

7 Kylie Cheung, "How Not to Get Arrested for Miscarriage or Abortion: A Practical Guide," Jezebel, April 11, 2022, https://jezebel.com/how-not-to -get-arrested-for-miscarriage-or-abortion-a-1848779647.

Chapter 10: Another World

1 Rebeca Martínez, "'The Feminism of the 1 Percent Has Associated Our Cause with Elitism': An Interview with Nancy Fraser," *Jacobin*, August 21, 2019, https://jacobin.com/2019/08/feminism-for-99-percent-nancy-fraser.

2 Kylie Cheung, "Ruth Wilson Gilmore Says Freedom Is a Physical Place— but Can We Find It?," Jezebel, June 21, 2022, https://jezebel.com/ruth -wilson-gilmore-says-freedom-is-a-physical-place-bu-1849079415.

3 Kaba, *'Til We Free Us*, 127.

4 "About S&P," Survived and Punished, https://survivedandpunished.org/about/.

5 Leigh Stein, "The End of the Girlboss Is Here," Medium, June 22, 2020, https://gen.medium.com/the-end-of-the-girlboss-is-nigh-4591dec34ed8.

6 Miller, *Know My Name*, 323.

INDEX

Dick's Sporting Goods' post-*Roe* corporate
   response, 238
Dickman, Samuel, 135
digital footprint, 243
Disney
   donations to Republican politicians, 239
   insurance coverage of abortion, 162
   post-*Roe* corporate response, 238
divorce, no-fault, 72–73
Dobbs v. Jackson Women's Health,
   160–161, 246
Doe v. Oberlin College, 195
Doe v. Purdue University, 195
Doe v. University of the Sciences, 195
domestic abuse and violence, 8, 16–28
   California definition, 19–20
   COVID stay-at-home orders, 23–26
   economic coercion, 20
   election outcomes, 73–78
   healthcare system, 28–31
   homicide, 21
   intimacy, 59–60
   mutual abuse, 43, 185–188
   normalized, 1–2
   Oklahoma "failure to protect" law, 22
   political candidates, 23
   police officers, 19
   political violence, 60–67
   reproductive coercion, 19–21, 126
   state domestic abuse rates, 72, 77
   victims seen as perpetrators, 35, 43–44
   Violence Against Women Act
      mandatory arrest provision, 99
   voter suppression and coercion, 13–19,
      27–28, 36–37, 60–67, 69
Domestic Shelters, 43
Douglas, L. Tomay, 227
drug use during pregnancy/postpartum, 7,
   99, 138, 142–144
The Duchess, 206
due process, 68, 113, 196
   campus sexual assault, 229
   Jane's Due Process, 117, 162
Duncan, Kyle, 88

E

economic coercion, 20
Eilish, Billie, 184
elections
   2016, 68
   2020, 16, 18, 26–28, 67, 79–80

candidates with allegations of sexist
   misconduct, 169–170
domestic abuse by political
   candidates, 23
domestic violence, 16
incarceration and criminalization of
   women and victims, 73–78
invocation of voting as cure-all, 167
language barriers, 80–81
no-fault divorce, 72–73
obstacles to voting, 79–81
oversimplified calls to vote, 109
protecting victims' voting rights,
   62–63, 67
sexual misconduct of politicians,
   38–39
shaping of public policy, 68–69
state reproduction coercion,
   69–72
voter fraud, 80, 82
voter intimidation, 83
voter suppression. *See* voter
   suppression and coercion
voting. *See* voting
electoral college, 64, 89
   disproportionate power to Republican
      candidates, 84
   ratio of domestic abuse rate–electoral
      college representation, 84
Ellison, Keith, 181
embryos
   custody battles, 127
   laws conferring personhood
      upon, 143
emergency care costs, 134–135
emergency contraception, 135
   hoarding of, 163
Emergency Medical Treatment and Active
   Labor Act (EMTALA), 30
Enough, 206
Epstein, Jeffrey
Equal Rights Amendment, 246
Esposito, Cameron, 222
Everard, Sarah, 99
evidence
   "clear and convincing evidence" vs
      "beyond a reasonable doubt",
      123, 231
   rape kit misuse, 22, 93, 95
executive branch, 85–86
Exonerated Five, 68
Expose Fake Clinics campaign, 152

ABOUT THE AUTHOR

Photo by Biata Shem-Tov

KYLIE CHEUNG is a journalist and the author of two other books on gender and power, *A Woman's Place* and *The Gaslit Diaries*. Currently a staff writer at Jezebel, she previously worked at the culture desk at Salon and at several nonprofits where she researched reproductive health policy. Cheung holds a BA in political science from the University of Southern California and lives with her pit bull-chihuahua, Bucky. In their free time together, they enjoy watching NBA games and superhero movies. You can follow Cheung's work at www.kyliewrites.net and her Twitter, @kylietcheung.

About North Atlantic Books